Escaping Slavery

Escaping Slavery

A Documentary History of Native American Runaways in British North America

Antonio T. Bly

LEXINGTON BOOKS
Lanham • Boulder • New York • London

Published by Lexington Books
An imprint of The Rowman & Littlefield Publishing Group, Inc.
4501 Forbes Boulevard, Suite 200, Lanham, Maryland 20706
www.rowman.com

86-90 Paul Street, London EC2A 4NE

Copyright © 2022 by The Rowman & Littlefield Publishing Group, Inc.

All rights reserved. No part of this book may be reproduced in any form or by any electronic or mechanical means, including information storage and retrieval systems, without written permission from the publisher, except by a reviewer who may quote passages in a review.

British Library Cataloguing in Publication Information Available

Library of Congress Cataloging-in-Publication Data

Names: Bly, Antonio T., author.
Title: Escaping slavery : a documentary history of Native American runaways in British North America / Antonio T. Bly.
Description: Lanham : Lexington Books, [2021] | Includes bibliographical references and index.
Identifiers: LCCN 2021046907 (print) | LCCN 2021046908 (ebook) | ISBN 9781793632708 (cloth) | ISBN 9781793632722 (paperback) | ISBN 9781793632715 (ebook)
Subjects: LCSH: Indian slaves—United States—History—Sources. | Fugitive slaves—United States—History—18th century—Sources. | Slavery—United States—History—18th century—Sources. | Indians, Treatment of—United States—History—Sources. | Julian, approximately 1700-1733. | Indians of North America—History—Colonial period, ca. 1600-1775—Sources. Classification: LCC E98.S6 B59 2021 (print) | LCC E98.S6 (ebook) | DDC 973.04/97—dc23
LC record available at https://lccn.loc.gov/2021046907
LC ebook record available at https://lccn.loc.gov/2021046908

To my indigenous ancestors.

Contents

Acknowledgments	ix
Introduction: Social Death in the Lands of Their Forefathers	xi
A Note on the Notices	xxxiii
A Note on Newspapers	xxxv
1 New England Colonies	1
2 Mid-Atlantic Colonies	77
3 Southern Colonies	115
Appendix A: Advertisements for Mustees	123
Appendix B: As the Law Directs: Social Death in Julian's Massachusetts	133
Appendix C: Julian's Story as Broadsides Ephemera	145
Appendix D: Julian's Story Memorialized	149
Appendix E: A Timeline of Julian's Story	157
Appendix F: Julian the Indian in Court Records	161
Appendix G: Graphic Representation of Advertisements for Native American Fugitives	171
Appendix H: Public Days in Julian's Massachusetts: Advertising Native American Slavery, Servitude, and Social Death in Eighteenth-Century America	173

Glossary	185
Name Index	193
Subject Index	197
Subscribers	199
About the Author	203

Acknowledgments

I would like to thank my students. Over the years, your questions have proven invaluable. In my tireless efforts to answer them, you have inspired me. In exploring your curiosities about the past you have allowed me to discover something more about this thing we call *history*.

I would also like to thank my research assistants, Ms. Vivian Tang and Mr. Arthur Henry, whose help was instrumental in the completion of this volume; Elizabeth C. Bouvier, Head Archivist, Division of Archives and Records Preservation, Massachusetts Supreme Judicial Court and Christopher J. Carter, the Judicial Archivist, Massachusetts Supreme Judicial Court Archives, whose help proved invaluable in helping me develop more fully Julian's story.

Lastly, I would like to thank the outsider readers who reviewed this work, Eric Kuntzman, Jasper Mislak, Madeline Kogler, Monica Sukumar, and the editorial staff of Lexington Books.

This work was made possible by Elizabeth Shattuck and the Peter H. Shattuck Endowment in Colonial American History. Thank You.

Introduction
Social Death in the Lands of Their Forefathers

> In every human Breast, God has implanted a Principle, which we call Love of Freedom; it is impatient of Oppression, and pants for Deliverance.[1]

September 14, 1732. An unnamed Indian man who belonged "to one Mr. [Thomas] Howard of Bridgewater" absconded from his master's place in Boston.[2] Like most fugitives of his day, the New England runaway had grown weary of the conditions in which he lived. Captive in the land of his forefathers, a stranger among strangers, he probably thought of his predicament as nothing short of being a person who had fallen from grace. His native deities had forsaken him. Or so he might have thought, if only for a moment. Before he decided to run, before he elected to protest his situation with his feet, he had been the *subject* of at least one other whom he would call master. Before Howard, the fugitive Indian had once been the property of one "Major [John] Quincy," Esquire, of Braintree. Like most servants, he had been subject to sale, transfer, or trade. In his effort to own himself, the unnamed Indian man documented, albeit unintentionally, one of many aspects of what Orlando Patterson would characterize as social death.[3]

Like most bondservants and slaves in early America, the Native American man did not own himself. Without the consent of his owner, he could not move about freely. He could not own a horse or a watercraft. For such possessions could facilitate escape. Without the permission of his master, he could not hire himself out. He could not achieve a sense of automony. Like other servants in British North America, he had been forbidden from drinking spirituous liquors. Because consumption could compromise a master's investment. The fugitive also could not legally marry, engage in sexual intercourse, or produce children without the permission of his said master. Consequently, within this context, the fugitive Indian man had been reduced to a type of chattel, a mere piece of property subject to someone else's prerogatives as opposed to his own.[4]

But like most fugitives, the runaway thought his freedom a birthright, one implanted in him by God, long before Thomas Jefferson came to believe liberty a quintessential right of all men. In his pursuit of happiness, he judged the act of absenting himself from his owner justifiable. When he left, he left alone. In the dead of night, he took his flight, as the retiring evening would have provided the colored manservant a protective hedge of sorts. Like most fugitives, when he left, he carried with him only the clothes he wore that day. He left in the autumn, maybe anticipating that the change of season would perhaps assist him in his bid to be free. Bad weather, he might have reasoned, coupled with his knowledge of the terrain would aid him in his exodus. For several days, he managed to elude capture. In that time, the Native American man traveled over 20 miles to the town of Braintree, the township of his former master and conceivably the home of a dear loved one, if not family, friends, or someone else he could trust.

Not long after his bondservant had declared his independence and stole himself away, Howard had a manuscript advertisement posted. Between Bridgewater and Braintree, he got the word out. One of the notices attracted the attention of Mr. Rogers, who at the time had been at Weymouth. Enticed by Howard's promise of a reward, and, of course, payment for all necessary charges incurred in the business of securing the runaway, the Pembrook resident took down the advertisement from the bulletin and proceeded to look for the "Indian Fellow." After making several inquiries, he discovered the whereabouts of the fugitive. He secured his bounty and began to make his way back to Mr. Howard's place to collect his payment.[5]

But the unnamed Indian refused to go idly. No longer would he serve another whom he would call master. Rather, the man had plans of his own. In his insistence on the subject of being his own master, he ran away from the would-be bounty hunter. One night, while the two were lodging at Braintree, he escaped. Finding him gone, Rogers offered the local residents of the town a reward of "Ten Shilling" if they helped him secured the determined fugitive. His public solicitation did the trick. He hired a *deputy*, and with his assistance, Rogers took up the runaway again. After he settled his accounts, he resumed his trip back to Howard's place in Bridgewater.

Five miles into the journey, the man hunter got tired and decided to stop by a neighboring community to refresh himself. At Mr. Scot's place, he ordered "a Dram," a spirituous beverage whose liquor he had hoped would revive him for the long trek ahead. But Scot had no whiskey, a reasonable expenditure in the business of taking up runaways. A conversation ensued. As the two men talked, the Indian man seized on the occasion. He freed himself of his restraints and resumed his journey to freedom. To make his escape, he fled to a nearby cornfield. He would have his freedom, he thought, as he proceeded to steal himself away again. But before he could get to the field, someone alerted the bounty hunter that his man was trying to escape his custody.[6]

Determined to receive his just reward, which by that time included a not so small debt of his lodgings for the night before, "Ten Shillings for the services of a deputy-for-hire," and of course the price of the "Dram," that is had he been able to secure one, Rogers pursued the Indian who fled toward the outlying field. Before the Native son could reach his destination, the bounty hunter closed the distance between the two—like a wolf hunting a deer. But, just before he could grab his prize, the runaway Indian suddenly turned around, opened a Jack-Knife he had in his possession, and plunged the blade deep into Rogers's left breast. Initially, unaware that he had been stabbed, Rogers grabbed hold of the knife. For what might have been only a few seconds, the two struggled over the weapon. As they wrestled, neither of the men seemed to be aware of what just occurred. Onlookers, however, did grasp the full nature of what had just transpired. After witnessing the fight and its grisly conclusion, John Scot and a Negro in the House ran up to the two men. Upon seeing the blood, that stained the shirts of both men, Scot asked the bounty hunter three times: to whom did the red, vital fluid belong? "I am either stab'd or wounded," Howard said, before he fell down and "dy'd immediately."[7]

As his would-be catcher fell to his death, the Indian fugitive turned and ran away. Quickly, he tried to resume his flight toward the cornfield. His efforts to own himself again, however, were to naught. The Negro man who witnessed the assault and followed the innkeeper to the scene of the "barbarous Murder" chased the runaway down and caught him. While the black bondservant or slave prevented the Indian from escaping, Mr. Scot went for help in order to secure the fugitive.[8]

As several residents of "Brantrey" [sic] took the Indian into custody, the body of Mr. Rogers laid on the ground—lifeless and very dead. In his case, the risks inherent in the business of catching fugitives proved deadly. The entrepreneur had been a widower, "of about 43 years of age." Back home, at Pembrook, he left "three Children" behind. As his body became stiff, people throughout New England probably took a moment to reflect on the "melancholy Account" that appeared in the pages of John Draper's *Boston News-Letter*.[9] After hearing of the tragic incident regarding the bounty hunter read aloud, they likely talked about it. In public places like ordinaries or taverns, if not in the streets, they mourned. A few, perhaps most specifically those who were known for engaging in the precarious business of hunting servants and slaves, probably considered seriously the subtle message concealed in the many public warnings affixed to most advertisements for runaways.

Precarious indeed can be the business of hunting such human beings who clearly prized their freedom above all others.[10]

Days following the incident, additional details began to appear in several newspapers in New England. The *Boston News-Letter*, for example, printed a follow-up story, one that disclosed the names of the main actors of the tragedy. Before the "Superior Court" of the county of Suffolk, John Draper informed the *readers* of his newspaper, "Julian" stood on trial for the murder of "Mr. John Rogers, of Pembrook." After Mr. Scot and others (possibly even the unnamed Negro who assisted the innkeeper in apprehending the runaway) testified as to what they had witnessed about the episode involving the two men, the jury deliberated. After "Two Hours and a half," the panel of judges returned. Their verdict: Guilty.[11]

During the proceedings, Julian did not speak. He did not abject; he did not cry out in protest. He did not speak out. He did not dispute Scot's damning testimony. He did not demonstrate any sign of remorse for his actions. Instead, according to a notice that appeared in Bartholomew Green and John Boydell's *Boston Gazette*, the Indian man's appeared well "behav'd with undaunted Courage." Stoic had been his demeanor. Still was his countenance.

All of that changed, however, when Julian heard his sentence. In addition to announcing a verdict of guilty for the crime of murder, the jury pronounced judgment on the Native American man. Because he had taken a life, they decided that his actions had warranted that he be put to death. Upon hearing this sentence, Julian's steely resolve turned. After the words of the jury sunk in, he fainted. Eventually, he would confess and become "very penitent."[12]

The *Weekly Rehearsal*'s account of the trial differed from the one offered by the *Boston Gazette*. While Julian did in fact faint at the end of the proceedings, the Indian man did attempt to defend himself against the charge made against him. Before those who attended the court scene, he rebutted Scott's testimony. He presented for the jury a different account of the incident that occurred that September afternoon. Mr. Scot, Julian reminded his judges, had testified that before stabbing Rogers, that he, the defendant, had threatened the man with the knife beforehand. What is more, when he stabbed the man, he refused to let go of the blade. The wound was, in the words of the innkeeper, "very deep and open." Only after tussling with the Indian had Scot and the Negro been able to take the knife, bent in the scuffle, away from the hands of the strong and determined man. To this dramatic characterization of the final moments that led to Mr. Rogers's death, Julian objected. He denounced Scot's account as hyperbole. Indeed, by his account, it did not happen in that way. Before he left the inn, he explained to the jurors, while Rogers tried to get himself a drink, he did in fact come across a knife. He put the open blade in his pocket. He intended to use it to *maintain* his freedom, if not to secure some form of sustenance during his sojourner. To the cornfield, he made his way. But before he could get there, Rogers threw him down and with such force that Rogers himself inadvertently fell upon the escaping fugitive. It was during that moment when the blade, open and in Julian's "Jacket Pocket," entered Rogers's chest and ended the bounty hunter's life. Contrary to the testimony given in court by Mr. Scot, Julian insisted, Rogers lost his life as the result of an unfortunate accident. Instead of a verdict of guilty, he pleaded with the jurors, that they find him "not Guilty." Julian hoped for the Wisdom of Solomon.[13]

After the Native American man rested his defense in the proceedings, the jury adjourned to consider the case. As the Indian waited in the county jail to hear his sentence, they deliberated. They reviewed the testimony of all of the witnesses. They pondered the somber account made by the defendant himself. But at the end of discussions, they still found the Indian guilty of murder, and hanging as a suitable punishment.[14]

After Julian fainted, after he recovered himself, after he had been carried back to his jail cell, he likely requested the *benefit of clergy*. The benefit of clergy is a special provision in which the defendant in capital crime cases pleads with the court for leniency—a pardon to escape execution. In a last ditch effort to save his life, he asked that the jury consider his case an exceptional one. In that request, Julian did not try to absolve himself of the act of killing Rogers. Instead, he might have asked the jurors to consider the unusual way in which he insisted the Pembrook resident lost his life and grant him clemency. The finality of execution, he thought, was too extreme a punishment, because he did not assault the man. Rather Rogers's death had been the result of mishap, a horrible accident.[15]

The court did not concur. They refused his request. Perhaps drawing upon their religious convictions, they thought an eye for an eye fair. Because he had "confessed the whole Matter, which agreed *exactly* with what the Witness had deposed against him," that is, that the bounty hunter died in the process of trying to secure his person, the court held fast to their verdict of death. The question of the open blade in Julian's possession might have played some part in their decision. His race might have played a part in their decision as well.[16]

As death weighed heavy on his mind, before the administration of his execution, Julian asked to speak to a priest. The afternoon following his sentence, the townsfolk allowed the Indian the benefit of attending church. The first minister he went to hear was Reverend Byles. On that particular occasion, the New England minister used the Indian's unfortunate story and a passage from Psalms to address not only his congregation, but also to offer consolation to the condemned man. In the fifty-first chapter, fourteenth verse, "Deliver me from bloodguiltiness, O God, thou God of my salvation: *and* my tongue shall sing aloud of thy righteousness," Byles entertained the members of his church with a message of mercy and redemption. Using David's plea with God to show him forgiveness for his transgressions as the model of his sermon, the Congregationalist preacher offered the Indian absolution. Like David, Byles advised Julian to seek salvation by demonstrating contrition and by beseeching God for clemency in the next life. The "next Lord's Day" the residents of Suffolk County allowed the death row inmate to hear two sermons by "Rev. Mr. Chickley." In the forenoon, the minister recounted the story of Cain and Abel. In the afternoon, he preached from the Book of Isaiah. At his "Meeting House," Chickley used the first chapter, eighteenth verse of the King James Bible to reassure the Indian man that salvation and restoration would be his if he repented and trusted in God. According to several accounts that appeared in the newspapers, the Native American appeared in church "very penitent." At Rev. Dr. Coleman's church in Brattle Street, he sat in attendance and listened to a sermon based on the Gospel of Luke, chapter twenty-three, verse forty-three, in which Jesus offered a condemned man, during the very moment of his own crucifixion and transformation, Grace: "Verily I say unto thee, To day shalt thou be with me in paradise."[17]

While well intended and received, neither of the sermons offered by Byles, Chickley nor Coleman succeeded in reassuring the Indian. As the hour of his execution neared, Julian became depressed. His melancholy grew. With his pleas for reprieve denied and his hopes for a pardon coming to naught, the Indian trembled in his cell as his mind turned to the impending subject of his execution. His public displays of remorse did not succeed in convincing the residents of the local community to reconsider mercy. Instead, despite "all the unwearied Pains taken with him by the Reverend Ministers of the Town," the people of Suffolk were not moved to grant the man a stay. Quite the opposite; they demanded justice, and justice meant death—a life for a life. Having exhausted every possible avenue to save his own life, the New England felon called for the Rev. Mr. Byles and asked him "to instruct him and pray with him at the Place of [his] Execution." The minister complied.[18]

Before being put to death, the condemned man also requested of his jailer a quill, ink, and paper that would be sufficient for him to share his life story for the benefit of the living. In his cell, he sat. He reflected. He wrote. He revised. Ultimately, he committed the following account of his life:

> "From my Childhood to Twenty Years of Age, I liv'd in a Family where I was learnt to Read and say my Catechism, and had a great deal of Pains taken with me.—And in my younger Years I was under some Convictions and Awakenings, and concern'd about the Condition of my Soul;—and I had many Warnings in the Providence of God to turn from my Sins—But I have (and I desire to lament it) abused God's Patience and Goddness to me, and apostatised

from God and good Beginnings, and now I have forsaken God, he has forsaken me, and I acknowledge he has been just in leaving me, so that I have gone from bad to worse, till for my Sins I am now to die.

Whereas I have been charged with and tried for burning my Master's Barn, I now declare as a dying Man that I did not do it, nor was I any way privy to it.

I acknowledge I deserve to die, and would confess especially my Drunkeness and Sabbath-breaking, which have led me to this great Sin, for which I now die.

I desire therefore that all, and especially Servants, would take Warning by me; I am a dying Man, just going to leave this World, and the Thoughts of it terrify me, knowing how unfit I am to appear before my Judge.

O beware of sinning as I have done.—Beware of Drunkenness, of Sabbath-breaking, and of running away from your Masters, and don't put away the Thoughts of Death and Judgment: I once put these Things far away, but now they are near. And I am going to appear before my great and terrible Judge, which surprizeth me beyond what I am able to express.

If you have been Instructed and catechized from your Childhood, and joined your selves to Assemblies in which the Lord Jesus Christ is most purely worshipped, then let me warn and charge you to beware of casting off the Things that are good, lest God leave you to your selves, and you go in Sin till you come to the greatest Wickedness.

O take Warning by me all of you, I intreat you—See and fear and do no more so wickedly as I have done.

O let me once more intreat you all, especially Servants, as beware of the Sin of Drunkenness, and be obedient to your Masters; don't run away from them, nor get Drunk, for if you do it will bring you to Harme as it has done me.

I call to you now as one come from the Dead, to turn from your evil Ways while you have time, and not put off your Repentance to another Day, lest you then call and Good will not answer you.

My Master often told me that my Sins would bring me to this, but I little thought that it would be so.

I return my hearty Thanks to the Rev. Ministers who have taken Pains to assist me in preparing for my latter End. And as I desire to be forgiven, so I forgive all Mankind.

These Things declare freely and voluntarily, and desire Mr. Fleet to Print the same for the Benefit of the Living: And I do hereby utterly disown and disclaim all other Speeches, Papers or Declarations that may be printed in my Name, as Witness my Hand this 21st of March, 1733. Julian."[19]

Not long after these pages were penned, Thomas Fleet collected Julian's papers. In his print shop, he typeset the manuscript and published the Indian's life story in his *Weekly Rehearsal*. The printer also began working on Julian's story in broadside form that he would offer, of course, for a modest fee for his work in preserving the Indian's tragic tale for the instruction of others.[20]

On March 22, 1733, four o'clock in the afternoon, Julian the Indian was executed for the murder of Mr. John Rogers of Pembrook. It was an odious day. Notwithstanding "the Severity of the Weather, occasioned by a hard Wind . . . and Snow," death seemed to loom. Before the man was hung, he talked with Reverend Byles about his impressions of Dr. Coleman's stirring sermon. In Christ's promise, he found peace. He discovered strength, forgiveness, and serenity. After their discourse, Byles walked with the convicted man to the gallows. At the base of the structure, the two men prayed—one final time. The minister took his leave of the repentant congregant. After ascending the platform, a contrite Julian turned to the spectators, who elected to brave the cold to witness the conclusion of the spectacle, and "warn'd [them to find meaning in] his untimely End." As he had explained before, in his published life story, the convicted man offered the onlookers his life story as a cautionary tale. Forsake, he reminded them, the "Sins of Drunkenness, Sabbath-breaking, rash Anger and Passion." Such behavior would only lead one down a dark path toward despair. To his fellow servants, he repeated the advice he had offered them previously. Be forewarned "against absconding from their Masters Service and keeping bad Hours." The doomed man then thanked the community's religious leaders for ministering to him. He also forgave his would-be trespassers. Before he had been "turned off into an awful Eternity," the Indian prayed in solitude. As he prayed by himself, the executives of the gallows did their part. And a little thereafter, Julian was no more.[21]

In addition to revealing a tragic tale of murder in British North America, Julian's story reveals another, one almost concealed underneath the "melancholy Account" that appeared in Thomas Fleet's *Boston News-Letter*. For in the backdrop of the "barbarous" scene in which John Rogers lost his life while attempting to apprehend a bondservant who absented himself from master is the equally tragic story about Native Americans who were made into strangers in lands they considered their ancestral homes. To be sure, before Columbus, fifty-four million lived in the Americas, reflecting hundreds, if not thousands of unique and distinct communities. Over five million lived between the Hudson Bay and the Gulf of Mexico, the Atlantic and the Pacific Oceans. Along the eastern part of the North American continent, these indigenous communities went by many names: Pequot, Delaware, Creek, Seminole, Susquehannock, Catawba, Mohawk, and Erie.[22]

But with the discovery of the New World, life for indigenous peoples would never be the same. Over the course of three centuries, Native Americans would be forcibly remade into one group of homogenized people: the Indians. As the Portuguese, the Spanish, the English, the Dutch, and the

French began to migrate to the Americas, chasing dreams of New Canaans—lands that flowed with milk and honey, Native Americans began to lose their cherished Eden. Their paradise had been lost. To make matters worse for Julian's forebearers, the discovery of the Americas brought with it "possibly the greatest demographic disaster in the history of the world."[23]

Joined by geography and circumstance, the conjoined twins of war and disease robbed North America of its original inhabitants. In the aftermath of Columbus's *discovery*, most of the indigenousness populations died precipitously from smallpox, as well as from other Old World diseases. As they bore witness to the destruction of their civilizations, several groups parlayed their resources. They formed pan-Indian confederations. In an effort to preserve their traditions, they powwowed; they settled old disputes. They found common ground with one another. Out of many, they became one. Other Indians, however, fled from the lands of their ancestors. Migrating out in all directions, they sought refuge elsewhere. Some assimilated. Increasingly, most adopted the technology, values, and customs of their new landlords as a way to fight back, as a means to prevent their destruction.[24]

Between the seventeenth and eighteenth centuries, the numbers of Indians in North America dropped as the numbers of Europeans in the continent increased. By 1600, the indigenous population in what would later become Canada and the mainland of the United States of America declined dramatically. In the ensuing decades following the arrival of the Nina, Pinta, and the Santa Maria, less than four million Indians resided in the lands northward of the Rio Grande.[25] For much of the eighteenth century, there were barely two million Indians in the North American continent. By the advent of the 1800, that number continued to fall. Not long after the Shawnee, the Delaware, the Ohio, the Michigan, the Indiana, the Illinois, and the Wisconsin peoples signed the Treaty of Greenville in 1795, under one million Native Americans resided within the borders of the mainland of the United States.[26]

As these social, cultural, and geopolitical currents crashed against the uneven rocks of the new republic, Native Americans like Julian found themselves not only outnumbered, but also lost in a world in which the memories of their indigenousness traditions were rapidly fading away. Like the four winds, the names of America's first inhabitants faded: Ahone, Okee, Blackfoot, Abenakiand, Hahgwehdiyu, and Cautantowwit. So that they might remember, so that they might remain close to the lands of their forefathers and to the bodies of their honored dead, some Indians married Europeans. Some even married persons of African descent.

Reduced to being strangers in their own lands, other Native Americans adopted Christianity as their new religion. As the names of their Gods seemed to disappear, one of the first ways in which Indians demonstrate their new faith was by taking on names foreign to their culture and their birthright. In their awareness of the politics in which names signify not only power, but also social and cultural currency, indigenous men took names like John, Thomas, Isaac, and Peter. As they became Christians, the names of their ancestors were no longer considered prudent. Waning were names like Calian, Anakin, Alo, and Dakota. In order to survive the complete eradication of their culture, Native American women also adopted new names, names like Mary, Sarah, and Hannah.

This embrace of the white man's magic, however, was not in total. Native American culture persisted. They did not forget, at least not in full, who they once were. Their appropriation of the *religions* of the Old World did not mark the end of their indigenous ways. Rather, as it had been the case with other peoples who had been colonized, Christendom, as it had been revealed to them, with its pantheon of heralded figures and patriarchs and their parables, offered the indigenous people of North America an opportunity to maintain the ideas and the beliefs of their forefathers. The Great Spirit, for example, lived on in the form of Yahweh. Like Joseph's coat of many colors, their beatific visions of the world that existed beyond the horizon of the living differed from that of the colonizers in that theirs included men and women who looked like them. Moreover, when Jehovah spoke, the God of the Old and the New Testament spoke not in a language they considered foreign or strange. Instead, when He spoke, the great "I am" spoke in the language of their people: the Powhatan, the Wampanoag, the Cayuga, the Tuscarora, the Pawnee, the Honniasont, the Massachusetts, and the other ethnic groups who believed North America their ancestral homelands.[27]

As early as the 1660s, this reimagining of Protestantism would be reinforced by the bilingual publication of John Eliot's Indian Bible, his *Indian Primer, Or, The Way of training up of our Indian Youth in the good Knowledge of the Scriptures and in an ability to Reade*, and other instructional texts. In the minds of many Indians, for example, the printing of the Anglican Book of Common Prayer in both English and in the language of the Mohawk only confirmed their reinterpretation of Christianity. Throughout the colonial period, the efforts made by groups like the Society for the Propagation of the Gospel in Foreign Parts encouraged further this process of *scripturalization*. By learning something of the indigenous peoples' language and culture, as a part of a larger plan to establish schools to convert Indians, these societies, that advocated biblical literacy, unwittingly provided Native Americans with the tools to maintain parts of their indigenous ways of life at the very moment when the tide seemed to have turned against them. Like their enslaved, black neighbors, they read the Bible and remade the Christian faith in their own image. In his effort to appeal to the jurors of the superior court of Suffolk and to the residents of the local New England community for leniency, Julian embodied this bold reinterpretation of the scriptures. Because "God is no respecter of persons," he fought for his life, not as an Indian, but as a man. In court, he demanded justice. In God's impartiality, Julian found inspiration. He defended himself. He vindicated his unintended actions on that September day. "Ye shall not respect persons in judgment; but ye shall hear the small as well as the great; ye shall not be afraid of the face of man; for the judgment is God's: and the cause that is too hard for you, bring it unto me, and I will hear it." Despite the convictions of the court that he belonged to a "sinful" and "wicked Race," Julian stood upright before his judges. He dared to see himself as the equal to any man.[28]

His unsuccessful cry for mercy notwithstanding, Julian's story also highlights the calamity that had been Native American bondage in the land of their forebearers. Before indentured servants and African slaves were brought to the New World, Indians were seen, by their Old World interlopers, as inferiors. Caught somewhere between servitude and slavery, the Indian man, and likewise his people, were systematically reduced to a state of social death within their own homelands. Marked first by their color, second by their ethnicity, they were considered strange and alien in the lands of their birth.[29] Before European children were spirited away, before poor, unsuspectingly adults who filled the streets of the Old World were lured away across the Atlantic by promises of land or the opportunity to start life anew, Native Americans were condemned for *being*. Before Africans were violently transported in loose and tight packed vessels destined for the New World, indigenous peoples in North America were made into a captive people whose captive status would be used to justify their annihilation. The extant records regarding Julian's life captured this unique story. In the extant court documents, newspaper accounts, and half penny broadsides about the awful incident in which the Native American man killed another emerges two tales in which Indian bodies and minds were colonized.[30]

By his own account, Julian had been made into an Indian. At an early age "to Twenty Years of Age," he explained, he had been taken in by a New England family who "learnt [him] to Read and say [the] Catechism." For a time, they considered him a fictive member of their family. Within the larger Massachusetts community in which he lived, he became their kin. Before reaching the age of his majority, he learned how to read the Bible. Not long after he learned to read, he began to study the Church's catechisms. He learned the governing tenants of Protestantism through the Book of Common Prayer. Like other catechists, he memorized his lessons before he learned to read. When asked, for example, "What is thy duty towards thy Neighbour," Julian learned the proper reply. "To honour, and obey the King. . . . To submit myself to all my governors, teachers, spiritual pastors and masters. To order myself lowly and reverently to all my betters . . . and to do my duty in that state of life, unto which it shall please God to call me." As a result, after receiving these lessons, over the course of his "younger Years," the Native American man grew increasingly concerned about the "Condition of [his] Soul." In this way, Julian started his journey toward becoming a Christian and an Indian.[31]

In that transformation, literacy played an important role. Because if writing restructures consciousness, as Walter Ong and other Book historians have suggested, reading prepared Julian's young mind for the radical process of being transmuted from an Amerindian into a noble savage. Through the act of learning his letters and eventually learning to read, he became aware of distant places. As he discerned his ABCs, nouns, verbs, and adjectives, he became exposed to disparate ideas and beliefs. Through reading Julian acquired knowledge; he gained information, information that he, in turn, weighed and evaluated. What is more, with this introduction to a world on paper, Julian came to see himself and his people as being different. Consequently, whether intentionally or not, the mind of the Native American man had been refashioned and in terms that were not necessarily his own.

To be certain, reading involves a complex process of naming, identifying, categorizing, and conceptualizing life into a series of useful texts. While he learned of the biblical story of Genesis, where Adam had been given the task of naming all of the things in Yahweh's Creation, or as it had been described in one of the broadsides about Julian—God's "good Beginnings," the Native American man also learned how literacy played an essential role in bringing order to what appeared to be an otherwise unstructured cosmos. In other words, in the act of naming the various aspects of the physical manifestations of God's thoughts turned into utterances, Adam achieved dominion; he attained stewardship over the Earth. In time, with the publication of the Bible, the descendants of the father of mankind, millenniums later, realized agency. For reading signified at once knowledge and comprehension. The act of writing would transform that knowledge into power or at the very least the inability to perceive the worlds revealed in print beyond the sacredness of words set in black and white.[32]

At the beginning of Julian's transformation, the indigenous youth rejected the efforts of those who wished to convert him. Of his New England family, he explained, "a great deal of Pains taken with me." Perhaps sensing that his introduction to Christianity threatened the beliefs, traditions, and practices of his indigenous ancestors, Julian might have resisted learning to read. If not but for a short time, he might have tried to hold on to the beliefs of forefathers. He may have sought to preserve something from his Native American parents—possibly the rudiments of the language of his native people. In this manner, Julian elected to remember them. He might have fought against the eventuality of setting aside, if not forgetting his indigenous past. Consequently, other historical accounts confirm this, demonstrating how other Native peoples, who were brought, sold, and adopted, managed to maintain aspects of their previous lives.[33]

Sometime before his twentieth birthday, however, Julian relented. He yielded to the instructions he received. He discovered God and turned from his "Sins." He turned from his native past. During that revelation, he learned not only how to read and say the catechism, but also how to write. He became an eighteenth-century exemplar of a Praying Indian. As a confirmation of his new found faith, he probably put on the clothes of those who introduced him to Christianity. Rebuked were the garments that reflected native heritage—the apparel of his former savagery and barbarism. Censured were the feathers, the buckskins, the moccasins, the embroidered bracelets and belts. Admonished were those articles that honored the Indian family or race or paid homage to the indigenousness past and what seemed to most New Englanders strange practices, antithetical to "the Christian Faith." In the place of those symbols of his Indian past, Julian took on the dress of his Christian teachers.

To demonstrate his new faith, he wore a castor, if not a felt type of hat. He sported a colored jacket and possibly an undercoat. Like most New Englanders, he probably wore a cotton or a linen shirt, a pair of leather breeches, yarned stockings, and round or square toed shoes or boots. Among his native people, these new articles of clothing signified his loss of position. They signified both real and imagined symbols of his transformation into a thing.[34]

Gone also was his native name that likely signified much in a few words. In its place, the young man accepted the name Julian. With his new name, his former self died. In the Latin tongue, the name Julian is derived from Iulianus or Julius, the name of a prominent family in ancient Rome. It is also a name associated with Jove. In Roman mythology, Jove had been the god of the sky and of thunder. Prior to the emergence of the Roman Empire, the name had been an alternative designation for Jupiter (i.e., Zeus): the "Father of gods and men." In English, however, the name Julian came to mean youthful or downy. In the context of colonial American slavery and bondage, it represented a classical name. Derogatory in its intent, it was a name that could be given to either a boy or a girl. Not discounting the exact nature of its origins, its etymology, Julian's new name embodied his conversion. It reflected his transformation into an Indian.[35]

Much like his seventeen-century predecessors, and possibly to his own dismay, the Praying Indian man learned that, despite the sincerity of his conversion, not all Christians were treated alike, and that he did not like that particular distinction. While it is uncertain if he would have preferred the systems of bondage practiced among his indigenousness people, one thing is clear: vehemently, he did not care for bondage by any name. Like the Ancient Israelites in the Old Testament, his preference had been for deliverance from his modern Egyptians. He longed for the prerogative of calling himself his own master. In spite of his best efforts, however, the disillusioned Indian struggled to observe the Apostle Paul's instructions in the New Testament to "obey in all things your masters." Confronted with the absurdity of their conduct with respect to how they treated Native Americans and others of his "Race," he judged their words and actions diametrically opposite to one another.[36]

Not surprisingly, before he killed John Rogers for the act of coveting his freedom for profit, Julian proved an unruly bondservant. Unhappy with the state of his life as a servant, he turned to drinking. He became a drunkard. At the bottom of the bottle, he sought refuge. He tried drowning his sorrows but to no avail. Purportedly, the strong liquors were not enough to erase the knowledge of his captivity. Instead, the spirits might have heightened further his awareness of his condition. As his melancholy grew, he turned away from the church. Once a devout Christian, one who attended service regularly, Julian broke the Sabbath. By his own account, he broke the day of religious observance and abstinence repeatedly. He lost confidence in his master's administration of religion. "I have forsaken God," he wrote in his own hand, and "he has forsaken me." As he struggled to reconcile his Christian faith with the harsh realities of his life, the bounded or enslaved Indian found little in the way of consolation with what might have seemed the church's contradictory, if not conflicting messages of brotherhood and bondage, universal amity and veracious xenophobia. Confronting these dueling expressions of religiosity from his fellow Christians, particularly those with lighter hues who considered Native Americans a "sinful" and "wicked Race," the Indian man protested his plight with his feet and ran away. Extant documents suggest that he might have run away on several occasions. In one particular instance, he might have even engaged in act of day-to-day resistance by destroying the property of one of his two masters. Not long after he had converted to Protestantism, he noted, he had been charged with and tried "for burning" his "Master's Barn." Despite his claim that he had nothing to do with the act of arson, that bold action probably explains why the Native American man might have been made the subject of two different owners. That is, before his death, Julian proved to be hard to govern.[37]

After his execution, the Indian man's troubles continued. They followed him to his grave. In both life and in death, the Indian had been thought a socially dead person. After his body had been removed from the gallows, the *Weekly Rehearsal* reported, the "Physicians of the Town" took possession of Julian. For two full days, they studied its lifeless form. For two full days, they "busily" dissected it for benefit of the "young Students in Physick and natural Philosophy." It is "remarkable," they reported, "altho he had lain in Prison above Six Months," he was well maintained during the time of his imprisonment. Impressed with the physical condition of the body of the Indian man, the physicians extoled Julian's jailers: The "Praise of his Keeper be is spoken," they noted. As they "Anatomize" Julian, one doctor recalled how he "cut at least two Inches thick of Fat on the Breast, and much thicker on the Belly." He was a fit specimen for their purposes. At the end of the autopsy, after the Indian's organs were removed and his flesh had been detached of its frame, the "Bones" of the executed man were "preserv'd, in order to be fram'd into a Skeleton." And with that notice, that appeared in the *Boston News-Letter*, the story of Julian, the bondservant, the slave, the runaway, the fugitive, the murderer, the felon, the Praying Indian came to a close.[38]

While his is a story that is unique, it is not an unusual one. Far from it. While no extant advertisement for his apprehension appears to have survived the vestiges of time, indeed it might have disappeared when Rogers removed the notice from the bulletin, what has endured in the pages of early American newspapers, the extant court records, and in broadsides are nonetheless representative of the complex narratives of Native American peoples who, like Julian, boldly protested bondage with their feet. In the volume that follows are their life stories, the stories of hundreds of Indians who proved steadfast in their dogged determination to be their own masters. Like Julian, they too rejected the terms of their incarceration in the lands that once belonged to their forebearers. In that peculiar context, their stories, stories of absconding servants, deserters, and slaves of Amerindian descent are seemingly incomparable. Hostage in the lands of their birth, nothing short of social death captures the enormity of the tragedy they experienced.

NOTES

1. Slave-poet laureate of Boston, Phillis Wheatley to Samson Occom, Mohican, Minister of Brothertown, and Indian missionary. *The Connecticut Gazette*, March 11, 1774. The correspondence between the two had been part of a larger discussion regarding the questionable piety of white Christians in early America. Neither Wheatley nor Occom believed them truly sincere in their work among the dispossessed. For a fuller account of Phillis Wheatley, see William H. Robinson. *Phillis Wheatley and Her Writing* (New York: Garland, 1984); Vincent Carretta, *Phillis Wheatley: Biography of a Genius in Bondage* (Athens: University of Georgia Press, 2011). For a fuller account of the Occom and the Brothertown Indians, see Brad D. E. Jarvis. *The Brothertown Nation of Indians: Land Ownership and Nationalism in Early America, 1740–1840* (Lincoln: University of Nebraska Press, 2010); Craig N. Cipolla. *Becoming Brothertown: Native American Ethnogenesis and Endurance in the Modern World* (Tuscan: University of Arizona Press, 2013); David J. Silverman. *Red Brethren: The Brothertown and Stockbridge Indians and the Problem of Race in Early America* (Ithaca: Cornell University Press, 2015).

xxvi *Introduction*

2. New Englanders often used the terms slaves and servants interchangeably, making ultimately the question of the status of bound people seemingly nuanced. Within the context of bondage in eighteenth-century Massachusetts, Rhode Island, Connecticut, and New Hampshire, both were nonetheless thought conditions of social death. Julian's story, for example, the story that is central to this introduction of Native American slavery, embodies this complexity. In some instances, in other extant records, he is referenced as a servant; in other instances, a slave. On one occasion, he is described as a Negro. See Appendix F. For a comprehensive account of the natal alienation, most, if not all, servants and slaves endured, see Lorenzo Greene, *The Negro in Colonial New England, 1620–1776* (New York: Columbia University Press, 1942), 124–143. Also, for a useful account of social death in eighteenth-century New England, see Appendix B.

3. This account regarding the fugitive's life is based primarily on the "melancholy Account of a barbarous Murder" that appeared in the *Boston News-Letter* and the subsequent notices that appeared in New England newspapers. For a fuller account of Julian's life story, see Appendices C, D, E, and F.

Julian has been subject to some scholarly attention. See Laura M. Stevens, *The Poor Indians: British Missionaries, Native Americans, and Colonial Sensibility* (Philadelphia: University of Pennsylvania Press, 2004); Lawrence W. Towner, *Past Imperfect: Essays on History, Libraries, and the Humanities* (Chicago: University of Chicago Press, 1993); and, Katherine Grandjean, "'Our Fellow-Creatures & our Fellow-Christians': Race and Religion in Eighteenth-Century Narratives of Indian Crime" *American Quarterly* 62.4 (December 2010): 925–950.

Julian might have had three masters. One of the broadsides about his tragic life story indicates that the Native American man had been sold to a New England family at age three. In the absence of the name of that New England family, it is possible that the Indian may have been the property of three masters. *Boston News-Letter*, September 14, 1732. Thomas Fleet. *Advice from the Dead to the Living; OR A Solemn Warning to the World. Occasioned by the untimely Death of poor Julian.* Boston: Thomas Fleet, 1733. Boston Public Library.

In his seminal study of slavery over time and space, Orlando Patterson identifies five symbolic instruments of a socially dead person's deracination. By way of an individual's name, clothing, hair, language, and religion, natal alienation of the enslaved is achieved. In Julian's case, all of these characteristics of social death are on full display. Patterson, *Slavery and Social Death: A Comparative Study* (Cambridge: Harvard University Press, 1982), 1–17; 35–76.

4. In the broadside, *Advice from the Dead to the Living; OR A Solemn Warning to the World. Occasioned by the untimely Death of poor Julian*, the lines, "By his Account he first was sold, When he was not quite three Years old," suggest that the Indian might have been a slave. By contrast, extant court documents suggest that his status in New England is inconclusive. See Appendix F.

Incidentally, Julian's *first* master was John Quincy (July 21, 1689–July 13, 1767), an influential New England politician. Between 1717 and 1740, he served as the Braintree representative of the Massachusetts General Court. From 1729 to 1741, he served as the Speaker of the Massachusetts House of Representatives. In the military, he achieved the rank of Major in the British Army. Julian's *second* master, Thomas Howard, sometimes spelled Hayward, was also a grandee in his own right. Like Quincy, Hayward had been a member of a prominent New England family. His father, for example, was one of the founding fathers of the town of Bridgewater.

5. According to the notice that recounted Julian's story, Roger took the advertisement with him which suggests that it might have been a manuscript notice. No extant advertisement of Julian's flight has yet discovered in the newspapers. *Boston News-Letter*, September 14, 1732.

6. *Boston News-Letter*, September 14, 1732.

7. Ibid.

8. Ibid. Because the black man, who assisted Mr. Scot, is not identified in the extant newspaper accounts, his status is unclear.

9. A month later, the story also appeared in a Pennsylvania newspaper: *American Weekly Mercury*, October 12 1732.

10. *Boston News-Letter*, September 14, 1732.

11. *Boston News-Letter*, February 22, 1733.

12. *Boston Gazette*, February 26, 1733; *New England Weekly Journal*, February 26, 1733; *Weekly Rehearsal*, February 26, 1733; *Rhode Island Gazette*, March 1, 1733.

13. Extant court records suggest that the wound Julian inflicted on Rogers had been 3 inches in depth and 1 inch in width. See Appendix F.

14. *Weekly Rehearsal*, February 26, 1733.

15. Daniel R. Coquillette, Robert J. Brink, and Catherine S. Menand, eds., *Law in Colonial Massachusetts, 1630–1800* (Boston: Colonial Society of Massachusetts, 1984), 236–239; Colonial Society of Massachusetts, *Publication of the Colonial Society of Massachusetts* (Boston: Colonial Society of Massachusetts, 1904), 332; Roger Lane, *Murder in American: A History* (Columbus: Ohio State University, 1997), 58.

16. *Weekly Rehearsal*, February 26, 1733.

17. *Weekly Rehearsal*, February 26, 1733; *Weekly Rehearsal*, March 12, 1733.

18. *New England Weekly Journal*, March 26, 1733.

19. *Weekly Rehearsal*, March 26, 1733.

20. In addition to the two broadsides printed by Thomas Fleet, B. Gray and A Butler printed a broadside memorializing the Indian's story. Unlike the two printed by Fleet, this broadside was published without Julian's consent. See Appendix C. The broadsides probably sold for a halfpenny or a penny. Patricia Fumerton, *The Broadside Ballad in Early Modern England: Moving Media, Tactical Publics* (Philadelphia: University Pennsylvania Press, 2020), 147–148.

21. *Weekly Rehearsal*, March 26, 1733; *New England Weekly Journal*, March 26, 1733.

22. Russell Thornton, *American Indian Holocaust and Survival: A Population History since 1492* (Norman: University of Oklahoma Press, 1987), 15–41; William M. Denevan, "The Pristine Myth: The Landscape of the Americas in 1492" *Annals of the Association of American Geographers* (September 1992) 82.3: 369–385.

While scholars are divided on the subject of the size of the Native American population in the New World, there is consensus on the subject of the impact of contact. Denevan, *The Native Population of the Americas in 1492*, 1–7; Alan Taylor, *American Colonies* (New York: Viking, 2001), 4.

23. Peter C. Mancall, ed., *Envisioning America: English Plans for the Colonization of North America, 1580–1640* (Boston: St. Martin's Press, 1995). For the quote, see William M. Denevan, *The Native Population of the Americas in 1492*, 2nd edition (Madison: University of Wisconsin Press, 1992), 7.

24. Michael McDonnell, *Masters of Empire: Great Lakes Indians and the Indians and Making of America* (New York: Hill and Wang, 2016); Woody Holton, *Forced Founders: Indians, Debtors, Slaves, and the Making of the American Revolution in Virginia* (Chapel Hill: University of North Carolina Press, 1999); Colin G. Calloway, *The American Revolution in Indian Country: Crisis and Diversity in Native American Communities* (Cambridge: Cambridge University Press, 1995); Taylor, 39–47; 330–350.

25. Alexander Laban Hinton, Andrew Woolford, and Jeff Benvenuto, eds., *Colonial Genocide in Indigenous North America* (Duke University Press, 2014); David E. Stannard, *American Holocaust: Columbus and the Conquest of the New World* (Oxford: Oxford University Press, 1992); Colin G. Calloway, *New World for All: Indians, Europeans, and the Remaking of Early America* (Baltimore: Johns Hopkins University Press, 1997).

26. Thornton, *American Indian Holocaust and Survival*, xvii; Wiley Sword, *President Washington's Indian War: The Struggle for the Old Northwest, 1790–1795* (Norman: University of Oklahoma Press).

27. E. Jennifer Monaghan, *Learning to Read and Write in Colonial America* (Amherst: University of Massachusetts Press, 2005), 65; Michael D. McNally. "The Practice of Native American Christianity" *Church History* 69.4 (December 2000): 834–859; Joel W. Martin and Mark A Nicholas, eds., *Native Americans, Christianity, and the Reshaping of the American Religious Landscape* (Chapel Hill: University of North Carolina Press, 2010); Linford D. Fisher, "Native Americans, Conversion, and Christian Practice in Colonial New England, 1640–1730" *The Harvard Theological Review* 102. 1 (January 2009): 101–124.

28. E. Jennifer Monaghan, *Learning to Read and Write*, chapters 5–6. Scripturalization is a complex process wherein people, across societies, time, and space, reread, reinterpret, and appropriate religious texts to communicate useful meanings about themselves and the world. For the passages from the Bible, see Deuteronomy 1: 17 and Acts 10:34. King James Version. For a fuller account about scripturalization as an articulation of resistance, agency, and culture, see Vincent L. Wimbush, *White Men's Magic: Scripturalization as Slavery* (Oxford: Oxford University Press, 2012). For the references to Julian's race, see Thomas Fleet. *Advice from the Dead to the Living; OR A Solemn Warning to the World. Occasioned by the untimely Death of poor Julian*. Boston: Thomas Fleet, 1733. Boston Public Library.

Julian defense of himself suggests that the Native American man thought himself the equal of those who tried him for the death of Rogers. To be sure, extant court records depict him as a competent man, one more than able to speak for himself and on his own behalf.

29. Thomas Fleet. *Advice from the Dead to the Living; OR A Solemn Warning to the World. Occasioned by the untimely Death of poor Julian.* Boston: Thomas Fleet, 1733. Boston Public Library; Peter C. Mancall, ed., *Envisioning America*.

30. Abbot Emerson Smith, *Colonists in Bondage: White Servitude and Convict Labor in America, 1607–1776* (Chapel Hill: University of North Carolina Press, 1947); David W. Galenson, *White Servitude in Colonial America: An Economic Analysis* (Cambridge University Press, 1981); Don Jordan and Michael Walsh, *White Cargo: The Forgotten History of Britain's White Slaves in America* (New York: New York University Press, 2007); Philip D. Curtin, *Atlantic Slave Trade: A Consensus* (Madison: University of Wisconsin Press, 1969); Sowande M Mastakeem, *Slavery at Sea: Terror, Sex, and Sickness in the Middle Passage* (Urbana: University of Illinois Press 2016).

31. [Church of England], *The Book of Common Prayer and Administration of the Sacraments & Other Rites and Ceremonies of the Church* (1662; reprint, Oxford: The University Press, 1927), 273; John Lewis, *Church catechism explained, by way of question and answer, and confirmed by Scripture proofs: divided into five parts, and twelve sections: wherein a brief and plain account is given of I. The Christian covenant. II. The Christian faith. III. The Christian obedience. IV. The Christian prayer. V. The Christian sacraments* (London: 1700; reprint, New York, James Oram, 1800), 40 & 42. Mark 12: 17 (King James Version).

According to Fleet's authorized broadside regarding Julian's life, the Indian had been adopted or enslaved at age three. While it is unclear whether or not his Indian parents maintained any type of relationship with their son, it is nonetheless possible that the Native American man had some type of connection with his native family, if not other indigenous people. Like most Indians, Julian had to be aware of the racial animosity that existed between himself and those who held him in bondage and did not look like him. References in the broadside highlight further that inescapable fact. Moreover, the woodcut included in the broadside depicted an Indian with long hair. Among native peoples, hair signifies status and culture. Early New Englanders concurred. As early as 1675, they enacted legislation that prohibited men from having long hair or using a periwig to achieve a similar effect. Such displays were considered prideful. Such displays also signified status. In 1702, New Englanders revisited the subject of periwigs and hair and passed similar legislation. In this setting, Julian's hair tells us something about him and his connection to his Native American culture. Throughout this volume, masters remarked on Indian hair as a source of pride and heritage. Fleet, *Advise from the Dead to the Living*; *The General Laws and Liberties of the Massachusetts Colony: Revised and Re-printed* (Boston, 1672), 233; *The Acts and Resolves, Public and Private, of the Province of the Massachusetts Bay* (1692–1714; Boston, 1869), 1:501; Carl Degler, *Out of Our Past: The Forces That Shaped Modern America* (New York: Harper & Row, Publishers, Inc., 1984), 9–22; Richard Godbeer, "Perversions of Anatomy, Anatomies of Perversion: The Periwig Controversy in Colonial Massachusetts" *Proceedings of the Massachusetts Historical Society* 109 (1997): 1–23.

32. Walter J. Ong, *Orality and Literacy* New York: Methuen & Company, 1982), 77–114; David R. Olson, *The World on Paper* (Cambridge: Cambridge University

Press, 1994); Peter J Rabinowitz, *Before Reading: Narrative Conventions and the Politics of interpretation* (Ithaca: Cornell University Press, 1987); Henry Louis Gates. Jr., *The Signifying Monkey: A Theory of African-American Literacy Criticism* (Oxford: Oxford University Press, 1988), chapter 4.

33. *Weekly Rehearsal*, March 26, 1733. In her study of biblical literacy in colonial America, E. Jennifer Monaghan noted, Indians, as early as the 1670s, maintained many of their indigenous practices, such as healing, powwows, and naming practices (64–65). Also, see Linford D. Fisher, "Native Americans, Conversion, and Christian Practice in Colonial New England, 1640–1730" *Harvard Theological Review* 102.1 (January 2009): 101–124; Lee Irwin, "Freedom, Law, and Prophecy: A Brief History of Native American Religious Resistance" *American Indian Quarterly* 21.1 (Winter 1997): 35–55; Douglas L. Winiarski, "Native American Popular Religion in New England's Old Colony, 1670–1770" *Religion and American Culture: A Journal of Interpretation* 15.2 (Summer 2005): 147–186; Joel W. Martin, Mark A. Nicholas, and Michelene E. Pesantubbee, Native Americans, Christianity, and the Reshaping of the American Religious Landscape (Chapel Hill: University of North Carolina Press, 2010).

34. Fleet, *Advice from the Dead to the Living*; Patterson, *Slavery and Social Death*, 55–59. For a useful analysis of how conversion signified social death, see John Eliot and Kenneth M. Morrison, "'That Art of Coyning Chrisitians': John Eliot and the Praying Indians of Massachusetts" *Ethnohistory* 21.1 (Winter 1974): 77–92.

35. Mary Ann Dwight, *Grecian and Roman Mythology*, 3rd edition (New York: A.S. Barnes & Burr, 1864), 114; Mike Dixon-Kennedy, *Encyclopedia of Greco-Roman Mythology* (Santa Barbara: ABC-CLIO, 1998), 181.

36. Alan Gallay, *Indian Slavery in Colonial America*, Illustrated edition (Lincoln: University of Nebraska Press, 2015); Alan Gallay, *The Indian Slave Trade: The Rise of the English Empire in the American South, 1670–1717* (New Haven: Yale University Press, 2002); Christina Snyder, *Slavery in Indian Country: The Changing Face of Captivity in Early America* (Cambridge: Harvard University Press, 2010); Jared Ross Hardesty, *Black Lives, Native Lands, White World: A History of Slavery in New England* (Amherst: University of Massachusetts Press, 2019), chapters 2 and 3. For a useful account of the Praying Indians and the praying towns, see Kenneth Lockridge, *A New England Town* (New York: W.W. Norton & Company, 1985); Kathryn N. Gray, *John Eliot and the Praying Indians of Massachusetts Bay: Communities and Connection in Puritan New England* (Lanham: Bucknell University Press, 2013); Richard W. Cogley, *John Eliot's Mission to the Indians before King Philip's War* (Cambridge: Harvard University Press, 1999). For the reference to the Old and New Testament, see Exodus 1–13: 3 and Colossians 3:22–24 King James Version.

37. *Weekly Rehearsal*, March 26, 1733.

The extant records regarding Julian's story suggest that the Native was born sometime around 1700. By the time he had reached the age of twenty, he was probably aware of the ill treatment converted natives received at the hands of their white benefactors. One of the extant broadsides characterized Native Americans as a "sinful" and "wicked" Race. For a fuller account of the Praying Indians, Praying Towns, and their treatment, see Lockridge, *A New England Town*. For a fuller explanation of day-to-day resistance, see Raymond A Bauer and Alice H. Bauer, "Day to Day Resistance to Slavery" *Journal of Negro History* 27.4 (October 1942): 388–419. Here, I would also like to acknowledge my debt to Phillis Wheatley whose letter to Samson Occom informed this part of my reconstruction of Julian. *Connecticut Gazette*, March 11, 1774. For the references regarding Julian's "Race," see Fleet's *Advice from the Dead to the Living* broadside.

Julian and a Negro named Jeffery were suspected of arson. While the Indian would eventually be cleared of the charge of burning the Barn, Appendix F reveals nonetheless an interesting story regarding the incident. Incidentally, the two men were suspected of having burnt more than just one barn.

38. *Weekly Rehearsal*, March 26, 1733; *Boston News-Letter*, March 30, 1733.

A Note on the Notices

The original wording, spelling, punctuation, and capitalization of the advertisements have been maintained. The original vernacular, that is the use of the word "Indian" or occasionally the word "Negro," was also retained. Only modest alterations were made to the original text. Illegible words are indicated by bracket, as are letters added for clarity. A glossary has been included to define many of the contemporary terms that appear in the notices.

The notices are printed chronologically and by region. Reprints and variants are noted at the end of each notice.

While I have tried to be both thorough and diligent in documenting all of the notices, I would remiss if I did not acknowledge the possibility of human error.

A Note on Newspapers

In the creation of this documentary history of fugitive Native Americans who absconded from their masters between 1700 and 1789, all of the extant copies of colonial newspapers on microfilm at the Library of Congress and the Readex, America's Historical Newspapers database, were consulted. If the newspapers enumerated below were printed by different printers over time in newspapers that shared the same names, those versions are indicated by the date ranges that follow the name of the newspaper in the list below.

All of the newspapers consulted are listed alphabetically by colony and by the name of the paper.

LIST OF NEWSPAPERS

Connecticut

- American Mercury, 1784–1789.
- Connecticut Courant, 1764–1789.
- Connecticut Gazette, 1763–1789, 1755–1767.
- Connecticut Journal, 1767–1789.
- Fairfield Gazette, 1786–1789.
- Litchfield Monitor, 1784–1789.
- Middlesex Gazette, 1785–1789.
- New-Haven Chronicle, 1786–1789.
- New-Haven Gazette, 1784–1786.
- New-Haven Gazette, and Connecticut Magazine, 1786–1789.
- New-London Summary, 1758–1763.
- Norwich Packet, 1773–1789.

Delaware

- Delaware Gazette, 1785–1789.

Georgia

- Gazette of the State of Georgia, 1783.
- Georgia Gazette, 1763–1770.
- Royal Georgia Gazette, 1788–1789.

Massachusetts

- American Gazette, or, the Constitutional Journal, 1776.
- American Herald, 1784.
- American Herald and the Worcester Recorder, 1788–1789.
- American Recorder, 1785–1787.
- Berkshire Chronicle, 1788–1789.
- Boston Chronicle, 1767–1770.
- Boston Evening-Post, 1735–1775.
- Boston Evening-Post and the General Advertiser, 1781–1784.
- Boston Gazette, 1719–1789.
- Boston News-Letter, 1704–1776.
- Boston Post-Boy, 1735–1775.
- Censor, 1771–1772.
- Continental Journal, and Weekly Advertiser
- Courier de Boston, 1789.
- Essex Gazette, 1768–1775.
- Essex Journal, 1784–1789, 1773–1777.
- Hampshire Chronicle, 1787–1789.
- Hampshire Gazette, 1786–1789.
- Hampshire Herald, 1784–1786.
- Herald of Freedom, 1788–1789.
- Independent Chronicle, 1776–1789.
- Independent Ledger, 1778–1786.
- Massachusetts Centinel, 1784–1789.
- Massachusetts Gazette, 1785–1788.
- Massachusetts Spy, 1775–1789, 1770–1775
- New England Chronicle, or Essex Gazette, 1775–1776.
- New-England Chronicle, 1776.
- New-England Courant, 1721–1726.
- New-England Weekly Journal, 1727–1741.
- Plymouth Journal, and the Massachusetts Advertiser, 1785–1786.

A Note on Newspapers

- Publick Occurrences, 1690.
- Salem Chronicle, and Essex Advertiser, 1786.
- Salem Gazette, 1781–1785.
- Salem Mercury, 1786–1789.
- Weekly Rehearsal, 1731–1735.
- Western Star, 1789.

New Hampshire

- Exeter Journal, 1778–1779.
- Freeman's Journal, 1776–1778.
- Freeman's Oracle, and New-Hampshire Advertiser, 1786–1789.
- New-Hampshire Gazette, 1756–1789.
- New-Hampshire Mercury and General Advertiser, 1784–1788.
- New-Hampshire Recorder, 1787–1789.
- New-Hampshire Spy, 1786–1789.
- New Hampshire Gazetteer, 1789.

New Jersey

- New-Jersey Gazette, 1778–1786, 1777–1778.
- New-Jersey Journal, 1786–1789.
- Political Intelligencer, 1783–1785.
- Political Intelligencer and New-Jersey Advertiser, 1785–1786.

New York

- Albany Gazette, 1788–1789.
- Albany Journal, or, the Montgomery, Washington and Columbia Intelligencer, 1788–1789.
- Albany Register, 1789.
- Constitutional Gazette, 1775–1776.
- Country Journal, 1785–1789.
- Daily Advertiser, 1785–1789.
- Gazette of the United States, 1789.
- Impartial Gazetteer, and Saturday Evening's Post, 1788.
- Independent Gazette, 1783–1784.
- Independent Journal, 1783–1788.
- Independent New-York Gazette, 1783.
- Independent Reflector, 1752–1753.
- New-York Chronicle, 1769–1770.
- New-York Daily Gazette, 1788–1789.

- New-York Evening Post, 1744–1752.
- New-York Gazette, 1759–1767.
- New-York Gazette, and Weekly Mercury, 1768–1783.
- New-York Gazette, or Weekly Post-Boy, 1747–1770.
- New-York Gazetteer, or, Northern Intelligencer, 1782–1784.
- New-York Journal, 1766–1776, 1784–1789.
- New-York Mercury, 1752–1768.
- New-York Morning Post, 1783–1789.
- New-York Packet, 1783–1789.
- New-York Weekly Journal, 1733–1750.
- Poughkeepsie Journal, 1789.
- Rivington's New York Gazetteer, 1773–1775.
- Rivington's New-York Gazette, and Universal Advertiser, 1783.
- Rivington's New-York Loyal Gazette, 1777.
- Royal American Gazette, 1777–1783.
- Royal Gazette, 1777–1783.
- Weekly Museum, 1788–1789.

North Carolina

- State Gazette of North Carolina, 1787–1788.

Pennsylvania

- American Weekly Mercury, 1719–1746.
- Carlisle Gazette, 1785–1789.
- Federal Gazette, 1788–1789.
- Freeman's Journal; or, the North-American Intelligencer, 1781–1789.
- Germantowner Zeitung, 1763–1777.
- Independent Gazetteer, 1782–1789.
- Neue Unpartheyische Lancaster Zeitung, 1787–1789.
- Pennsylvania Chronicle, 1767–1774.
- Pennsylvania Evening Herald, 1785–1788.
- Pennsylvania Evening Post, 1775–1784.
- Pennsylvania Gazette, 1736–1775.
- Pennsylvania Journal, or, Weekly Advertiser, 1742–1789.
- Pennsylvania Ledger: or the Virginia, Maryland, Pennsylvania, and New-Jersey Weekly Advertiser, 1775–1778.
- Pennsylvania Mercury, and Universal Advertiser, 1784–1789.
- Pennsylvania Packet, 1771–1778, 1777–1778.
- Pennsylvanische Fama, 1750.
- Royal Pennsylvania Gazette, 1778.

- Story and Humphreys's Pennsylvania Mercury, 1775.
- Wochentliche Philadelphische Staatsbote, 1762–1779.

Rhode Island

- American Journal and General Advertiser, 1779–1781.
- Gazette Francoise, 1780–1781.
- Newport Gazette, 1777.
- Newport Herald, 1787–1789.
- Newport Mercury, 1758–1789.
- Providence Gazette, 1762–1789.
- Rhode-Island Gazette, 1732–1733.
- United States Chronicle, 1784–1789.

South Carolina

- Charleston Evening Gazette, 1785–1786.
- Charleston Morning Post, 1786–1787.
- Chronicle of Liberty, or the Republican Intelligencer, 1783.
- City Gazette, 1787–1788.
- Columbian Herald, 1784–1789.
- South-Carolina Gazette and General Advertiser, 1783–1785.
- South-Carolina Weekly Advertiser, 1783.
- South-Carolina Weekly Gazette, 1783–1786.
- State Gazette of South-Carolina, 1785–1787.

Virginia

- Norfolk and Portsmouth Chronicle, 1789.
- Norfolk and Portsmouth Gazette, 1789.
- Norfolk and Portsmouth Journal, 1787–1789.
- Virginia Gazette, 1736–1746, 1750–1778, 1766–1776, 1775–1778, and 1779–1780.
- Virginia Gazette and Alexandria Advertiser, 1789.
- Virginia Gazette and Weekly Advertiser, 1782–1789.
- Virginia Herald, 1787–1789.
- Virginia Journal and Alexandria Advertiser, 1784–1789.

Chapter 1

New England Colonies

MASSACHUSETTS NEWSPAPERS

Boston News-Letter, June 19, 1704.

Ran away from Capt. John Aldin of Boston, on Monday the 12th Currant, a tall lusty Indian Man call'd Harry, about 19 Years of Age, with a black Hat, brown Ozenbridge Breeches and Jacket: Whoever will take up said Indian, and bring or convey him safe either to John Campbell Post master of Boston, or to Mr. Nathaniel Niles of Kingstown in Narraganset, Master to said Indian, shall have a sufficient Reward.

Boston News-Letter, November 13, 1704.

Ran away on Wednesday last, the 8th. Currant from his Master in Boston, a Sirranam Indian Manslave, named Prince, aged about fourteen years old, black short hair, markt upon his breast with the Letters AP joyned at the foot: has on a black broad Cloath Jacket, under that a frize Jacket and Breeches, a Crocus Apron, gray yarn Stockings and Mittens, and a speckled Neckcloth: Speaks little or no English Whosoever shall take up and apprehend said Indian Boy, and him Convey to John Compbell Post master of Boston, or give any true Intelligence of said Boy, so as his Master may have him again, shall have a sufficient reward.

Boston News-Letter, October 8, 1705.

Ran away from his Master, Samuel Niles, of Kingstown, in Narraganset; an Indian Man Servant, age about 26 Years, he is a short and indifferent thick fellow, with a broad flatt Nose, he has had the Small Pox: He has on a grayish Coat, a Castor Hat, Ruffet coloured Stockings, and old Shoes: Whosoever shall take up said Indian, and brings or convey him safe to his said Master, or secure him and send notice of him, shall be well satisfied for his pains.

Variant Reprint: Boston News-Letter, July 29, 1706.

Boston News-Letter, December 10, 1705.

Lately Deserted Her Majesties Service in the Province of Maine, an Indian Man (under the Command of Cap. Joseph Brown) named Isaac Pummatick, was seen at Newbury, in Company with the above Runaway Negro; he is a short Fellow not very thick, speaks very good English, he lived formerly with Mr. Samuel Thackster of Hingham; he has on English Cloaths, a fad coloured old coat, or else a new light coloured drugget Coat, with buttons, holes and lining of black, black breeches, gray yarn Stockings, a black hat almost new, Whosoever shall apprehend Said Indian, & him convey to his said Captain, or to Andrew Belcher Esqr. at Boston, shall have a sufficient reward besides his Charges.

Reprints: Boston News-Letter, December 17, 1705; Boston News-Letter, December 31, 1705.

Boston News-Letter, January 20, 1707.

Ran-away from her Master Nicholas Jamain in of New York Merchant, the beginning of September last, A short thick Indian Girl, named Grace, aged about 17 years, her face is full of Pock holes, very few hairs on her Eye-brows, a very flat Nose, and a broad mouth; She speaks English, Dutch and French, the last best. Whosoever than apprehend and take up the said Servant, and deliver her unto Mr. Andrew Faneuil Merchant in Boston: If taken up in the Provinces of the Massachusetts and New-Hampshire; if in Connecticut-Colony, to Mr. John Clark at Saybrook; If at Rhode-Island Colony, to Mr. William Barbutt; In Pennsylvania to Mr. Benj. Godfrey ; In Carolina to Messieurs Guerard and Pacquerau, If in the Province of New-York at Albany to Col. Peter Schuler; any other part of said Province to her Master Jamain, 3 pounds, shall forthwith be paid to any one that shall deliver the said Indian to any of the persons abovementioned, besides reasonable Charges.

Reprints: Boston News-Letter, February 3, 1707; Boston News-Letter, February 17, 1707; Boston News-Letter, March 3, 1707.

Boston News-Letter, February 3, 1707.

Advertisements.

Ran-away from his Master Capt. James Pitts of Boston about a Month agoe [*sic*], An Indian Young Man, named Daniel Hump, aged about 18. years, has on a dark gray Coat, a double breast Jacket, dark gray Stockings, and a black Hatt; one of his Legs being Sore looks like a Bandy Legg. Whosoever shall apprehend and take up the said Servant and deliver him unto his said Master, or Mr Barnabas Lathrop at Barnstable; or Capt Simon Davis at Bristol, or Mr. Augustus Lucas at Rhode-Island, shall be sufficiently rewarded and paid, besides all reasonable cost and charges.

Reprint: Boston News-Letter, February 10, 1707.

Boston News-Letter, February 3, 1707.

Ran-away the Last Spring from her Master John Otis Esq. of Barnstable, is the Province of the Massachusetts-Bay in New-England, an Indian Girl named Hannah Wapuck, aged about 20 years, middle sized, full fac'd, a comely Countenance, she speaks good English, not very perfect of the Indian Language; had on English Apparel: Whosoever shall apprehend and take up the said Servant, and deliver her to her said Master, or give any true Intelligence of her unto John Campbell Post master of Boston, or unto her said Master, so as that he may have her again, shall be sufficiently rewarded, besides all reasonable Cost and Charges said.

Reprint: Boston News-Letter, March 17, 1707.

Boston News-Letter, September 29, 1707.

Advertisements.

Ranaway from his Master, Samuel Wentworth of Boston Merchant, on Saturday the 20th Currant, An Indian Man, Servant, named John Elles, aged about 23 years, of low Stature, a round well favour'd face, short hair: Having on a round puffc [*sic*] and quilted Cap, a double breasted Kersey Jacket, and round toe'd Shoes; he was bred at Mr. Ebenezar Billings's on the Road between Boston and Rhode-Island, and bought by his Master of Mr. Ephraim Pray. Whoever shall apprehend the said Servant, and him safely convey to his said Master, or give any true Intelligence of him, so as that he may have him again, shall be well rewarded, besides all necessary Charges paid.

Boston News-Letter, October 6, 1707.

Ran away from her Master, Nathaniel Baker of Boston, Baker, on the 22d of August last, a Tall Lusty Carolina Indian Woman named Sarah, aged about five or six and twenty years; having long straight black Hair, tyed up with a red hair-lace, very much mark'd or cut in the hands and face: Had on a striped red blue and white Homespun Jacket, & a red one, a black and white silk Crape Petticoat, a white Shift, as also a blue one will, her, and a mixed blue and white Linsey Woolsey Aprons: Whoever shall apprehend the said Servant, and her safely Convey to her said Master; or give any true Intelligence of her, so that he may have her again, shall have Four Pounds Reward, besides all necessary Charges paid.

Boston News-Letter, May 10, 1708.

Ran away from her Master James Berry of Boston Mariner, about Nine a Clock on Sabbath day night, being the 2d Currant, a young Indian Woman Servant, Named Pegg, about 20 years of Age, speaks broken English, full Visage, and pretty Tall; She hath a Mark or Branch made in the flesh on her right Arm with Powder, or something else black: hath on two Jackets, one Greenish, and two Petticoats, one Red, yellow Stockings, with Shoes on. Whosoever shall apprehend the said Runaway Servant, and her safely Convey to her above said Master, in Black-horse-lane in the North-End of Boston, or to Mr. Jonathan Mountfort, Shop-keeper near the North-Meeting-house in said Boston, or give any true Intelligence of her, so as that he may have her again, shall have Satisfaction to content, besides all necessary Charges paid.

Boston News-Letter, June 11, 1711.

Ran-away from William Gardner of Kingstown in the Colony of Rhode-Island, on the 28th of May last past A Molatto Man of Middle stature Branded on the Cheek with the Letter G about five or six & twenty years of Age having A gray Homspun Jacket Linnen Breaches Flannel Shirt, Speakes English well, & an Indian Squa his Wife with a Child. Whoever shall take up & Convey said Runawaies [sic] to their said Master or give any Intelligence so that he may have his said Servants again shall be sufficiently Rewarded for their pains besides all Reasonable Charges paid.

Boston News-Letter, August 13, 1711.

Ran away from her Master, John Jenkins of Boston Mariner, the 8th of thus Instant August, a Carolina Indian Maid-Servant, Named Moll, Aged about 20 years, Speaks good English, a short thick fat Wench, having short Hair, is Lame in one of her Hips & goes Wadling; she has carried away Considerable Money, & a bundle of Cloaths. viz. A Pladd Stuff Jacket, broad Check'd a Peticoat small Check'd; an old dark Home-spun Jacket, a dark colour'd Kersey Peticoat, & a strip'd Home-spun Peticoat Cotton & Wool; several Cotton & Linnen Shifts, with some others, several pair of Stockings, & several Lace Caps; blue Gloves, and Shoes about half wore out. Whoever shall take up the said Run-away, & her safely Convey to her above said Master, or give any true Intelligence of her, so as her Master may have her again who Lives at the North End of the Town in Shipstreet, shall be sufficiently rewarded besides all necessary Charges Paid.

Reprint: Boston News-Letter, August 27, 1711.

Boston News-Letter, September 17, 1711.

Ranaway from their Master at Boston on Friday last the 14th of this Instant September the following Indians, via. From the Reverend Samuel Myles, a Carolina Indian Man nam'd Toby, Aged about 20 years of a middle stature, hath with him a light colour'd Suite edg'd with black, a dark homespun Suite, edg'd and fac'd with black, a Hatedg'd with Silver lace, several Shirts and other cloathing. From the Hon. Col. Thomas Savage, a Carolina Indian Woman nam'd Jenny aged about 40 years, a pretty thick set Woman, with a flower'd Callico Jacket, blue and whote chequer'd plad petticoat and a lac'd night Cap. From Mr. John Staniford Taylour, a Carolina Indian Woman named Phillis, well set Aged about years, [missing text] years, has on a white Linnen Jacket a speckled calico Pettycoat, and a flowered serge one, a lac'd night Cap, red and white Stockings. From Mr. John Beanchan Leather Dresser, a Spanish Indian Man named Manaway Aged about 19 year of a middle stature, has on a whitish Druget coat and westcoat, Leather Breeches, black and white worsted Stockings, a black felt Hat, Cotton and Linnen Shirt. From Mr. Daniel Loring, a Spanish Indian Lad named Boston Aged about 18 years, a streight body'd Indian, has on a Kersey coat, a white Jacket, Leather Breaches, and felt Hat. Whoever shall apprehend the said Runaways, or any at them, and them or my of them safely convey to their respective Masters, or give any true Intelligence of them again shall be sufficiently rewarded besides all necessary Charges paid.

Boston News-Letter, October 15, 1711.

Advertisements.

Ran-away from their Master and Mistress at Marblehead, on Wednesday night, the 3d of this Instant October the following Indians, viz. from the Honorable Nathaniel Norden Esq.

An Indian Man, named Toney, a thin favour'd Man, of a middle Stature, and pretty elderly Countenance; he carry'd with him a new fad coloured Kersey Coat, not lin'd; a pair of red Breeches, a coloured Cap, cloth Coat and Breeches, a black Hat, a pair of fad coloured yarn Stockings, and new French-fall Shoes.

From Mrs. Elizabeth Brown Widow, an Indian Woman, named Rose, a thick short Woman, her Neck, Arms and Leggs Marked with Flowers, after the Indian manner, and some stoaks in her Cheeks; with a red Jacket, bound with edging, and a white Flannel Petticoat, aged about Forty Years.

Whoever shall apprehend the said Runaways, or either of them, and him or she safely convey to their Master or Mistress, or give any true Intelligence of them, or either of them, so as that their Master or Mistress shall have them, or either of them again, shall be sufficiently Rewarded, besides all necessary Charges paid.

Boston News-Letter, December 17, 1711.

A Carolina Indian Woman of Middle Stature, Speaks very little English, Aged about 40 years. Taken up as a Runaway; Inquire at the Post Office in Boston, and know further.

Boston News-Letter, July 28, 1712.

Taken up by Mr. William Troop of Bristol a Spanish Indian Woman aged between 30 & 40 years. Whoever can lay any Just claim to the said Indian paying the necessary charges may have her again.

Boston News-Letter, August 18, 1712.

Ran away from the Masters in Connecticut Colony the following Negro's and a Spanish Indian, viz from Mr. George Phillips in Middle-town Two

Negro Men one Named Trankile aged about Thirty years, of middle Stature, speaks good English, well Apparelled, one finger of one hand Stump'd. The other Negro Named Harry aged about 20 years streight Lim'd, has on a blew Shirt, Red Jacket, Castor Hat, Speaks broken English, and well Apparelled.

Ran away also from Mr. Jabiel Hauley of Durham, A Spanish Indian Man, Named Peter aged about Twenty years, of Middle Stature, Cheridary Wastcoat, A Soldiers blew Coat fac'd with red, the Cape taken off, he speaks very good English.

And on the 18th of July, Ran away from Mr. Ebenezar Hubbard of Middletown, a Negro Man nam'd Peter, aged about 18 years, a Slim Fellow, thin fac'd, having a Skare on the back of one of his hands near the Nuckles, with a Slit on one of his Ears, speaks good English.

Whoever shall apprehend said Run-aways or any of them, and him or them safely convey to his or their said Masters, or give any true Intelligence, of them or either of them. So as their Masters may have them again shall have Fourty Shilling reward, for each Servant, besides all necessary Charges paid.

Boston News-Letter, September 14, 1713.

Ran way on the Third of September Currant, from his Master, Richard Draper of Corn-Hill, Boston, Shop keeper, A Spanish Indian Man-Servant, Named James, a Tall, Well fellow, about 20 Years of Age: he had on when he went away a course broad cloth Jacket, with a large Patch in the back, and linen strip'd Breeches.

Ran away also with him, another Indian Man, Named Toby, Tall, Slimb fellow. thin Visage: he had on when he went away a Home-spun strip'd Jacket, leather Breeches, home-spun Stockings. New Shoes.

Whoever shall apprehend the said Run-aways, or either of them, and him or them safely convey to Mr. Richard Draper aforesaid, or give any true Intelligence of both or either of them, so as that the said Master Draper may have them again, shall have Forty Shillings reward for each, besides all necessary Charges paid.

Boston News-Letter, October 25, 1714.

Ran away from his Master, Gilbert Ash of the City of New-York Merchant; A Lusty Indian Man, Named Joseph Emery, aged about 26 Years, he has bushy Hair, a squinting look, with a Cinamon coloured Coat lin'd with Red, a white Cotton Wastcoat, and speckled Shirt. Whoever all apprehend the said Run-away, and him safely convey to his said Master at New-York, or give any true Intelligence of him, so as his Matter may have him again, shall have Twenty Shillings reward, besides all reasonable Charges paid.

Boston News-Letter, May 9, 1715.

Ran away from his Master, William Borden Ship-Carpenter of Newport on Rhode-Island, on the 23d of April, a very likely Spanish Indian Lad, without any Marks on his Face, had long Hair, looks very like our Indians, named Caesar, speaks Indifferent good English, aged about Eighteen Years, had on a brown Kersey Jacket, a pair of old Broad-Cloth Breeches pretty near the same Colour, an old Beaver Hat, and a course Linen Shirt. Whosoever shall apprehend the said Indian Lad, or give any true Intelligence of him so as his said Master may have him again, shall be Rewarded to their Satisfaction, besides all Necessary Charges paid.

Boston News-Letter, July 30, 1716.

This is to give Notice, That on the 16th of July 1716. Run-away from his Master, David Lyell, An Indian Man Named Nim, he lately belonged to Mr. James Moore, he is about One and Twenty years of Age, and is a short broad shouldred [sic] Fellow, his Hair hath been lately cut off, he has a swelling on the back of his right hand, and can do something at the Carpenters Trade, he hath with him two new Shirts, a new Waste-coat and Breeches of white course Linnen, and the same of Blew striped: a home-spun Coat, wears a Hat, Shoes and Stockings; it is believed he endeavours to get on board some Vessel. Whoever takes up the said Indian in the Jerseys, & brings him to his said Master shall have Forty Shillings and Charges; and if in any other Government Five Pounds, if they give but Notice where he is, so that his Master may have him again. Direct to David Lyell in New Yor, or at Amboy in New Jersey.

Boston News-Letter, August 27, 1716.

Ran away from Mr. David Hillard of Stonington, a Negro Man, called Mingo, aged about Thirty one Years; with an Indian Squaw, called Milly, that ran from Mr. John Swan of said Town, both speak good English, the Negro Man is of a pale colour, he has on Home-spun Clothes of a Ruffet colour. Whosoever takes up said Negro Man, and him safely keep, so that his Master may have him again, or give true Intelligence of them, shall have Three Pounds Reward, besides all necessary Charges paid.

Boston News-Letter, September 24, 1716.

Ran away from their Masters in Boston, the 15th of this instant September, at Night, Three Carolina Indians, viz. Two Men Servants and One Woman, they speak but broken English, about 30 Years of Age or above; one from Mr.

Samuel Adams Master, named James, well sett, he hath a Leather Jacket, black Stockings. Another of them Servant to Mr. Nehemiah Yoals Ship Carpenter, named Robin, with double Breasted Jacket, Leather Breeches; they both have other Cloaths with them. The Indian Woman Servant to Mr. Thomas Salter Cordwainer, named Amareta, pretty Lusty, the hath a strip'd homespun Jacket, blue Petticoat. Whosoever shall take up the abovesaid Runaway Servants, and them or either of them Convey to their abovesaid Masters in Boston, shall have Forty Shillings Reward besides all necessary Charges paid.

Boston News-Letter, July 22, 1717.

Advertisements.

Ran away on the 24th of June last, from their Masters Samuel Vernon and William Bourden, both of Newport on Rhode Island, two Carolina Indian Men-Servants, of about 20 Years of Age each, one of them is branded with W on one Cheek, and B on the other; one of them is a short Fellow, full Fac'd, has on a dark Gray Coat, trim'd with black, and Jacket with brass Buttons. Whoever shall apprehend the said Runaways, and them or either of them safely convey to their said Masters, or to Mr. Barrat Dyer in Boston, or give any true Intelligence of them to as that their Master may have them again, shall have Forty Shillings Reward for each, besides all necessary Charges paid.

Boston News-Letter, April 14, 1718.

Ran-away from their Masters Capt. John Knight and Mr. Clemant Hughes of Piscataqua, on the 9th of April Currant, two Marthas Vineyard Indian Women, one Named Desiah Chin, middlesize about Twenty Years Old, her Right Thumb has been hurt; she had on when she went away away a black Crape Gown and a striped Stuff Jacket; The other named Rachel Choho, much about the same Age. something Taller she had on a blew Flannel Petticoat, a dark Estamine Gown and a double striped Gown, Any Person that shall take up and secure them so that their Masters may have them again; or either of them, shall have Three Pounds Reward for each and all necessary Charges Paid, upon their giving Notice thereof to their said Masters.

Boston News-Letter, January 4, 1720.

A Stray Spanish Indian Woman Named Sarah, Aged about 40 Years taken up, which the Owner may have paying the Charges, and be informed by John Campbell of his House in Cornhill.

Boston News-Letter, June 9, 1720.

Advertisements.

Ran-away from his Master James Palin at the Rainbow Coffee House in Corn hill, Boston, on Monday the 6th of this Instant June, An Irish Man Servant, Named Richard Evelin, of a middle Stature, about 22 or 23 years old had on a dark coloured Drugget Jacket, a pair of Leather Breeches, white thread Stockings, but no Coat.

Also went away with said Servant, an Indian Woman, born at Rhode-Island, Named Zipporah, about 30 or 35 Years old of short Stature, hath on a stuff Gown and Petticoat, also a yellow quilted Petticoat, and a plain round Cap. Whoever shall take up said Servants, or either of them, bring them to their Master, or give any true Intelligence of them, so as their Master may have them or either of them again, shall be well Rewarded for their Pains, and all necessary Charges paid.

Boston News-Letter, September 11, 1721.

Ran-away the 5th of this Instant September from Mr. Nathanael Kanney, of Boston, Butcher, A Boy named Charles Crouch. Aged about Fifteen Years, small of Stature, white Stort hair, large Lips, has on a good Felt Hat, a dark gray Coat lin'd with blue baze, a dark and yellow striped pair of Breeches, round to'd Shoes, and has with him several pair of Stockings, and other Cloaths.

Runaway also at the same time, a Carolina Indian Man named Will, a slim tall Fellow, about Thirty Years of Age speaks good English, has a dark spot on one Cheek, has with him a light colour'd broad Cloth Coat, and several Jackets, and several pair of Breeches, and several pair of Stockings, & Shoes: He is suppos'd to have a considerable quantity of Paper Money.

Whoever shall take up the said Runaways, and them safely bring to their abovesaid Master Mr. Nathanael Finney at Boston, or if unwilling to come to Boston, they are desir'd to bring them to Roxbury or Charlstown, or some other near Town, and send Word, so they may be had again, and they shall receive Three Pounds Reward, and all necessary Charges paid.

N. B. Whoever takes them up are desir'd to search them.

Boston Gazette, October 2, 1721.

Deserted from His Majesty's Ship' Sea-Horse, about the 10th of July last, an Indian Man named Hector, about 22 or 23 Years of Age, Speaks very good English; wears his own Hair, being of a middle Stature, spare in Body, and thin in the Face, Whoever shall apprehend and Safely convey him to the next

Country Goal shall have 5 1. Reward, and all necessary Charges paid. Note, The said Indian is a very good Seaman and is suppos'd to be gone to Sea: Whoever can truly discover the Ship or Vessel that carry'd him off shall have 20 s paid by Cape. Wentworth Paxton of Boston.

Reprint: Boston Gazette, October 9, 1721.

New-England Courant, June 24, 1723.

Advertisements

RAN away from his Master Mr. Thomas Byles of Newport on Rhode-Island, on the ninth of this Instant June, a Spanish Indian Man Servant, named Sassidillah, but 'tis thought he will change his name: He is about 21 Years of Ages about 5 Foot 8 Inches high, and pretty Slim; his Hair pretty long, and somewhat curled. He has an Indian mark of Blue across the Temples on the right Side of his Face.

N. B. His Cloaths were found lying by the Water Side on the Day he went away, and 'tis thought he has stole some other Cloaths from on board a vessel.

Whoever shall apprehend the abovesaid Runaway Servant, and him safely convey to his said Master in Newport, shall have Five Pounds Reward, and all necessary charges paid.

New-England Courant, August 26, 1723.

Ran away from his Master, Mr. Job Bissel of Newport on Rhode Island, Blacksmith, on the 20th of July last, a Carolina Indian Boy, called Bristow, about 16 or 17 Years of Age, of a short Stature, well set, full Faced, with big Eyes, and thick Lips; he had on when he went away a gray Jacket, and striped Breeches. Whosoever shall apprehend the said Runaway, and him safely convey to his abovesaid Master, or give true intelligence so that his said Master may have him again, shall have Forty Shillings Reward, and all necessary Charges paid.

Boston News-Letter, September 30, 1725.

On Saturday Night last, the 25th Instant, Three Indian Men, (being Captives) Cloth'd in English Habits like Servants, Ran-way from Dorchester in a Canoe, Intending (as is supposed) to Travel thro' the Country to the Eastward, and by that Means to escape out of the hands of the Government: His Majesty's good Subjects are Desired to enquire after, and if they may be found, to Apprehend and Convey them to His Majesty's Goal in Boston; And such Persons shall be rewarded to their Content.

New-England Courant, October 2, 1725.

On Saturday Night last three Indian Captives, who were at work at Dorchester, ran-way from thence in a Canoe, and have not been since heard of.

Boston News-Letter, October 14, 1725.

On Friday Night last, Saccaristis, one of the Indian Hostages, and one other Indian, (who was taken Captive by Capt. Lovewell) Cloathed in English Habit of a Red Colour, Ran-way from His Majesty's Castle William, in a Canoe, Intending (as is supposed) to Travel through the Country to the Eastward, and so to escape out of the Hands of the Government: His Majesty's Subjects are desired to enquire after, and if they may be found, to Apprehend and Convey them to His Majesty Goal in Boston; and such Persons shall be satisfied to Content.

New-England Courant, October 16, 1725.

On Wednesday last one of the Indian Hostages, and another Indian, who ran away from His Majesty's Castle on Friday the 8th Instant, surrender'd themselves at Ipswich, and were brought to Town. They had caught only a Rackoon for their Subsistence since their Escape, and the late Rains had so swell'd the River Merrimack, that they could not pass it.

New-England Weekly Journal, October 16, 1727.

Ran away from his Master Mr. Josiah Bacon of Boston, Sawyer, on the 4th Instant, an Indian Man Servant Named Jo Daniels, about 20 years of Age, a tall slim Fellow, has strait black Hair, had on an old Castor Hat, a double breasted Orange colour'd Jacket, with a strip'd woolen one under it, a Cotton & Linnen Shirt, an old pair of Leather Breeches, grey yarn Stockings.

Whoever shall take up the abovesaid Runaway, and him safely convey to his abovesaid Master at the North End near the Salutation, shall have Forty Shillings Reward, and all necessary Charges paid. Boston. October 16, 1727.

New-England Weekly Journal, June 26, 1727.

Ran away from his Master Mr. Benj. Muzzy of Lexington in the County of Middlesex, on the 11th of this Instance June, a Spanish Indian Man-Servant, named Beneto Furnace, about 26 years of Age, speaks very good English, and has a Blood-Wart under the left side of his Nose; is a well-set Fellow. Had on when he went away, a Kersey jacket of a Cinnamon colour, with Pewter Buttons; a pair of gray home-spun Cloth Breeches, with only one Button at each Knee: A Woollen Shirt, black and white Yarn Stocking, round to'd Shoes, but no Hat. He had on an Iron Horse-Lock on the small of one of his Legs.

Note, He was lately a Servant to Mr. John Muzzy of Mendon.

Whoever shall apprehend the said Runaway and him convey to his said Master at Lexington, shall have Five Pounds Reward, and all necessary Charges paid. Boston, June 26, 1727.

Boston News-Letter, August 22, 1728.

On the 19th of July last, An Indian Woman, Named Lydia Charles, bound by Indenture for several Years yet to run, to John Menzies Esq; Deserted his Service from his House in Boston; she is a Tall Lusty Woman, and has on a narrow stript Cherrederry Gown, turned up with a little flowred red & white Callico, a stript homespun guilted Petticoat, a plain Muslin Apron, & a suit of plain Pinners, and a red & white flower & Knot, also a pair of green Stone Earrings, with white Cotton Stockings & Leather heel'd Shoes. Whoever shall discover her so as she may be apprehended & delivered to the said John Menzies Esq; at his House in Summer Street in Boston aforesaid, shall have Forty Shillings reward.

Dated, Boston, Aug, 21st. 1728.

Reprint: Boston News-Letter, September 5, 1728.

Note: Lydia Charles appeared in the Boston Gazette on August 18, 1729. By the time the advertisement was published, however, William Lambert became the owner of the Native American woman.

Boston News-Letter, September 26, 1728.

Ran-away from the Gray hound in Roxbury, on the Lord's Day the 15th Instant, A lusty Indian Woman, Named Bersheba Larrens, she had on a Red flower'd Callico Jacket & Peticoat, a quilted Peticoat. Whosoever shall take up the said Runaway and Convey to Roxbury, shall have 20 Shillings reward & necessary Charges paid.

Boston Gazette, November 4, 1728.

Ran away the 6th of October from his Master Elisha Green of Warwick in the Colony of Rhode Island, an Indian Man Servant Named Simon George, of a middle Stature and a pale Complexion, he had with him a Cinnamon Coloured Jacket, and a pair of Long breeches, a Woolen Shirt, and a pair of Black Worsted Stockings, and an old Hat: Whoever shall Apprehend Said Runaway and him Convey to his abovesaid Master shall have Forty Shillings Reward, and all necessary Charges paid.

Reprints: Boston Gazette, November 11, 1728; Boston Gazette, November 18, 1728.

New-England Weekly Journal, December 2, 1728.

Ran away on the 13th of Novemb. Instant, from their Master Mahuman Hinddell of Deerfield. Two Men Servants. The one John Griffin, a White young Man, about 16 years of Age, something pock broken, short brown hair, had on a Castor Hat, a Kersey Coat, homespun Jacket with Pewter Buttons Leather Breeches, and gray yarn Stockings.

The other a Pequot Indian, named Peter Put, alias Pompey, of middling stature, hair about 3 Inches long, has a remarkable Scar on the midst of his Forehead, had on a blue Broad cloth Coat, Kersey Jacket with Pewter Buttons, and leather Breeches, speaks good English. They carried away with them 2 Guns, 2 Silver Spoons, & 2 Duffil Blankets.

Whoever will take up and convey the said Runaways, or either of them, to their abovesaid Master at Deerfield, shall have Five Pounds Reward for each of them, and all necessary Charges paid. Boston. Novemb 18, 1728.

Reprint: New-England Weekly Journal, December 9, 1728.

Boston Gazette, August 18, 1729.

Whereas Lydia Charles a lusty well set Indian Woman about 25 Years of Age, Ran away from her Master William Lambert of Boston Esq; on the 14th Instant, and carry'd with her a purple and white Callico Gown and Petticoat, the Gown fac'd with a small checker'd purple and white Callico, a white striped cherrydery Gown and Petticoat, the Gown fac'd with red & white Callico, and sundry other Cloths: she was formerly servant to Shubal Gorham of Barnstable Esq; and by him disposed of to the Hon. John Menzies Esq; deceas'd: If any Person secures her and bring her to the said William Lambert in Boston shall have Forty Shillings Reward, and all Charges paid. 18th of Aug. 1729.

Boston Gazette, August 18, 1729.

Ipswich, August 16, 1729.

Pursuant to an Advertisement of Shubal Jones and Joseph Bursley of Barnstable, I have taken up their two Indian servants, Solomon Wampum and Joseph Wampum, and they are in his Majesty's Goal in Salem, ready to be delivered, agreeable to the Tenour of the Advertisement. By Philemon Dane.

Reprint: Boston Gazette, August 25, 1729.

Boston Gazette, October 13, 1729.

Ran away from his Master Mr. Henry Laughton of Boston, Taylor, on Friday the 12th of this Instant September, a tall slim Indian Boy named Tom, about 18 Years of Age: his Hair is not above half an Inch long, has a Scar over his left Eye, occasioned by a Wound lately cured; also a Scar on each Leg, about the Small. He bad on a double breasted Drab Coat with small Buttons and small Sleeves, blue Drugget Breeches, black Stockings, round to'd Shoes, a black Neck-Cloth, and a white Shirt. Whoever shall take up the said Servant and bring him to his said Master, living near the Town House in Boston, shall have Three Pounds Reward and all necessary Charges paid. Dated, Boston, Sept. 22.

New-England Weekly Journal, August 3, 1730.

Ran away on the 26th Instant July, from Mr. Christopher Phillips of North-Kingstown, a Spanish Indian Man named Warmick, about 24 Years of Age, of a middle Stature, and slim, Short Hair, a Tanner by Trade.

And a Mallagasco Negro Man, Named Cato, about 21 Years of Age, a Thick Short Fellow of a Tawney Complection, long Bushy Hair if he has not since cut it off, a Currier by Trade; They both Speak good English. Whoever shall take up the abovesaid Servants and them convey to their abovesaid Master, shall have Five Pounds Reward, besides all necessary Charges paid by Christopher Phillips.

North-Kingstown, July 31, 1730.

Boston Gazette, May 31, 1731.

Ran away from his Master Capt. Richard Brown, of Newbury, on the 15th of May, an Indian Man Servant Named Nero, about 22 Years old, near six Foot high, well Sett; he had on when he went away, a gray Pea-Jacket, lin'd with homespun Striped Flanel, a Cotton and Linnen Shirt, Leather Breeches, and gray Yarn Stockings. Five Pounds Reward if taken up and convey'd to his Master.

Reprints: Boston Gazette, June 7, 1731; Boston Gazette, June 14, 1731.

New England Weekly Journal, August 30, 1731.

Ran away on the 2d of this Instant August, from his Master, Mr. Com[fort] Carpenters, Rehoboth, a Spanish Indian Man Servant, named Caesar, about 23 years of Age, of a middle Statute, his Hair lately cut off. Had with him when he went away, an old Felt Hat, a Cloth colour'd Serge Coat black Calaminco Jacket, Ozenbrigs Shirt & Trousers, and strip'd Cotton Breeches. He had Iron Pot hooks about his Neck when he went away, and has a Scar on his right Elbow. Whoever shall apprehend the said Runaway & him convey to his said Masters, or secure him in any of His Majesty's Goals, shall have Three Pounds Reward & all necessary Charges paid.

Boston Gazette, October 11, 1731.

Ran away from his Master, the Rev. Mr. Johnson of Stradford, in Connecticut, Sept. 17th an Indian Man named Pallas, aged about 19 Years, a good looking Fellow, with short Hair, and a worsted Cap, a good grey homemade plain cloath Coat full trim'd with black, and linnen Breeches, speaks pretty good English, and had with him two Bags with some Provision in them, marked with Ink S I. If anyone shall secure the said Indian that he may be recovered by his said Master, shall have Four Pounds Reward, and all necessary Charges paid.

Reprints: Boston Gazette, October 18, 1731; Boston Gazette, November 1, 1731.

Boston News-Letter, March 9, 1732.

Ran away from his Master, Mr. Nath. Dole of Newbury, the 26th of January Last, A Spanish Indian Man Servant, Named James, about 26 Years of age, speaks good English, Middling Stature, with streight black Hair, not very long, & a Scar in his Forehead: He had on when he went away, A dark coloured Homespun Pee Jacket, with round Pewter Buttons, a pair of long Trowsers over his Leather Breeches, a good Felt Hat, a pair of Yarn Stockings, and round to'd Shoes.

Whosoever shall take up the abovesaid Run away, and him safely Convey to his said Master at Newbury, shall have Forty Shillings Reward, and all necessary Charges paid.

Reprint: Boston News-Letter, March 16, 1732.

Boston News-Letter, September 14, 1732.

We have the following melancholy of a barbarous Murder committed at Brantrey on Tuesday last, about Noon, as related by some that were of the jury of Inquest, viz. An Indian Fellow belonging to one Mr. Howard of Bridgewater, (formerly to Maj. Quincy of Brantrey having Run-away, Advertisements were issued out after him, and a Reward to take him up, and bring him home, one Mr. Rogers of Pembrook, being at Weymouth, on his way home happen'd to see one of the Advertisements, took it, and returned back to look for the said Indian, and on Monday Evening last, after some enquiry, found him; and lodging that Night at Brantrey, the Indian got away again on Morning Mr. Rogers, finding the Indian was gone, he offered Ten Shillings to a Man to find him again, who accordingly went, and soon brought him back: Mr. Rogers, having the Indian with him, set out on his Journey homewards, and when they had got about Five Miles, Mr. Rogers stopt and went into the House of one Mr. Scot with the Indian, and call'd for a Dram, but they had none; and while they were talking together in the House, the Indian went and stood outside by the Door; and Mr. Scot seeing him pass by the Window, told Mr. Rogers, the Indian wou'd get away; upon which he went out, and seeing him at a little Distance from the House, going towards a Corn Field, he ran after him: the Indian looking back and seeing him coming, took a Jack-Knife and open'd it, as Mr. Scot tho't by the Motion of his Arms, and when Mr. Rogers had got near, the Indian suddenly turn'd about, and made up to him, and then stab'd the knife into his left Breast, as 'tis tho't, up to the Haft, the Wound being very deep and open: Mr. Scot and a Negro in the House seeing Mr. Rogers assaulted, ran up to assist him, and finding the Indian with the knife in his Hand, which Mr. Rogers had then hold of and let go, they with much difficulty, after bending the Knife double, got it from him : Mr. Scot seeing them both bloody, ask'd Mr Rogers whether it was his, or the Indians blood, three times before he made any Answer, and then only said, I am either stab'd, or wounded, and fell down and dy'd immediately. The Indian got away again, while they were looking after Mr. Rogers, but the Negro pursu'd him, and soon catch'd him and held him, till Mr. Scot went and brought others, and then secur'd him. Mr. Rogers was a Widower, of about 43 Years of Age, and has left three Children. The Coroner's Inquest charges the said Indian with the Murder, and he was Yesterday towards Evening brought to Town, and committed to Goal.

Reprint: American Weekly Mercury, October 12, 1732.

New-England Weekly Journal, August 6, 1733.

Run from Bermuda July 3d, 1733. in an open Boat built with Cedar, with two Masts, and two Sails, about 16 feet Keel, Three Soldiers, one Negro Man, and one Indian, whose Names &c. as follows, viz.

William Frary was born in Suffolk a Smith by Trade, aged about 30 Years, of a middle Stature, fair complexion, wears his own hair, had on when he departed a strip'd ticken Wastcoat and Breeches, and an Oznabrigs Frock, white yarn Stockings, Square to'd Shoes, and an old Hat.

John Hunter was born in Lancashire, was bred a Country Man, aged about 27 Years, of middle Stature, brown Complexion, speaks very Country, very Freckled, has on his own hair, has three Jackets, a red one, a brown Fustian one, and a strip'd Ticken, white yarn Stockings, and round to'd Shoes.

Thomas Mawkins was born in Cambridgeshire of short Stature, fair Complexion, a flat Nose and pretty red, aged about 21 Years, had on a white Canvas Frock, a strip'd Ticken Jacket and Breeches, white yarn Stockings, and round to'd Shoes: They had all Lace round their Hats being thick Felts.

One young Negro Man named Hazard, he speaks broken English being born in Guinea, a spare Body with a long Visage, one of his Legs has been broke, had on Oznabrigs Cloathing.

One young Indian Man named Will, a short well set Fellow, with a very round smooth face, bad on a dark colour Kerzy Jacket, and Oznabrigs Shirt and Breeches.

If any Person fall take up any of the said Persons and deliver them to Capt. John Compton in Boston, shall receive & Reward for each White Man, two Pistoles, and for each Slave four Pistoles.

Reprints: Boston News-Letter, August 9, 1733; American Weekly Mercury, August 23, 1733; New-England Weekly Journal, August 27, 1733; American Weekly Mercury, August 30, 1733.

Boston News-Letter, August 9, 1733.

Ran away from her Master, Mr. Samuel Allaen of Newbury, the 17th of July past, an Indian Maid-Servant, named Keziah Wampum, about 19 or 20 Years of Age, a tall, lusty Wench, Speaks good English, but Stutters. She had on when she went away, a striped homespun Gown and Coat, a pair black Shoes with wooden Heels. She took with her also a new striped bought Stuff Gown, and a Silk Crape quilted Coat. Whoever shall take up the abovesaid Maid Servant, and her convey to her said Master at Newbury, or to Mr. Boylstone of Charlstown, shall have Forty Shillings Reward, and all necessary Charges paid.

Boston Gazette, November 11, 1734.

Ran away from his Master Stephen Sawyer of Newbury, the 7th of April last, an Indian Man Servant named Peter, middle stature, upwards of 30 Years, he had a small bunch on his Forehead, speaks with Small Voice. He had on when he Ranaway, a Homespun brownish plain Coat, a homespun sea-green Jacket with pewter Buttons, a Speckl'd woolen Shirt, Trowzer Breeches, yarn stockings, and good shoes. Whoever will take up abovesaid Ranaway and him convey to his said Master, shall have Ten Pounds Reward, and all necessary charges paid them.

Reprint: Boston Gazette, November 18, 1734.

Boston Post-Boy, August 11, 1735.

Advertisement.

Run-away from Capt. John Corney's Ship lying at Cape Ann, an Indian Man Servant named Silas Quanomp, belonging to My, Samuel Staniford of Ipswich: He is a well set Fellow, has a large Scar on his Right Check down toward his Chin: His Hair is newly cut off. The said Staniford hereby forbids all Masters of Vessels carrying of the said Indian on the Penalty of the Law.

Reprints: Boston Post-Boy, August 18, 1735; Boston Post-Boy, August 25, 1735; Boston Post-Boy, September 1, 1735; Boston Gazette, September 8, 1735.

Boston News-Letter, October 9, 1735.

Ran away from Mr. Abijah Wheeler of Ipswich, on the 7th Instant, a Spanish Indian Man, named Jack, about 30 Years of Age, a well set stubbed Fellow, full Face, long thick black Hair, wears an Orange colour'd Jacket, thick Leather Breeches, with a Patch in the Crotch of Shoe Leather, Checker'd Woollen Shite, light gray Stockings, with tops sew'd on of another sort, pretty good Shoes, and a Felt Hat. He took with him a coarse Bag, with some Provision in it. He speaks good English.

Whoever takes up the said Runaway, and him convey to his Master at Ipswich, shall have Five Pounds Reward, and all necessary Charges paid.

Reprints: New-England Weekly Journal, October 14, 1735; Boston News-Letter, October 16, 1735; Boston News-Letter, October 23, 1735.

Boston Gazette, December 22, 1735.

Ran away from Mrs. Grizel Catton, on Wednesday the 3d Inst. An Indian Girl Named Jenny, about 16 Years of Age, lusty and well set, remarkable for her Limping as she walks she had on a stript homespun Jacket and Petticoat, a Cap, Shoes but no Stockings, 'tis suppos'd she's entertain'd somewhere in this Town. If any Person will discover and secure said Runaway, so as her Mistress may have her again shall have Three Pounds Reward, and all necessary Charges paid.

Boston News-Letter, December 25, 1735.

Marblehead, Dec. 23. 1735.

Ran away from the Snow Sherburn, Obed Hussey Master, now lying at Marblehead, an Indian Man about Twenty two years old, an Irish Lad about Twenty Years old, both Indented Servants to the said Hussey : They took with them the Snow's Long-Boat, with two Masts and Sails, a Case of Bottles with Rum, sundry Cloaths, &c.

Whoever shall convey the said Run-aways, Boat, &c. to the said Hussey at Marblehead, shall have Five Pounds Reward, and all necessary Charges paid, by Obed Hussey.

New-England Weekly Journal, August 10, 1736.

Ran away from his Master Mr. Joseph Mansfield of Lynn, Shipwright, on the 22d of July past, a Spanish Indian Man Servant, named Peter, about 26 Years of Age, a sturdy well set Fellow, of middle Stature, speaks good English, has lately clip off his Hair, & wears a black Natural Wigg; had on a good Castor Hat, Cinnamon colour'd Coat pretty short, a striped linsey woolley Jacket, white homespun Trousers, Yarn Stockings, and a good pair of single sole shoes with flat Pewter Buckles therein. Whoever shall take up the abovesaid Runaway and him safely convey lo his abovesaid Master at Lynn, shall have Four Pounds Reward, and all necessary Charges paid.

Boston Gazette, November 8, 1736.

On Tuesday the 12th of October, Ran away from his Master Ebenezer Brenton of South Kingston, in the Colony of Rhode Island, a Mustee Man: servant, named Abel, aged about 23 Years, a sort thick set Fellow, something stooping in his shoulders, bare Leg'd, short Hair a little Brown, he shews something of white in his Completion ('tis supposed that Father was a Dutch man, his Mother a Spanish Indian) He had on when he went away, a Grey Kersey Great Coat & Jacket, Linnen Frock & Trousers, New Felt Hat, and New Shoes ; he took with him a Gun. Whoever shall apprehend said Runaway, and convey him safe his Master shall have Ten Pounds reward &d all necessary Charges paid by Ebenezer Brenton.

Reprints: Boston Gazette, November 15, 1736; Boston Gazette, November 22, 1736.

Boston News-Letter, September 29, 1737.

Ran away from his Master Nathanael Holbrook of Sherburn, on Thursday the 15th of September Instant, an Indian Lad about Sixteen Years of age, named John Pittome, he is pretty well set and full Fac'd : He had on an old grey Coat, a new dark grey Jacket with large Brass Buttons, white Linnen Breeches, no Stockings, old shoes and an old Felt Hat. Whosoever shall take up the abovesaid Runaway and bring him to his Master of Sherburn, shall have Forty Shillings Reward, and necessary Charges paid.

Variant Reprints: Boston News-Letter, October 11, 1739; Boston News-Letter, October 18, 1739.

Boston Evening-Post, January 23, 1738.

Ran away from his Master, Mr. Andrew Gilman of Exeter, on the 18th of November last, an Indian Man Servant named Covy, about 27 Years of Age: He is a shore thick Fellow, has a very grum Voice, and smooth Face, speaks very good English, can both Read and Write, and plays on a Viol [sic]. He has a large scar on one of his Knees, and a Scar on the upper part of one of his Feet. He had when he went away, two Jackets, one a dark coloured Kersey, the other a blue and white striped woollen Cloth, a white woollen Shirt, a new Felt Hat, a pair of Indian dress'd Leather Breeches, a new pair of gray Yarn Stockings. Whoever takes up said Runaway, and conveys him to his said Master, shall have Five Pounds Reward, and all necessary Charges paid.
   Andrew Gilman, Exeter, December 26th, 1737.

Reprints: Boston Evening-Post, January 30, 1738; Boston Evening-Post, February 6, 1738.

Boston News-Letter, February 2, 1738.

Ran away from her Master, Mr. John Wilson on Friday the 13th of January past, An Indian Woman, named Ann Warwick, about 22 or 23 Years of age, speaks good English: She had on who she went away. A homespun Gown, strip'd Blue and Grey, Cotton and Linnen Shift, blue Stockings and wooden heel shoes. She had also with her, an English Stuff Gowri, strip'd White, Green and Red. Whoever shall take up the said Indian Woman and convey her to the above said Mr. Wilson in Roxbury, shall have Three Pounds Reward and all necessary Charges paid.

Reprints: Boston News-Letter, February 9, 1738; Boston News-Letter, February 16, 1738; Boston News-Letter, February 23, 1738.

New-England Weekly Journal, April 4, 1738.

Ran away from his Master Mr. Thomas Choat jun. of Ipswich, the 19th Instant, an Indian Man Servant, named Primus, about Thirty Years of Age, middling Stature, well set, full Face, wears his Hair; He had on when he went away, a Homespun double-breasted gray Jacket, his Breeches of the same, bluish yarn Stockings, check'd Drugger Shirt, and Flat Hat almost new, round to'd Shoes. He can Read pretty well. Whoever shall take up the abovesaid Runaway Servant, and him convey to his said Master at Ipswich have Five Pounds Reward, and all necessary Charges paid. And all Matters of Vessels and others, are hereby caution'd against concealing or carrying off said Servant, on Penalty of the Law in that Case made and provided.
  Boston March 21st. 1737,8.

Reprint: New-England Weekly Journal, April 11, 1738.

New-England Weekly Journal, September 26, 1738.

Broke out of His Majesty's Goal in Boston, the last Night, nine Persons, as follows, viz Thomas Dwyer an Irish Man, being a lusty full fac'd Fellow, of a pale Complection, having long strait black Hair; he had on when he went away, a dark blue Coat, about 25 Years of Age.
  John Maccarty, a tall slim pock broken Fellow with a Scar upon his right Temple, about 30 Years of Age, he had on a green double breasted Jacket with Mettal Burtons.
  Michael Hair, about 28 Years of Age, of middle Stature, short black Hair, down look, he had on a dark colour'd Coat; a Turner by Trade.
  Alexander Maccarty, about 20 Years of Age, a likely Fellow, wears a light Wig, and a Cloth colour'd Coat.
  One - Hambleton, about 30 Years of Age, wears his own Hair, his fore locks are White and is a short Fellow small Face, he had on a dark colour'd Coat, This fellow together with the aforegoing are Irish Men.
  Thomas Myby alias Thomas Manning, an English Man, a lusty well set Fellow, about 40 Years of Age, he had on a dark colour'd Coat & Great Coat.
  And one Elizabeth Decoster about 30 Years of Age, a very likely Woman, she had on a strig'd Callimanco Gown.
  An Indian Fellow named John Baker, a short Fellow, and who has but one Arm.
  A Negro Fellow Named Jocco, about twenty Years of Age, a well set Fellow, speaks very good English, and is Servant to Capt. Sigourney

Whoever shall apprehend the said Absconded Prisoners, and bring them to the said Prison, shall have Three Pounds Reward for each or either of them, paid by me, William Young.

New-England Weekly Journal, October 24, 1738.

Ran away from her Master George Dolbeare of Colchester in Connecticut, on the 18th Instant, in the Night, an Indian Woman named Pegg, about 25 Years of Age, she is of a middling Stature, pretty thick set, very much pock-broken, has a small Mole on her Neck, has a wadling Gate, speaks good English, stutters a little when talking earnestly, she can read and write well: She carried away with her a check'd Cotton and Linnen Shirt, and two fine Garlick Shirts, a large Great Coat of a brownish colour with large flat metal Buttons, a pair of Mens sharp to'd Calf Skin Shoes, a pair of new Steel Buckles: She is suspected to have changed her Woman's Dress to Man's; or dress'd with Blankets, Indian like, she having run away once before, and was found in a Man's Apparel.

Whoever shall take up said Run-away, and bring her to her said Master, shall have Five Pounds Reward, and all necessary Charges paid by George Dolbeare. New London, October 19. 1738.

New-England Weekly Journal, February 6, 1739.

Deserted from the Sloop Mary, Josiah Thacher Commander, on Wednesday Last the 31st of January, an Indian Man named John, about 22 Years of Age, of middling Stature, short Hair He had on a grey Kersey double Breasted Jacket with flat Mette Buttons, Breeches of the same, and a speckled Woollen Shirt. Whoever shall take up the abovesaid Indian Fellow and bring him to Dr. Stephen Greenleaf, in Boston, or to Mr. Hezekiah Usher, of Newport, or to the abovesaid Thacher at Norwalk, shall have Forty shillings Reward, and all necessary Charges paid.

Boston, Feb. 6. 1738,9.

Boston Gazette, March 19, 1739.

Ran away about two Months ago, from his Master, Moses Gombauld, of the City of New York, Merchant, one Indian Boy named Pero, about Eighteen Years of Age, speaks French, English and Spanish, but all bad. He had on when he went away, a lap'd double Breasted blue Jacket and Breeches, and has thick bushy Hair.

Whoever shall take up the said Indian Boy, and bring him to his abovesaid Master in New York, or to Mr. Stephen Bontineau, Merchant in Boston, or secure him so that his Master may have him again, shall have Three Pounds Reward New York Money, or Nine Pounds our Currency.

Variant Reprints: Boston Gazette, March 26, 1739; Boston Gazette, April 2, 1739; Boston Gazette, April 9, 1739; Boston Gazette, May 7, 1739; and Boston Gazette, May 21, 1739.

Boston Gazette, March 19, 1739.

Ran away from her Master William Wall of Prudence Island, on the 20th of March last, an Indian Woman named Mary, she had with her when she went away two Gowns, one of a homespun Drugget of red and yellow Colour, the other of a strip flannel and black Duroy quilted Coat and a blue Callico Apron; she hath lost her Toes on one Foot. Whoever shall take up the said Runaway, and bring her to Dr. Aaron Bourne of Bristol, or to her Master on Prudence Island, shall have 40 s. Reward, & all necessary Charges paid.

Reprints: Boston Gazette, April 9, 1739; Boston Gazette, May 7, 1739.

Boston Post-Boy, May 19, 1740.

Ran away from his Master John March, Esq; at Newbury, on the 8th Day of May Instant, an Indian Man named Primus, a short Fellow about 40 Years of Age, speaks very good English and can read and write very well: He had on when he went away, a yellowish coat with Brass Buttons, and a dark brown Coat with Pewter Buttons, a strip'd Wastcoat, and Leather Breeches.
    Whosoever shall take Said Indian and convey him to his aforesaid Master shall have Forty Shillings Reward and all necessary Charges paid by John March.
    Dated at Newbury, May 17th, 1740.

Variant Reprints: Boston Post-Boy, May 26, 1740; Boston Post-Boy, November 3, 1740.

Boston Gazette, June 9, 1740.

Ran away from his Master the Rev. Mr. Johnson of Stratford, a pretty handsome Indian Man named Pallas Worrison, about 27 Years old: He speaks good English, is apt to get in Drink, and then affects much to be thought a Scholar, and to talk about Religion, and Preaching to the Indians: He had on a white Linnen work'd Cap, a brown Camblet Coat lined with red, a lightish Drugget Jacket, and Tow Breeches, and had with him a good Fiddle on which he delights to play.

Whoever shall take up said Fellow, and bring him to his said Master, shall have four Pounds Reward and all necessary Charges paid.

Variant Reprints: Boston Gazette, June 23, 1740; Boston Post-Boy, June 23, 1740.

Boston Post-Boy, June 23, 1740.

Ran-away from Andrew Davis, of Groton in Connecticut, the 16th Day of March, last, an Indian Man Servant, Named James Wright, a well Set Fellow of a midling Stature, he had on when he went away, a yellowish Coat and Jacket. a new Beaver Hat, a worsted Cap a fine Holland Shirt, a pair of thread Stockings, his Hair cut off. He Stole a white Mare, Bridle and Saddle. Whoever shall take up said Fellow and convey him to the said Andrew Davis at Groton, or secure him so that his said Master may have him again, shall have Ten Pounds Reward, and all necessary Charge paid by me Andrew Davis.

New-England Weekly Journal, September 16, 1740.

Ran-away from Mr. Thomas Norton of Boston, the 10th Instant, an Indian Man Servant named Silas Charles, about 35 Years of Age, a tall well set Fellow, can speak good English: He had on when he went away an old Hat bound and painted red round the Button in Imitation of a Cockade, has short Hair and has an old Wigg with him, two short Jackets, a pair of old Trousers tarr'd and something colour'd with red Paint, a pair of yarn Stockings, and a pair of English Shoes half worn.

Whoever shall rake up said Runaway Indian, and shall convey him to Mr. William Baker, at the South side of the Town House in Boston, shall receive Ten Pounds Reward, and all necessary Charges paid.

Boston. September 15th 1740.

Boston Post-Boy, September 22, 1740.

Boston, September 5, 1740.

Ran away an Indian Man Servant, named Paul Abraham, of whitish Complexion, short black Hair, and a good Set of Teeth, about Thirty Years of Age, speaks pretty good English, a middle statured Fellow, He had on when he went away, a striped spotted Swan Skin red and white Jacket, a new blue and white Linen

Check Shirt, a Pair of old Trouzers, a Cinnamon or Chocolat colour'd pair of Cloth Breeches, with Linen Linings, and flowered yellow Mettle Buttons, very handsome ones, Worstead Stockings, new Shoes, and White Mettle Shoe-Buckles. He was seen on the Road going towards Barnstable.

Whoever takes up the said Runaway, and conveys him to his Master Caleb Philipps on Dock Square in Boston, shall have Five Pounds and all Charges paid by Caleb Philipps.

Boston Evening-Post, September 29, 1740.

Ran away from his Master, Capt. Edward Stewart of Newport on Rhode Island, the 27th of this Instant September, an Indian Man Servant named Moses Thomas, about 25 Years old, of middle Stature but slender, and a good looking Fellow, that speaks very good English, and has short Hair. He had on a brown Drug get Coat, pair of striped Breeches and a pair of Trouzers over them, an Oznabrigs Frock, and a Felt Hat, but neither Shirt, Jacket, Shoes or Stockings. Whoever shall take up the said Servant, and bring him to Mr. Martin Howard in Newport, of to Mr. John Tuckerman in Boston, shall have Three Pounds Reward, and all necessary Charges paid. N B. A Masters of Vessels and other persons are hereby cautioned against harbouring Concealing or carrying of the said Servant, as they will avoid the Penalty of the Law.

Reprint: Boston Evening-Post, October 6, 1740.

Boston Post-Boy, April 6, 1741.

Ran away from her Master John Bazin, the 8th an Indian Woman named Betty Paun, about 25 Years of Age, a pretty lusty well-set Woman, has several Scratches in her Face which she got by Fighting. She had on when foe went a red and white Callicoe Gown pretty much wore, a coarse Tow-[Colour'd] Shift, an upper Petticoat of a brownish Colour, patch'd with an ironing Cloth, and a blue Duffle under Petticoat.

Whoever shall apprehend said Run-away and convey her to said Master in Newport shall have Forty Shillings Reward and all necessary Charges paid. Newport, March 10. 1740.

Boston News-Letter, May 7, 1741.

Ranaway from his Master, Joseph Perry of Sherburn, An Indian Servant named Joshua Waban, about 19 or 20 Years old, of middle Stature: He bad on when he went away, a white woollen Shirt with a cotten Collar, a Bluish colour'd Cloth Coat, a brown Linnen Jacket, blue yarn Stockings, a Pair of new double sol'd Shoes, and a Castor Hat not much worn, Whoever shall take up said

Servant and bring him to his Master again, shall have all necessary Charges paid. All Masters of Vessels and other Persons are hereby cautioned against harbouring, concealing or carrying off the said Servant, as they would avoid the Penalty of the Law. He left his Masters Service the 15th Day of April last.

Reprint: Boston News-Letter, May 14, 1741.

Boston News-Letter, January 7, 1742.

Ran away from his Master Capt George Ruggels of Boston, on the 1st Inst. an Indian Man Servant, named Sylvanus Charles, alias Venus, about 22 Years of age, a tall lusty Fellow, with short Hair, had on a Seaman's Dress. Whoever shall take up said Runaway and him safely convey to his abovesaid Master in Wing. Lane, Boston, Mall have Five Pounds Reward, and all necessary Charges paid All Masters of Vessels are hereby caution'd against carrying of said Servant, on Penalty of the Law.

Reprint: Boston News-Letter, January 14, 1742.

Boston Gazette, July 13, 1742.

Ran away from his Master, Capt. John Guynn of Boston, Mariner, on Thursday the 8th of this Instant July, a Spanish Indian Slave named John Francies alias Jaun Francisco, about 26 Years of age, short well set Fellow, short Hair, speaks pretty good English; he had on when he went away a blue Waistcoat, Oznabrigs Frock and Trousers, Worsted Cap, Felt Hat, a reddish Handkerchief, a new Pair of grey Yarn Stockings, and a pair of large Shoes

Whoever shall take up the above said Runaway, and brick him to his said Master, in Boston, shall have Three Pounds (Old Tenor) Reward, and all necessary Charges paid.

All Masters of Vessels and others are hereby caution'd against concealing or carrying of said Servant, on Penalty of the Law in that Case made and Provided.

Boston News-Letter, October 14, 1742.

Ran away from Nehemiah Allen of Sturbridge, on the 5th Day of September last, An Indian Man Servant, named James Coochuck, about 20 Years of Age: He is a slim spare Fellow: Whosoever shall take up said Run away, and bring him to his said Master shall have Twenty Shillings Reward, old Tenor.

N.B. All Masters of Vessels and other Persons are forbid concealing or carrying off said Servant, as they would avoid the Penalty of the Law.

Boston Post-Boy, December 13, 1742.

Ran away from his Master Paskee Whitford of North-Kingston, Rhod-Island Government on the 22d of September last, an Indian Boy, named James, about 17 Years of Age, and suppos'd by some to be part White, of a middle Stature, about five Feet and an half high: He has had one of his great Toes cut off and joined on again, and stands something crooked: He had on when he went away, a thick Kersey cinnamon coloured jacket, a pair of black and white strip'd Breeches, a Flannel Shirt, new Shoes, yarn Stockings folded half way up his Leg, and a new felt Hat. Whosoever will take up said Run-away Boy, and secure him in one of His Majesty's Goals; or deliver him safely to his Master, shall have Six Pounds, old Tenor, Rhode Island Currency Reward, and all necessary Charges paid by Paskee Whitford.

Reprint: Boston News-Letter, December 16, 1742.

Boston Gazette, April 19, 1743.

Deserted on Thursday the 14th Instant, from the Brig Industry, now lying in the Harbour of Boston, Andrew Gardner Commander, and Indian Man named Eli Moses, about 30 Years of Age of middle Stature, long. Hair, speaks good English. He had on when he went away a bluish colour'd Coat &c. Whoever shall take up said Deserter and bring him to Me Samuel Jackson on Minots T shall have forty Shillings (old Tenor) Reward.

Boston Post-Boy, May 2, 1743.

Ran away on the 25th of November last past from his Master Mr. Caleb Bennet of Portsmouth on Rhode Island an Indian Lad named Absalom Jennings, about 16 Years of Age of a middle Stature and well set; had on when he went away a dark mors-colour'd Wastcoat, another grey Wastcoat, with Flannel Sleeves, striped red and blue, a flaunel Shirt strip'd blue and White, a Pair of Breeches made out of a Sheep-Skin, a Pair of Trowsers, a Pair of good Stockings near the Colour of his upper Wastcoat, and an old Hat cut round like a jockey Cap: He has a Scar upon the outside of one of his Legs, about half way from his Knees to his Ankle, right across his Leg. He can work at the Weavers's Trade. Whosoever shall apprehend the said Run away, him safely convey to his said Master, or secure him in any of his Majesty's Goals so that his said Master may have him again, shall have Five Pound's Reward old Tenor, and all necessary Charges paid. Portsmouth, April 22d 1743.

Reprints: Boston Post-Boy, May 9, 1743; Boston Post-Boy, May 16, 1743.

Boston Post Boy, July 25, 1743.

Ran away the 14th Instant from Thomas Parkes of New Castle in the Province of New Hampshire, an Indian Man, named Samuel Cozens, a thick set Fellow, with short Hair: He had on when he went away, a strip'd homespun Jacket, long Trowsers, a new Felt Hat, Jersey knit Stockings: Any Person that shall take up said Run away and convey him to the Goal of said Province, or to said Parker, shall have Six Pounds Reward old Tenor. Thomas Parkes. New Castle, July 14th 1743.

Boston Gazette, November 1, 1743.

Ran away from Capt. Philip Wheeler Rehoboth the 28 Instant, an Indian Fellow, nam'd Nathan Harris, about 19 Years of Age, a stout well set Fellow, has short Hair, one of his Fingers crooked; he had on a blue worsted Jacket lin'd partly with blue Shalloon; & partly with striped Flannel, also two Flannel Jackets striped blue red & white, took with him two Shirts, one Toe & Linnen, the other checker'a blue & white Cotten & Worsted, Leather Breeches, worsted Stockings new Shoes, felt Hat the brim crop'd. Whoever mall take up said Indian, & bring him to his Master in Rehoboth, or secure him so he may be had again, shall have three Pounds Reward old Tenor, and necessary Charges paid.

And all Masters of Vessels are caution'd against carrying off said Servant, on Penalty of the Law.

Rehoboth, Octob. 29. 1743.

Boston News-Letter, August 23, 1744.

Ran away on the 12th of this Instant August, from Mr. Timothy Draper of Dedham, an Indian Fellow, about 20 Years of Age, named Thomas Scoggins, of middle Stature, has short Hair, his Face something scabby: He had on when he went away, & light colour'd Duroy Coat, a striped Jacket, a linnen Shirt, Leather Breeches, yarn Stockings, round told Shoes, a felt Hat about half worn. Whoever shall take up said Servant, and him convey to his said Master in Dedham, shall have Twenty Shillings, old Tenor, Reward, and all necessary Charges paid.

All Masters of Vessels are hereby caution'd against concealing or carrying off said Servant, as they would avoid the Penalty of the Law. Dedham, Aug. 18. 1744.

Boston Evening-Post, January 21, 1745.

Ran away from the Brigantine Happy Return, Richard White Master, two Indian Men, the one named Samuel Attakin, the other Jacob Harry. This is to give Notice, that if the said Indians will return to their Duty on board the said Vessel at Col. Hutchinson's Wharf at the North End, they shall be kindly received, otherwise deem'd as Deserters. Boston, December 29th, 1744.

Boston News-Letter, May 16, 1745.

Ran away from his Master Mr. James Howell of Boston, an Indian Molatto Man, aged about 20 Years, he had on when he went away a green Jacket, and yellow Leather Breeches, he left his Hat behind him, but I am inform'd He has got two Hats since. Whoever shall take up said Run away, and bring him to Ms. Alexander Thorpe's near the Common shall receive Three Pounds Reward, Old Tenor, and all necessary Charges paid by me, James Howell.

Reprint: Boston News-Letter, May 23, 1745.

Boston News-Letter, October 2, 1746.

Deserted from his Majesty's Service, a lusty well-sett Indian Man, named John Holborn, aged 26 Years, wears his own Hair, and had on him a striped Jacket, and a wide pair of Trowsers: Whoever will take up the said Deserter, and bring him to Henry Wendell in Boston, shall have Ten Pounds, old Tenor, Reward, and all necessary Charges paid.

Reprints: Boston News-Letter, October 9, 1746; Boston News-Letter, October 17, 1746.

Boston Gazette, November 11, 1746.

Ran away from her Master Thomas Stone of Lovewell's Island, on the first Instant, an Indian Girl named Ruth, born at Ipswich, a short well set Girl has a Scar over her right Eye, and another in her Throat; she went away with a light colour'd great Coat, without Cape or Cuffs, a bluish colour'd close body'd Coat smoak'd Leather Breeches, yarn Stocking, brass shoe Buckles; and 'tis suppos'd she has the said Cloaths on, having some time since inlisted in the Expedition, in such a Dress, but was soon discover'd and dismiss'd. Whoever shall take up and return the said Girl to be said Master on the Island, or to

Elias Stone of Charlestown, Jun shall have five Pounds, Reward, old Tenor, and all necessary Charges paid.

Boston Evening-Post, December 22, 1746.

Comfort Page, an Indian Woman, Wife of William Page of Newport, have Elop'd from Husband, and denies to live with him, therefore these are to desire all Persons not to Credit her, for he will not pay a Penny for her. Given under my Hand at Newport, the 19th of December, 1746. William Page.

Reprint: Boston Evening-Post, December 29, 1746.

Boston Post-Boy, March 2, 1747.

Portsmouth, Febr. 5 1746 .

Ran-away in Company two Indian Women, one of them named Experience, Servant to Aaron Eliot of Kellingworth, a large well-looking Wench, about 25 Years old, speaks pretty good English, a soft Voice, seemingly good-natured Behaviour; she carried with her two woolen Gowns of white Warp and striped in the filling with light Colours, one of them old, the other almost new, considerable of red, she hath since got a Blanket. The other named Patience, Servant to Nathaniel Chapman of Saybrook, about 27 Years old, a short thick fat Wench, her Arms scar'd with burning for the Gout, speaks but little, seldom any English and that broken, had on a green woolen Gown, striped Coat, leather-heal'd Womens Shoes, carried with her a dark colour'd streaked Bed blanket: They came both from Nantucket, and are not likely to part; they went in Company with a Negro Man. Whoever will take up said Runaways and return them home, or secure them and inform so that they may be had, shall have Fifty Shillings, old Tenor, per Head, and all necessary Charges paid for them by their respective Masters.

Reprints: Boston Post-Boy, March 9, 1747; Boston Post-Boy, March 16, 1747.

Boston Evening-Post, April 13, 1747.

Broke out of his Majesty's Goal in Taunton in the County of Bristol, the last Night, an Indian Man named Nathaniel Strum, alias Daniel James, a short slim Fellow, with a very flat Nose and short Hair: He had on a brown Great Coat and a blue close bodied Coat, old gray Stockings and old Shoes, and a Check Shirt. He was committed to said Goal for Theft. Whoever, shall take

up said Fellow, and secure him so that he may be remanded back again to Prison, shall have Five Pounds old Tenor Reward, paid by
   Sylvester Richmond, Sheriff of the County of Bristol. April 10, 1747.

Reprints: Boston Evening-Post, April 20, 1747; Boston Evening-Post, April 27, 1747.

Boston Evening-Post, March 7, 1748.

Ran away from his Master John Potter of South Kingston, an Indian Boy named James, about 14 Years of Age, a slim Fellow, and has an Impediment in his Speech. He had on when he went away, a light coloured Cloth Jacket and Breeches. Whoever shall take up said Boy, and convey him to his said Master in South Kingston, shall have Ten Pounds, Old Tenor, Reward, and necessary Charges paid by me. John Potter.

Reprints: Boston Evening-Post, March 14, 1748; Boston Evening-Post, March 21, 1748.

Boston News-Letter, November 3, 1748.

Ran away from Messieurs Dean & Mason of Boston, the 31st of last Month, an Indian Man named Justin, had on a Plaid under Jacket, and an outside white Kersey Jacket with brass Buttons figur'd with the Duke of Cumberland Bust, both new; he is middle aged, of low Stature speaks good French and but very little English. Whoever shall secure him so that his Masters may have him again, shall have six Pounds old Tenor Reward, and all necessary Charges paid by Messieurs Dean & Mason at their House near the Baptist Meeting. And all Masters of Vessels and others, are hereby caution'd against concealing or carrying off said Servant on Penalty of the Law. Boston. Nov 3, 1748.

Reprints: Boston Gazette, November 8, 1748; Boston News-Letter, November 10, 1748; Boston Gazette, November 15, 1748; Boston Gazette, November 22, 1748.

Boston Post-Boy, December 5, 1748.

Ran away from his Master Mr. Rowland Robinson of South-Kingston, on the 20th current, an Indian Boy Servant named Caesar, aged about eighteen Years, is a likely well looking Fellow, had on when he went away a coarse Kersey Jacket & Breeches of a Sheep's grey colour, Yarn Stockings of the same colour, an under Jacket of blue Duroy, lin'd with red, a new Felt Hat, and a strip'd worsted Cap. It is supposed he stole from his Master a dirty black colour'd Mare. Whoever will take up said Servant and convey him to his said

Master in South Kingston, shall have Fifteen Pounds old Tenor Reward, and all necessary Charges paid by Rowland Robinson. Novemb. 25 1748.

Boston Gazette, August 1, 1749.

Ran-away on the 13th Instant, from his Master David Nevins of Canterbury in Connecticut, a Spanish Indian Man Servant, named Cesar, about 18 Years of Age, tall well set Fellow, long Vissage, full fac'd, dark brown Eye [sic] with short Hair, speaks good English; had on a check'd Flannel Shirt, bold Leather Breeches, an old Felt Hat, without stockings or Sho[es].

Whoever shall take up said Run-away Servant and convey him to his abovesaid Master Canterbury aforesaid, or secure him in any of his Majesty's Goals, shall have twenty Pounds old Tenor Reward, and all necessary Charges paid by Timothy Green or Jonathan Dwight of Boston or of me the Subscriber. David Nevins.

And all Masters of Vessels and others are hereby caution'd aging conceal off carrying said Servant on Penalty of the Law.

Boston News-Letter, March 16, 1750.

Whereas an Indian Lad about 14 Years of Age, who was taken up at Attleborough, supposed to be a Run-away, goes by several Names, as Tom. Sam. Moses, &c. Whoever owns the said Lad may apply to Thomas Foster in said Attleborough, who will deliver him upon paying the Charges. March, 13. 1749,50.

Boston News-Letter, June 28, 1750.

Ran away on the 21st Instant from Daniel Amos of Boston, an Indian Girl, goes by the Name of Esther or Phebe, aged 16 or 17 Years: Had on when she went away, a homespun Petticoat, a short Osnabrigs Gown or a blue Calamanco one: Whoever will bring her to her said Master, shall have Forty Shillings old Tenor Reward. Daniel Amos.

Reprints: Boston News-Letter, July 5, 1750; Boston News-Letter, July 12, 1750.

Boston Post-Boy, July 2, 1750.

Ran away on the 17th of June, 1750, from Ichabod Goodwin of Berwick in the County of York, an Indian Woman Servant, about 20 Years of Age, named Sarah John, a fat thick short Woman; She carried away with her a silk Crape

Gown, she was seen to pass through Hampton on the 22d Inst. Whoever shall take up the said Runaway and secure her so that he may have her again, shall have 5 Pounds old Tenor Reward, and all necessary Charges paid.

Reprint: Boston Post-Boy, July 9, 1750.

Boston Post-Boy, July 23, 1750.

Ran away from Nathan Niles of Groton in the Colony of Connecticut, on the 16th Instant, an Indian Boy named Daniel, about 16 Years of Age, had on when he went away a new Felt Hat, a pair of light Duck Trowsers, and has lost two of his small Toes: Whoever shall secure the aforesaid Boy, so that his Master may have him again, shall receive Five Pounds Old Tenor Reward, and all Charges paid. Newport, July 18. 1750.

Reprints: Boston Post-Boy, July 30, 1750; Boston Post-Boy, August 6, 1750.

Boston Post-Boy, April 15, 1751.

Ran away from his Master Job Chase of Smithfield, in the County of Providence, on the 26th Day of March last past, an Indian Man Servant named Jeremiah Commoson, aged about 25 Years, of a middle Stature: Had on when he went away a good Felt-Hat one check'd and one white linnen Shirt, a pair of green Plush Breeches, yarn Stockings, square-toed Shoes, a light colour'd cloth Jacket, a striped double-breasted flannel Jacket under it.

Whoever shall take up the said Runaway and bring him to his said Master, or confine him in any of his Majesty's Goals, so that his said Master may have him again, shall have Seven Pounds old Tenor Reward, and necessary Charges paid by me Job Chase. Smithfield, April 8. 1751.

Reprints: Boston Post-Boy, April 22, 1751; Boston Post-Boy, April 29, 1751.

Boston Gazette, January 7, 1752.

Ran away from his Master Mr. Micah Havens of Framingham, on the 1st of Dec. last, Indian Man Servant, named Jonath. Pequeen, about 18 Years of Age, well sett Fellow, had on when he went away, long black Hair, an old Beaver Hatt, homespun Coat of a brown Colour with mettle Buttons, a Fustian Coat trim'd with the same, a pair of Leather Breeches, yarn Stockings, and a pair of double Channel Pumps: He speaks good English. Whoever shall take up said Run-away, and convey him to his aforesaid Master, shall have Two Dollars Rewards.

Boston Gazette, January 30, 1753.

Ran away from his Master John Battle of Dedham, on the 4th of November last, an Indian Lad, name Joshua Ephraim, about 19 Years of Age, strait and tall, with long black Hair: Had on a dark Coat & Jacket, old Leather Breeches, yarn Stockings, old Shoes, and an old Felt Hat: Whoever shall take up said Runaway, and convey him to his Master, shall have Four Dollars Reward, and all necessary Charges paid.

And all Masters of Vessels and others, are hereby caution'd against concealing or carrying off said Servant on Penalty of the Law. Dedham, January 29th 1752.

Reprint: Boston Gazette, February 6, 1753.

Boston Gazette, July 10, 1753.

Ran away from his Master Daniel Chickering of Dedham on the 7th Instant, an Indian Man Servant, named John Wamscom, about 18 Years of Age, a slim Fellow, with short black Hair; had on when he went away, a Felt Hat, a Leather Sheepskin jacket, white tow Shirt, white tow Trowsers yarn Stocking, but no Shoes. Whoever shall take up said Runaway, and bring or safely convey to his said Master, shall have four Dollars Reward, and all necessary Charges paid. And all Matters of Vessels and others are hereby caution'd against concealing or carrying off said Servant, on Penalty of the Law.

Boston Gazette, November 26, 1754.

Ran-away from Moses Marcy, Esq; of Sturbridge in the County of Worcester, on the 8th Instant, an Indian Woman, named Louis Wamscomb, aged 22, speaks English, well sett, has a Scar under her Chin. had on a green & white Russell Gown, a red Cloak, and took with her other Apparel.

Whoever shall take up and convey said Servant to her said Master, shall have two Dollars and all necessary Charges paid.

Sturbridge Nov. 25. 1754.

Boston Gazette, November 24, 1755.

Charlestown, November 21, 1755.

Run away on Wednesday Night last, from his Master Capt William Barber, of Charlestown, a Spanish Indian Boy, named Jack, about 17 Years of Age, a thick well-sett Fellow, with short Hair: Had on, a check Shirt, a dark Jacket, black Sheepskin Breeches, with Frock and Trowsers over them, a Pair of dark Yarn Stockings, and a Pair of half-worn Shoes, with Brass Buckles. Whoever shall take up the above Indian Boy, and convey him to his Master in Charlestown aforesaid, shall have Two Dollars Reward, and all necessary Charges paid. And all Masters of Vessels and others are hereby caution'd against harbouring, concealing or entertaining said Servant on Penalty of the Law.

Boston News-Letter, May 13, 1756.

Deserted from Capt. Nathaniel Blake's Company of Col. Bagley's Regiment, raised for the Expedition against Crown-Point, an Indian Man named Thomas Spywood, aged 25 Years, late belonging to Natick, a Person of middling Stature; had on when he went away a blue Coat and red Waistcoat. Whoever shall secure him, and cause him to be restored to the Service, or to be committed to any of His Majesty's Goals within the Province, so as that due Notice may be had thereof, within one Month from the Date hereof, shall be intitled to Four Dollars Reward, and all necessary Charges from Nath. Blake. Milton, 11th May 1756.

Boston Post-Boy, March 19, 1759.

Deserted from Captain Faulkner's Company of Rangers, the following inlisted Persons, viz. Joseph Anderson, Thomas Johnson, John Lewis, Thomas Southard, Isaac Omny, Isaac Umphry, an Indian, George Hawis, George O Donnel, James Daniel, John Quimbey, John Mc Donnald, Joseph Smith, Jacob Dockendorff, and John Nason. Whoever will apprehend any of the abovementioned Men, and commit them in any of his Majesty's Goals, and send word to the Commanding Officer at Boston, shall have Ten Dollars Reward for each Man.

Reprints: Boston Post-Boy, March 26, 1759; Boston Post-Boy, April 9, 1759.

Boston News-Letter, August 28, 1760.

Deserted from Col. Whetcomb's Regiment of Provincials, the following enlisted Soldiers, viz. John Williams, of Portsmouth, in Capt Taft's Company; Edward Soomin & John Biglow, of Boston in Capt. Gray's; Eli Nelson, of Boston, and Solomon Pain of Freetown, in Capt, Cowdin's.—Deserted also from Col. Ruggles's Regiment, Robert Trott, of Dorchester, Barnabas Evans of Woodstock, in Capt. MacFarland's Company; Jonathan Pegan, an Indian, of Dudley, in Capt. Small's; Peter Deforge, alias Allen, and John Gooden, of old York. Whoever shall apprehend the said Deserters, or any of them, and convey them to Timothy Paine, Esq; at Worcester, shall have Forty Shillings lawful Money Reward for each, and all necessary Charges paid, by Thomas Cowdin. Boston, Aug. 27, 1760.

One Phineas Goodwin, who has practised enlisting into many different Companies, and receiving the Bounty Money at each time, was taken up by the above Officer, and sent in Irons to the General Officers, where no doubt he will be made an Example of.—He enlisted six different Times, received the Bounty, and deserted, this Campaign.

Reprint: Boston Evening-Post, September 1, 1760.

Variant Reprints: Boston News-Letter, September 4, 1760; Boston News-Letter, September 11, 1760; Boston Evening-Post, September 15, 1760; Boston Evening-Post, September 22, 1760.

Boston News-Letter, October 30, 1760.

Ran away from his Master Ephraim Swift of Falmouth, on the 22d of October Instant, an Indian Servant Boy, about 17 Years of Age, named Jonas Moses, large of his Age: Had on when he went away, an Orange coloured Broadcloth Coat, with a narrow Cape, and a Flannel Jacket with narrow Stripes, a Cotton Shirt, and a large Pair of Ozenbrigs Trowsers, run through the Waistband with a String, a Beaver Hat, and had a Bundle of Cloaths with him; he has a large Scar upon his Nose between his Eyes. Whoever shall take up said Servant, and secures him in any of His Majesty's Goals, so that his Master may have him again, or brings him to his Master at Falmouth, shall have Three Dollars Reward, and necessary Charges paid by me Ephraim Swift.

Masters of Vessels and others are cautioned again harbouring, concealing, or carrying of said Servant, on Penalty of the Law. Falmouth, in the County of Barnstable, Oct. 27. 1760.

Variant Reprints: Boston News-Letter, November 6, 1760; Boston News-Letter, November 28, 1760.

Boston News-Letter, August 20, 1761.

Deserted from His Majesty's Garrison of Fort Frederick, St. John's River (commanded by Captain Lieut. Edmund Watmough) on Monday Night between the 15th and 16th of June, the Five following Persons, belonging to Maj. Gorham's Company of Rangers, viz. James Williams, 19 Years of Age, born in Annapolis-Royal, about five Feet six Inches in height, of a fresh Complexion, lately having the Small-Pox—John Durfoy, about Forty-one, born in Ireland, speaks good English, of a dark Complexion, about 5 Feet 8 Inches, pitted with the small-Pox.—Patrick Hendley, about Twenty-seven Years, born in Ireland, speaks good English, of a fresh Complexion, something Pock-broken, about 5 Feet 5 Inches, a thick, well-set Fellow:—Thomas Faulknot, an Indian Lad, born in Marthas-Vineyard, about Twenty seven Years of Age, a lusty Fellow, about 5 Feet 8 Inches, very much Pock-broken, lately having the Small-Pox, speaks very bad English: —Peter Warhonks, an Indian Lad, twenty four years Years of Age, born in Rhode-Island, a thick, well-set Fellow, about 5 Feet 5 Inches, lately having the Small-Pox, speaks good English, remarkably known by his frequently spitting in the relating of any Story, &c.—The above Persons were clothed in the Uniform of the Company, viz. Coats, red turn'd up with brown, with brown Capes and brown Insides, which may be worn either Side out; Waistcoats of the brown Colour; linnen Drawe[s]; leather Jockey-Caps, with Oak-Leaf or Branch painted on the left side, &c.

Whoever shall apprehend the above-named Deserters or either of them; and secure them in any of His Majesty's Goals, shall have Ten Dollars each; which Reward will be paid by Melatiah Bourn, Esq; in Boston.

Reprint: Boston News-Letter, August 27, 1761.

Boston Evening-Post, April 4, 1763.

On the first Inst. Ran away from his Master—Mayhew of Boston, an Indian indented Servant named Joseph Tallman, about 18 Years of Age, pretty well grown. He is supposed to have had on, when he went away, a blue Waistcoat and Breeches, Whoever takes him up, may expect a suitable Recompence from his said Master: And all Masters of Vessels are hereby warned against secreting, or carrying off the said Servant, on penalty of the Law.
Boston, April 4. 1763.

Reprints: Boston Evening-Post, April 11, 1763; Boston Evening-Post, April 18, 1763.

Boston Evening-Post, May 23, 1763.

Ran away from Col. Israel Putnam, on the Night between the 14th and 15th Instant, Two Men Servants, one named John Way a Melatto or Mustee, the other Charles Shawen, an Indian, each about 18 Years old : Carried away with them cloth colour'd lappell'd Coats cuffed and faced with Red, worsted Stockings and turn'd Pumps; said Way has a waste-coat red and part cloth colour, and short black curl'd Hair; said Shawen has a green or strip'd waste-coat; —they were in Col. Lyman's Regiment at the Havannah. Whoever will take up said Fellows and convey them to either of the Goals in Norwich, New-London, or Hartford, or convey them to their Master, shall have Five Dollars Reward for each, and all necessary Charges paid by me, Israel Putnam. Pomfret, May 16. 1763.

Reprint: Boston Evening-Post, June 6, 1763

Boston Gazette, August 27, 1764.

Twenty Dollars Reward.

Ran away from Col. Israel Putnam, on the Evening of the 18th of August Instant, a Spanish Indian Servant, named Charles, about 27 Years of Age, about five Feet ten Inches high, has long straight black Hair, small Eyes, high Cheek Bones, pretty slender made, speaks French well, also a little Indian and broken English; he has a small spot in the Forehead prick't in with Powder, and on one of his Arms has a Cross and the figure of a Cock, also prick't with Powder: He carried with him a blue strait bodied Coat lin'd with red, and a Waistcoat of the same, a Nankeen Waistcoat, one Pair of Leather Breeches, one Pair of red knit Ditto, one white Linnen Shirt, two Tow ditto, two Pair of mixt worsted Stockings, two Pair of Shoes, an old blue Surtout Coat trim'd with blue, with yellow Buttons speck'd with Steel, a yellow Button and Gold Loop on his Hat, is something pitted with the Small-Pox, he is more than common white, 'tis supposed that there is a Squaw part English gone with him and and that they carried off two or three Soldiers Blankets with them, and also a French Fowling Piece Iron mounted, but has a Silver Sight and Thumb Piece, and likewise a long Knife. He came from Canada, and was formerly the Property of Col. Lockorn of Montreal. 'Tis supposed he took a forged Pass with him. Whoever will take up and convey said Servant to his Master at Pomfret or secure him in any of his Majesty's Goals and give Notice thereof so that his Master shall have him again, shall receive the above Reward of Twenty Dollars, and all necessary Charges, paid by me Israel Putnam. Pomfret, Aug 20 1764.

N. B. All Masters of Vessels and others are hereby cautioned against harbouring, concealing, or carrying off said Fellow, as they would avoid the Penalty of the Law.

Reprints: Boston Gazette, September 3, 1764; Boston Gazette, September 10, 1764.

Boston Post-Boy, September 24, 1764.

Ran away from his Master, Thomas Ellis of Natick, on Tuesday the 11th of September, an Indian Fellow named Ephriam Sooduck, about 19 Years of Age, 5 Feet 7 Inches high, wore his own Hair.

Whoever will take up said Indian and bring him to his said Master shall have One Dollar Reward and all necessary Charges paid.

N. B. All Masters of Vessels and others are Cautioned against carrying off said Indian.

Reprints: Boston Post-Boy, October 1, 1764; Boston Post-Boy, October 8, 1764.

Boston Evening-Post, October 8, 1764.

Nantucket, September 29, 1764.

Run away from the Subscriber, in the Night of the 24th Instant, an Indian Servant Boy, about 14 Years of Age, named Jo Cash—
    Whoever will take up said Boy, and convey him to Nathaniel Wheatley in Boston, or Clothier Pierce in Newport, or to me here, shall have Five Dollars Reward, and all necessary Charges paid. George Hussey.
    It's supposed he landed near Hyannus.

Reprints: Boston Gazette, October 22, 1764; Boston Evening-Post, October 29, 1764.

Variant Reprints: Boston Evening-Post, October 15, 1764; Boston Evening-Post, October 22, 1764. In these reprints, the fugitive's first name is unabbreviated: Joseph.

Boston Evening-Post, October 22, 1764.

Ran away from his Master, Seth Dwight of Medfield, on the 12th Instant, an Indian Man Servant named Ebenezer Ephraims, of middling Stature, his own black Hair, aged nineteen Years ; had on when he went away, a blue Woollen Coat, a green Baize Waistcoat, Leather Breeches, grey Yarn Stockings, and a Pair of old Shoes. Whoever shall apprehend the said Servant and convey him to his said Master, shall receive One Dollar Reward, and necessary Charges paid by Seth Dwight. Medfield, Octob.15.1764.

Reprints: Boston Evening-Post, October 29, 1764; Boston Evening-Post, November 5, 1764.

Boston Gazette, April 7, 1766.

Ran away the 11th Instant, from me the Subscriber, an Indian Man, named Daniel Thomas, about 18 Years of Age—Had on when he went away, a Leather round Hat, brown Jacket, Woolen Shirt, Pair Deerskin Breeches, good Pair nail'd shoes, and has a Cut upon his Knee Pan, Whoever shall take up said Indian, and bring him to the Subscriber, shall have One Dollar Reward, by me, Daniel Morse.

All Masters of Vessels and others are hereby caution'd against harbouring, concealing or carrying off said Servant. N. B. Said Run-away stole and carried off a Gun with him. Natick, March 31, 1766.

Reprints: Boston Gazette, April 14, 1766; Boston Gazette, April 28, 1766.

Boston Evening-Post, February 2, 1767.

Broke away from an Officer on Wednesday Evening the 28th Instant, at Hardwick, in the County of Worcester, a Mollatto Fellow named Arthur, half Indian and half Negro, about 20 Years of Age: Had on when he escaped an old Grey Great Coat, three old lapell'd Jackets, one red and two blue, a pair of old Leather Breeches, and three Pair of Stockings; a good pair of Shoes with large Brass Buckles, and an old ragged white shirt; he wore short black Hair, and had on an old short brimm'd Hat, cock'd up on one side with a brass Button. He was hand-cuff'd, but at that Time only upon one Hand, and had a Rope about his Neck.

At the time of his Escape he rode off a Sorrel Horse, 14 Hands and an half High, with Bridle, Saddle and Saddle-Bags: The Horse has no artificial Mark, but is well carriaged, about 6 or 7 Years old, and Trots and Paces well.

The abovesaid Fellow was taken up for forcing two White Women in the most abusive Manner; he is an old offender, and a notorious Thief, and has broke Goal several times.

Whoever will apprehend said Criminal and Horse, and bring them to Nathaniel Jennison of Rutland District, in the County of Worcester, or secure him in any of his Majesty's Goals and give Notice thereof to said Jennison, shall have Ten Dollars Reward and all necessary Charges paid by me, Nathaniel Jennison.

Boston Chronicle, March 9, 1769.

Fifty Dollars Reward.

To be paid by the Subscriber onto William Cotton, who sailed from New-Haven in April A. D. 1757, in the Brigantine Minerva, Mr. Adam Babcock, owner, and William Sherman, master, who left said Brig in May following at St. Croix.—If he will attend the Hon. Superior Court to be holden at Norwich, in the county of New-London, on the 4th Tuesday of March inst. And also, Five Dollars to Samuel Robbins, (an Indian Boy about eighteen years of age) who entered on board said Brig soon after said Cotton left her, and come to New-Haven, upon his attending said Court: And a meet reward to said Cotton and Robbins, upon their applying to the Subscriber, in Stonington, in said county, any time afterwards. Phineas Stanton, jun.

Reprints: Boston Chronicle, March 13, 1769; Boston Chronicle, March 16, 1769.

Boston Gazette, May 27, 1771.

Ran away, on the 12th Instant, from the Subscriber, a Spanish Indian Man Servant, named Peter, about 28 Years of Age, speaks broken English, is well sett, about 5 Feet 8 Inches high, one of his Thumbs has a crooked stiff Joint, and has a large Scar, occasioned by a Cut, between the Wrist and Elbow of one of his Arms: Had on when he went away, an old Claret-colour'd Jacket, a striped Flannel ditto, a check Flannel Shirt, Buckskin Breeches, and long White Trowsers. Whoever takes up said Runaway, & conveys him to George Gordon, at Volentown, in Connecticut or commits him to any of his Majesty's Goals, so that his Master may have him again, shall have Ten Dollars Reward, and all necessary Charges, paid by me George Cordon.
 N.B. All Masters of Vessels are forbid to take off said Indian Servant, as they will answer the contrary at their Peril. May 18, 1771.

Reprints: Boston Gazette, June 3, 1771; Boston Gazette, June 10, 1771.

Boston Post-Boy, June 22, 1772.

Two Dollars Reward.

Ran away from the Subscriber, from on board Schooner Packet at Long Wharf the 19th Inst. an Indian Servant Boy, between 13 & 14 Years of Age, named George Poheag, had on when he went away a Red Duffil Jacket without Sleeves, an old Red Cap, Red patch'd Duffil Breeches, and a Check linnen Shirt, no Stockings or Shoes on when he went away. Whoever will take up the said George and deliver him to the Printers hereof, shall have Two Dollars Reward, and all necessary Charges paid. All Masters of Vessels and others are cautioned again harbouring, concealing, or carrying off said George Poheag, as they would avoid the Penalty of the Law. Daniel Folger. Boston, June 22, 1772.

Boston News-Letter, April 16, 1773.

Ran-away from his Master, John Caldwell, of Rutlant District, in the County of Worcester, Esq; a Mulatto Fellow, named Harry, Part Indian and Part Negro, aged about 23 Years, speaks good English, a straight limbed well-set Fellow, about five Feet ten Inches high, his Hair pretty long and curl'd but cut short on the fore Part of his Head: Had on when we went away, one large Jacket and one small Jacket, all Wool, a lightish Colour, and yellow Buttons, a Pair of old Shoes, a Castor Hat almost new, a Pair of old cloth Breeches near the same Colour of his Jackets, a Pair of Stockings a little darker than his Jackets, a striped all wool Shirt.—Whoever take up said Servant and conveys him to his said Masters or confines him in any of his Majesty's Goals, so that his said Master may have him again shall be handsomely Rewarded for their Trouble, and all necessary Charges paid by his said Master.

N.B. All Masters of Vessels and others are hereby cautioned against harbouring, concealing, or carrying off said Servant, as they would avoid the Penalty of the Law.

April 6th, 1773.

Reprints: Boston News-Letter, April 22, 1773; Essex Gazette, April 13 to April 20, 1773; Essex Gazette, April 20 to April 27, 1773; Essex Gazette, April 27 to May 4, 1773.

Massachusetts Spy, November 10, 1774.

Ran away from Elijah Allen, of Medfield, an Indian Boy, about 16 Years of Age, named Benjamin Thomas; had on when he went way, a white Frock, and Striped Jacket, white Shirt, short Trowsers, and short black Hair: Whoever will bring the said Runaway to said Allen, shall have Half a Dollar Reward, paid by me Elijah Allen.

New-England Chronicle, July 4, 1776.

Deserted from Captain Tresscott's Company, in the 6th Regiment of Foot, in the Continental Service, an Indian Man, named Enoch Cloas, about 6 Feet high; had on a blue out-Side Jacket, round-bound Hat. He belongs to Nantucket, and it is thought he has gone that Way. Whoever shall take up said Cloas, and return him to said Regiment, now in Boston, shall receive Five Dollars Reward, and all necessary Charges, paid by Lemuel Tresscott, Capt. Boston, June 19th, 1776.

Reprint: New-England Chronicle, July 11, 1776.

Continental Journal, and Weekly Advertiser, August 15, 1776.

John Potame, advertiz'd in No. IX. of this paper, is apprehended, and says that one Mol Thayer was with him when they broke open my House, and that she carried off all the Things there enumerated: She is part white and part Indian, has straight black Hair, about 5 Feet 6 Inches high, of a lofty

Look: —After they had plundered my House she went to Bunker's-Hill, from thence to the Castle; and I hear she is set out for New-York with the Army. Whoever will take up the said Mol Thayer and convey her to the Subscriber, or confine her, so as that she may be brought to Justice, shall have Five Dollars Reward, and necessary Charges paid, by Edward Buckman. Stoneham, July 30.

Reprint: Continental Journal, and Weekly Advertiser, August 22, 1776.

Boston Gazette, March 3, 1777.

Plymouth, February 12, 1777.

Ran away a Negro Boy named Pero, about 15 years old, (part Spanish Indian) five-feet high, had on when he went away a sky blue colour'd serge Coattees trim'd with metal buttons, a scarlet waistcoat, blue breeches, white yarn stockings, no hatt, one of his ancles is much larger than the other, remarkable flat nose, large lips and mouth. Whoever will take up said boy and bring him to me, or confine him in any goal, shall have Four Dollars Reward and all charges paid.—All masters of vessels are forewarned carrying off said negro Pero. Gideon White.

Reprints: Boston Gazette, March 10, 1777; Boston Gazette, March 17, 1777.

Independent Chronicle, March 20, 1777.

Deserted from my Company, Col. Bailey's Regiment, William Greenaway, 30 Years of Age, 5 Feet 4 Inches high, a Native of Rhode-Island, well built, but walks upright; had on when he went off a red Coat and Waistcoat; Moses Peter, an Indian, about 5 Feet 3 Inches high. Whoever will take up said Deserters, and bring them to Roxbury, or to lodge them in any Goal, so as I can have them again, shall receive for each Five Dollars Reward, and all reasonable Charges, paid by me, George Dunham, Captain.

Independent Chronicle, March 20, 1777.

Deserted from my Company, Col. Bradford's Regiment, the following Persons, viz. Barten [sic] Maker, of Haverhill, and Samuel Haney, Indian Fellow, belonging to Martha's-Vineyard. Whoever will take up and secure the said Deserters, shall have Ten Dollars Reward, for each Man, and all necessary Charges paid, by James Davis, Capt. Boston, March 19, 1777.

Boston Gazette, March 31, 1777.

Deserted from my company in Col. Marshall's regiment, an Indian Fellow, named John Almoquit, about 5 feet 10 inches high, belonging to Sandwich. Any person who shall commit him in any goal, or return him to me, shall have Eight Dollars Reward, and all necessary charges paid, by me, Amasa Soper, Captain.

Reprints: Boston Gazette, April 7, 1777; Boston Gazette, April 14, 1777.

Independent Chronicle, May 29, 1777.

Deserted from my Company, in Col. Wigglesworth's Regiment, Thomas Hopkins, an old Countrymen, 25 Years old, 5 feet 4 Inches high, dark Complexion, black hair, stammars in his Speech; John Wampy, an Indian Fellow, 6 Feet high, well drest, 27 Years old; also John Williams, an old Countryman, 24 Years old, 5 Feet 7 Inches high, a straight built Man, light Complexion, with defect in one Eye, had on, when he went away, a blue Great-Coat. Whoever shall take up said Deserters, and bring them to their Rendezvous, in Cambridge, shall have Ten Dollars Reward, for each, and all necessary Charges paid, by N. Alexander, Capt. Cambridge, May 28.

Reprint: Independent Chronicle, June 5, 1777.

Boston Gazette, June 16, 1777.

Deserted from me the subscriber, in captain Benjamin Warren's company, colonel Ichabod Alden's regiment, one James Harden, 25 years old, 5 feet 8 inches high, light complection, brown hair, grey eyes, born in Ireland, something pock-broken, well favour'd, a resident of Nantucket.—Also, one Isaac Barnabas, an Indian, 34 years of age, a native and dweller at Martha's Vineyard, with a down look, 5 feet 4 inches high. Had on when he went away, an old red great coat and other mean apparel.—Whoever will apprehend both or either of said Deserters, and deliver them to their regiment at Fort No. 2, Cambridge, or confine them in any goal, and send word so that they may be had, shall have Eight Dollars Reward for each of them, and all necessary charges paid by me, William Curtis, Lieut. Cambridge, June 11, 1777.

Reprint: Boston Gazette, June 23, 1777.

Boston Gazette, June 23, 1777.

Ticonderoga, June 9, 1777.

A Return of Deserters belonging to Captain John Chadwick's Company, in Colonel Samuel Brewer's Regiment, viz.

    Ichabod Sheffield of South Kingston, aged 32, 5 feet 6 inches, dark complexion, dark eyes, dark hair. Nathaniel Ring, of Worthington, aged 18, 5 feet 4, dark complexion, dark eyes, dark hair. Williams Phillips, an Irishman, aged 30, 5 feet 8, dark complexion, dark eyes, black hair. Nathaniel Day, of Wells, aged 23, 5 foot 8, the same description. Garshom Boston, of Wells, aged 19, 5 feet 4, dark complexion, black eyes, black hair. William Grady, of Boston, aged 20, 5 feet 9, light complexion, dark eyes, dark hair. Joseph Arter, of Truro, aged 17, 5 feet 4, dark complexion, dark hair. Israel Newport, of Sandwich, a Mulatto, aged 21, 5 feet 8. William Thompson, of Sandwich, an Indian aged 28, 5 feet 10. Samuel Wampee, of ditto, an Indian, aged 30, 5 feet 8. James Robbins, of ditto, an Indian, aged 27, 5 feet 6. Daniel Brown, of ditto, an Indian, aged 35, 5 feet 6. Moses Akins, of Great Barrington, a Dutchman, aged 22, 5 feet 10, dark complexion, dark eyes, dark hair, David Parday, of Nine Partners, aged 23, 5 feet 10, dark complexion, grey eyes, brown hair. Peter Patterson, of Stockbridge, aged 48, 5 feet 8, light complexion, grey eyes, dark brown hair. Edward Whigh, of Becker aged 25, 5 feet 4, dark complexion, dark eyes, dark hair. Silas Fay, of Becket, aged 22, 5 feet 7, dark complexion, dark eyes, dark hair. Benjamin Johnson, of Pomfret, aged 34, 5 feet 10, dark complexion, grey eyes, brown hair. Moses Brown, of Oblong, aged 24, 5 feet 7, light complexion, light eyes, light hair. Aaron Wright, of Brockfield, aged 22, 5 feet 9, dark complexion, dark eyes, dark hair. John Smith, of Hoosuck, aged 23, 5 feet 6, light complexion, light eyes, grey hair.

    Capt. James Donnell's Company.

    Samuel Lancaster, of Newbury, aged 37, 5 feet 10, dark. William, alias Solomon Jordan, of Cape-Elizabeth, aged 23; 5 feet 6, dark.

    Capt. Elisha Brewer's Company.

    Benja. Robinson, of Pomfret, an Irishman, aged 26, 5 feet 11, dark complexion, black eyes, brown hair. John Privart, of Stilwater, Age 21, 4 feet 8, light complexion, dark eyes, brown hair. John Troubridge, of Litchfield, aged 28, 5 feet 6, dark complexion, brown eyes, brown hair. Edward Fuller, of Northfield, aged 22, 5 feet 3, dark complexion, brown eyes, brown hair. David Horn, of Casco-Bay, aged 21, 5 feet 3, light complexion, dark eyes, dark hair. John Fullerton, of Westfield, aged 22, 5 feet 4, light complexion, dark eyes, black hair. Francis Sussa, of Pawnalboro, a French man, aged 18, 4 feet 9, dark complexion, black eyes, black hair. James Mecassatee, of Casco-Bay, an Irishman, aged 33, 6 feet, dark complexion, black eyes, black hair. John Mechurt, of Natick, aged 27, 5 feet 10, black complexion, white eyes, black hair. Moses Starr, of Danbury aged 23, 5 feet 7, black complexion, white eyes, black hair. James Wood, of Boston, aged 34, 4 feet 8, dark complexion, black eyes, brown hair. John English, of Lancaster, aged 25, 5 feet 8, black complexion, white eyes, black hair. Nathan Johnston, of Worcester, aged 19, 5 feet, light complexion, sandy eyes, brown hair. John Cook, of Lunenburg, Irish, aged 25, 5 feet 8, dark complexion, grey eyes, dark hair. Samuel Pool, of Lunenburgh, Irish, aged 23, 5 feet 4, light complexion, brown eyes, blue hair. Azel Goodridge, of Douglass, aged 19, 4 feet 4, light complexion, brown eyes, blue hair.

Capt. Enos Stone's Company.

Edward Edwards, of Stockbridge, aged 30, 5 feet 8, dark complexion, black hair, a scar on his arm. Jones Johnson, of Canaan, aged 15, 5 feet 7, dark complexion, brown hair, a blemish in one eye. James Sofield, a transient person, aged 23, 5 feet 7, dark complexion, brown hair. John Huffman, a transient person, aged 20, 5 feet 5, light complexion, brown hair. David Williams, aged 19, 5 feet 6, light brown complexion, brown hair. Richard Mitchell, aged 21, 5 feet 7, brown complexion, brown hair. Hugh Ames, of New Concord, in New York Government, aged 45, 5 feet 6, light complexion dark hair. Nathaniel Ames, a transient person, aged 35, 5 feet 7, dark complexion.

Captain Daniel Marril's Company.

James Ellison, of Boston, aged 40, 5 feet 3, light complexion, grey hair, light eyes.

Captain Josiah Jenkins's Company.

David Kilby, of Boston, aged 19, 5 feet 6, light.

Captain Nathan Watkins, Company.

Right Allen, of Scarboro, aged 24, 5 feet 8, dark complexion, dark hair, dark eyes. James Coolbuth, of Boxford, aged 21, 5 feet 10, light complexion, blue hair, brown eyes. Samuel Blood, of Concord, aged 21, 6 feet, black complexion, black hair, black eyes. John Patten, of Bodoinham, aged 26, 5 feet 8, dark complexion, dark hair, dark eyes. John Smith, of Kingston, aged 24, 5 feet 7, black hair, blue eyes, light complexion. Bigford Diah, of Gorham, aged 26, 5 feet 10, light complexion, dark eyes, dark hair, Rufus Hemingway, of Framingham, aged 18, 5 feet 7, light complexion, brown hair, blue eyes. Jacob Adams, of Boston, aged 21, 5 feet 8, light complexion, light hair, light eyes. Daniel Pribble, of Old-York, aged 24, 5 feet 8, light complexion, light hair, light eyes.

Elemuel Walsh, of North Yarmouth, aged 21, 5 feet 9, dark complexion, dark hair, dark eyes. Eli Hubbert, of Ware, aged 22, 5 feet 11, light complexion, light eyes, light hair. Samuel March, of Falmouth, aged 19, 5 feet 6, light complexion, light eye, light hair. James Whittam, aged 18, 5 feet 5, dark complexion, black hair, dark eyes. Edward Pakis.

Whoever shall apprehend the aforementioned Deserters, or either of them, and shall bring and confine them under the Main Guard at Boston, upon Certificate thereof, shall receive Five Dollars Reward, and all reasonable Charges paid, by the Deputy Pay Master General, agreeable to the Resolve of the honorable Continental Congress.

Reprint: Boston Gazette, June 30, 1777.

Boston Gazette, September 15, 1777.

Deserted from my Company in Col. Marshall's Regiment, Thomas Cuff and Ephraim Frost, two Indian Men, belonging to Dartmouth, in the Massachusetts State, a Reward of Five Dollars is offered to any Person who will secure said Deserters, so that they may be returned to their Duty or to Capt. Christopher Marshall, in Boston, who will pay the above Reward. All Officers, both Civil and Military, are desired to do their utmost in detecting such Robbers of the Public. Amasa Soper, Capt.

Hampshire Herald, November 30, 1784.

Whereas Sally the wife of me the subscriber, hath eloped from my bed and board and was stolen away by one Sip Willis, a negro man he stole with him when he went away about thirty dollars worth, he is about five feet six inches, well set talk's good english he has a brown great coat he is dress'd in blue cloaths he stole with him, forty shillings in cash, a red durant skirt, a black calamanco cloke, a chintz gown, a brown camblet gown, a pair of silver wash'd buckles, a pair of worsted stockings, a green baize gown, a red cotton handkerchief spotted with white, a bout three quarters square. I forbid all persons harbouring or trusting the said woman on my account. I shall pay no debts contracted by her after this date, she has some Indian blood in her, and some negro blood in her but will be taken for a white person unless strictly observed any person that will take up said woman and return information to the subscriber shall have five dollars reward, or any person that will take up both, or the negro man only, and give Information shall have twenty-five dollars reward and all necessary charges paid by me. Titus Vestpation, Westfield, November 2, 1784.

Reprint: Hampshire Herald, December 7, 1784.

Massachusetts Spy, August 7, 1788.

Ran away from the subscriber, on the 6th of July last, an Indian Lad, named Bill Wobin, about 18 years old, had a small face and a cross countenance, pretty well built, and speaks tolerable good English. Had on when he went away, frock and trowsers, and a good pair of shoes. Whoever will take up said runaway, and return him to the subscriber, shall have Half a Dollar reward. John Caldwell. Barre, July 12th, 1788.

Reprints: Massachusetts Spy, August 14, 1788; Massachusetts Spy, August 21, 1788.

CONNECTICUT NEWSPAPERS

New-London Summary, July 11, 1760.

Ran away from John Dodge, junr. of Colchester, on the 24th of June ult. an Indian woman named Betty, about 36 years of Age, of a very large stature; She had a scar on her left arm, and (I think) one on her neck; She talks very plain English, and nothing of the Indian tongue, (tho' she says she is three quarters Mohawk;)—Had on when she went away, a red quilt, and a streaked wrapper.—Whoever shall take up said Indian woman, and bring her to me the subscriber, shall have Three Dollars reward, and all necessary charges paid by John Dodge, Junior.

New-London Summary, August 22, 1760.

Whereas the following Persons, Soldiers duely enlisted in the Regiment under my Command, have deserted His Majesty's Service, by Willfully neglecting or refusing to join said Regiment, viz

Of the Colonel's Company,

Paul Blogget, Simeon Orcutt, Jonathan Yeomans, and John Johnson, all of Stafford; Edmund Chamberlain of Windham, Lemuel Root of Coventry, and William Goudy, and Alexander Aldridge, transient Persons.

Lieut. Colonel's Company,

Elias Clark of P[l]ainfield; John Cutler of Killingley, & David Brown a transient Person.

Major's Company,

Daniel Chapman and Hezekiah Wright of Norwich; Christopher Squibb, an Indian Fellow belonging to Lebanon, and John Ewes a transient Person

Capt. Smith's Company,

John Pour, John Smith, and Samuel Williams of New London.

Capr. Stanion's Company,

Elihu Babcock of Stonington.

Capt. Holme's Company,

Ebenezer Sterns of Douglass

Capt. Tyler's Company,

John Clark of Norwich, and Phineas Goodale of Marlborough.

Capt. Wheatley's Company,

Peter Tatlington & Denis Delanah of Colchester; and Thomas Still alias Samuel Hines of Lyme.

Capt. Butler's Company,

Samuel Kinne of New London, Joseph Hacket, and William Phelps of Lyme.

Capt. Palmer's Company,

Joseph Hewit, and Nathaniel Brown of Sonington; and John Shaw of New-London.

Capt. Durkee's Company,

Seth Burges of Coventry and Joseph Mamanath an India Fellow of that Place

Whoever shall apprehend the aforementioned Deserters or any one or more of them, and him or them safely Convey to Albany, and deliver to the Commanding Officer there, shall have a Reward of Eight Pounds Lawful Money for each Man they shall apprehend and Deliver as aforesaid.

E. Fitch, Col. of the 4th, Connecticut Regt. Camp at Fort Ontario, Aug. 4th, 1760

Reprint: New-London Summary, August 29, 1760.

New-London Summary, September 9, 1763.

Norwich, 29th of August, 1763.

Broke out of the Goal in Norwich, John Knight, Samuel Hill, and Hannah Elishua an Indian Woman.—Whoever shall take them or either of them and return them to said Goal, shall have Twenty Shillings Reward, and all necessary Charges paid by Joseph Peck, Goaler.

Reprint: New-London Summary, September 16, 1763.

Connecticut Gazette, August 31, 1764.

Twenty Dollars Reward.

Ran away from Col. Israel Putnam, on the Evening of the 18th of August Instant, a Spanish Indian Servant, named Charles, about 27 Years of Age, about five Feet ten Inches high, has long, straight black Hair, small Eyes, high Cheek Bones, pretty slender made, speaks French well, also a little Indian and broken English, he has a small spot in the forehead prick't in with Powder, and on one of his Arms has a Cross and the figure of Cock, also prick't in with Powder: He carried with him a blue strait-bodied Coat lin'd with red, and a Waste-coat of the same, a nankeen Waste-coat, one pair of leather Breeches, one pair of red knit Ditto, one white linnen Shirt, two tow Ditto, two pair of mix't worsted Stockings, two pair of Shoes, an old blue sertout Coat trim'd with blue, & yellow Buttons speck't with Steel, a yellow button and gold loop on His Hat, is something pitted with the Small Pox He is more than common White, 'tis supposed that there is a Squaw, part English gone with him, and that they carried off two or three Soldiers Blankets with them, and also a French Fowling Piece Iron mounted, but has a Silver Sight and thumb Piece, and likewise a long Knife. He came from Canada, and was formerly the property of Col. Lockorn of Montreal. 'Tis supposed he took a forged Pass with him. Whoever will take up and convey said Servant to his Master at Pomfret, or secure him in any of his Majesty's Goals and give Notice thereof so that his Master shall have him again, shall receive the above Reward of Twenty Dollars, and all necessary Charges, paid by me Israel Putnam. Pomfret, Aug. 20, 1764

N. B. All Masters of Vessels and others are hereby cautioned against harbouring, concealing, or carrying off, said Fellow, as they would avoid the Penalty of the Law.

Reprints: Connecticut Gazette, September 7, 1764; Connecticut Gazette, September 14, 1764.

Connecticut Gazette, January 31, 1766.

Ran away from her Master, Alexander M'Neill of New London, in the evening of the 21st Instant, an indented Indian Woman, about 26 Years old, is a very tall, likely, strait Limb'd, active Wench, both speaks good English and reads well; She was brought up by one Greene at Narraganset, and is called

Hannah Greene, but 'tis probable she will change her Name: she had on and carried with her, a dark striped flannel Gown, and a striped linnen Ditto, two Quilts, and sundry other Cloathing; 'tis probable she may have gone towards Albany & Crown Point, having, as she says, been in a Campaign.

Whoever will return said Servant, or give Information of her to her said Master, so that he may have her again, shall have all necessary Charges paid them, if to the amount of Ten Pounds lawful Money, besides a handsome Reward, in proportion to their Trouble, paid by Alexander M'Neill, New London, Jan. 23d, 1766.

Reprints: Connecticut Gazette, February 7, 1766; Connecticut Gazette, February 14, 1766.

Connecticut Courant, February 15, 1768.

Four Dollars Reward.

Run away from the Subscriber in September last, a Negro man named Stephen, born in Lebanon, in the colony of Connecticut, is a stout fellow, frouzled hair, is part Indian hath remarkable scars made by the king's evil breaking under his ears and chin, had with him an old fine black broad cloth coat. Any person that will bring him to me, or confine him in any of his majesty's goals, shall have the above reward, and all reasonable charges paid by Roswell Hopkins, of the Nine Partners.

N. B. All persons are forbid to harbour, conceal or carry him off.

Reprints: Connecticut Courant, February 22, 1768; Connecticut Courant, February 29, 1768.

Connecticut Gazette, March 10, 1769.

50 Dollars Reward.

To be paid by the subscriber unto William J Cotton, who sailed from New-Haven in April, A D. 1767, (in the brigantine Minerva, Mr. Adam Babcock, owner, and William Sherman, Master, who left said brig in May following at St. Croix) if he will attend the Hon. Superior Court, to be holden at Norwich, in the county of New-London, on the 4th Tuesday of March next—And also Five Dollars to Samuel Robbins, an Indian boy, about 18 years old, who entered on board said brig soon after said Cotton left her, and came to New Haven; upon his attending said court:—And a meet reward to said Cotton and Robbins, upon their applying to the subscriber in Stonington, in said County, any time afterwards. Stonington, Feb. 21, 1769. Phineas Stanton, jun.

Reprints: Connecticut Journal, March 10, 1769; Connecticut Gazette, March 17, 1769; Connecticut Journal, March 17, 1769; Connecticut Gazette, March 24, 1769; Connecticut Gazette, March 31, 1769.

Connecticut Gazette, July 21, 1769.

Ran away from last night, from the Subscriber in Groton, an indented Indian Wench, named Bilha, in her 17th year, is very thick fat, and rather more than common Height, has something of a down Look:—Had on striped red and yellow Cambleteen Gown, black Quilt, and black Hat. Whoever will return said Wench to the Subscriber in Groton, shall have One Dollar Reward, and all necessary Charges paid by me, Aaron Avery. July 19, 1769.

Connecticut Gazette, December 13, 1771.

Ran-away from William Stewart, on the Night of the 27th Ultimo, an Indented Indian Servant about Nineteen Years of age, named Warren Tatson, a lusty well-built Fellow, had on when he went away, a dark brown double: breasted Jacket, lined with red and brown striped Flannel, blue duffil Trowsers, yarn Stockings, and a blue buff cap : Carried off with him one or two Frocks, a new red Great Coat, and sundry other Cloaths: Whoever will apprehend said Run-away, and bring him to his Master, or secure him so that he may be had again, shall be handsomely rewarded therefor, and all necessary Charges paid.
    All Masters of Vessels and others are forbid secreting or carrying off said Indian, as they'll answer it at the Penalty of the Law.
    New-London, Dec. 5, 1771.

Reprints: Connecticut Gazette, December 20, 1771; Connecticut Gazette, December 27, 1771.

Connecticut Gazette, May 8, 1772.

Ran-away from the Subscriber on the 14th Instant, an Indian Servant Boy about 16 Years old, named George, a well set fellow; had on when he went away, a grey under Jacket without Sleeves, and a blue Jacket pach'd on the Sleeves with grey, a pair of Sheep Skin Breeches, and a full'd Cap, Whoever shall take up said run-away and return him to me the Subscriber in Ashford shall have One Dollar Reward, and no Charges paid by me Ebenezer Walker.
    Ashford, April 24, 1772.

Connecticut Gazette, March 19, 1773.

Ran away from the Subscriber in Stonington, on Monday Night last, an indented Indian Boy named David Job, about 15 Years old, likely and well made. Had on a blue Broadcloth Great Coat, two gray homespun Jackets, a striped flannel Shirt, a pair of brown cloth Breeches and gray cloth Cap with a patch of red in it; there followed him a large brindle Dog. Whoever will return the said Servant to his Master in Stonington, shall have Two Dollars Reward, and all necessary Charges paid by Elisha Williams. (March 18. 1773.)

Reprint: Connecticut Gazette, April 9, 1773.

Connecticut Gazette, May 14, 1773.

Ran away from the Subscriber, in New-London, on the First Day of Jan. last, an Indian Woman Slave named Mary, about 45 Years old, is very large made, limps with one of her Legs which is sore and much swelled. Had on a black and white drugget Gown. Is supposed to be in or near the Town of Plainfield.—All Persons are hereby forbid to entertain, harbour, or have any Kind of Dealings with the said Slave, on Penalty of the Law; and whoever will return her to me shall have Six Shillings Reward. Isaiah Bolles. New-London, May 6, 1773.

Reprint: Connecticut Gazette, May 28, 1773.

Connecticut Journal, October 8, 1773.

Messrs. Greens,

Reading in your Journal No. 308, an Advertisement sign'd Samuel Turner, offering Five Dollars Reward for taking up a Molatto Fellow, named Pero, whom the said Turner claims to be a Slave for Life. I esteem myself bound in Duty to inform the Public, That said Pero, was born free of an Indian Woman, called Hannah Moree, and bound to me by Advice of Authority by the Name of Aaron, per Indenture, bearing Date the 16th of Nov. 1750, the said Aaron being Twenty One Years of Age in Nov, 1768 -And do advise all who have the common Feelings of Humanity, to yield their Influence and Assistance to protect the said Indian against all Attempts upon his just Liberty.

Reprints: Connecticut Journal, October 15, 1773; Connecticut Journal, October 22, 1773.

Connecticut Gazette, September 2, 1774.

Ran away from the Subscriber in Colchester, on Friday the 22d of July last, an Apprentice Molatto Boy named Silas Free about 16 Years old, his

Complexion nearly as dark as a Negro, of midling Stature, has bulky Hair, a Star on his right Arm, occasioned by a scauld, in of middling Stature: Wore away a white tow Shirt and Trousers, a striped blue and white flannel Jacket without Sleeves, and an old Hat. Whoever will take up and return said Apprentice to me the Subscriber shall have Five Dollars Reward, and all necessary Charge paid by Daniel Clark. Colchesser, 13th Aug. A. D. 1774.

N. B. All Masters of Vessels and Others are forbid harbouring or carrying of said Apprentice, upon Peril of the Law.—He went of Company with an Indian Apprentice to Mr. John Tennant.

Connecticut Journal, September 16, 1774.

Manor of St. George, August 23, 1774.

Ran away from the Subscriber at the Manor of St. George, on the South Side of Long-Island, opposite to Brook-Haven, a Molatto Slave, half Negro and half Indian, named Dick, about 5 Feet 8 Inches high, full faced, thick Lips, bushy Hair, is about 23 Years of Age; carried away with him a Bundle of Cloaths that cannot be particularly described, except a red Cloth Jacket, blue Cloth Coat. Also,

Ran away with him from Col. Nathaniel Woodhull of the same Place, an Indian Fellow, named Joe, about 20 Years of Age, about 5 Feet 6 Inches high. Whoever takes up either of the said Fellows, and secures him or them in any of his Majesty's Gaols [sic], or shall bring one or both of them to their Masters, shall have Twenty Shillings Reward for each if taken up in this Colony, and Five Pounds for each if taken in any other Colony, and all reasonable Charges paid, by William Smith.

Reprints: Connecticut Journal, September 23, 1774; Connecticut Journal, September 30, 1774.

Note: Smith and Woodhull also advertised for Dick and Joe in the colony of New York.

Connecticut Gazette, January 27, 1775.

Ran away, on the 4th day of January, 1775, from Stephen Hassard, of South-Kingstown, in the Colony of Rhode-Island, a Mustee man slave, named Jo; about 20 years old; a thick, short fellow, long hair behind, a little curled, and on the top of his head cut short; his complexion is as light as an Indian, being part Spanish Indian; had on, when we went away, three jackets, his outside jacket and breeches were of a mill'd colour, but something faded, his jacket had pewter, and his breeches brass buttons; his middle jacket a very short one, one skirt of it worn off, and has been torn down the back seem by wrestling, his under jacket is an old red dufffl, much patched and faded; a good felt hat about half-worn; a pair of white yarn stockings, and an old pair of shoes. Whoever will take up said fellow, and secure him in any of his Majesty's Goals, so his master gets him again, or convey him to him, shall have Eight Dollars reward, and all charges, paid by Stephen Hassard.

N. B. If taken to the westward of, or near New-London, apply to Capt. Robinson Mumford, who will pay the above Reward, and necessary Charges.

Reprint: Connecticut Gazette, February 3, 1775.

Connecticut Gazette, September 29, 1775.

Abimeleck Uncas, a likely Indian Boy about 15 Years of Age, well set, comely, sensible, handsome spoken and ingenious, who has lived with the Subscriber this eight Years, took it in his Head to elope last Evening, and wore away a light colour'd cloth Jacket without Sleeves, a stript tow shirt, tow Trowsers, and felt Hat. His Master, desirous of having him again, will give Two Dollars Reward to any Person who will return him safe. Norwich, 14th Sept. 1775. Christo, Leffingwell.

Connecticut Courant, July 1, 1776.

Run away from David Brownson of Suffield, an Indian fellow, 20 years old, had on when he went away, an old pair of trowsers, woolen shirt, and carried away one pair of leather breeches one check shirt, one new castor hat, and an old felt ditto, a new homespun brown coat and vest, two pair shoes, and one pair large buckles, and calls his name William Thomas, is about 5 feet 10 inches high, a cooper by trade, has two teeth standing out each side of his nose, a small scar in his forehead. Whoever shall take up said Indian, and return him to me, shall have three dollars reward, and all necessary charges paid by David Brownson. Suffield, June 24, 1776.

Reprints: Connecticut Courant, July 8, 1776; Connecticut Courant, July 15, 1776.

Connecticut Gazette, October 4, 1776.

Deserted, last Friday, from the ship Oliver Cromwell, lying in the Harbour of New-London, an Indian named Oliver Blossom, who said he was born at Montauk, is tall and strait limb'd, pitted with the Small-pox, pretty Talkative, says he ran away from a Man of War, and has a Pass from Gen. Washington's

Aid de Camp: Had on a green short Jacket, striped Trowsers, a small round felt Hat, and a check'd woollen Shirt. Whoever will return him to said Ship shall have a handsome Reward, and all necessary Charges paid by William Coit. New-London, Sept. 26, 1776.

Reprint: Connecticut Gazette, October 18, 1776.

Connecticut Gazette, December 6, 1776.

Three Dollars Reward.

Ran away from the Subscriber in Plainfield, in Windham County, on the 25th Day of November Inst. an indented Indian Man Servant about 25 Years of Age, named James Simons; had on when he ran away a streaked linen Jacket with white linen Cuffs and Cape to it, had no Hat, and was very slightly cloathed. Said Indian was shipped on Board the Greenwich Cruiser,— Gardner, Commander, belonging to East-Greenwich. He was was [sic] taken into Custody for Stealing on the Night next after the 24th of November Instant, and on said 25th Instant made his Escape from his Keepers. He is used to the Sea, and says he was born at Martha's-Vineyard, and that he has sailed out of Nantucket. Whoever will take up said Indian and secure him in any of the Goals in the United States of America, or deliver him to the Subscriber in Plainfield, or on Board of said Privateer, shall have the above Reward, and all necessary Charges paid by Robert Kinsman.

Dated Plainfield, November 25th, 1776.

Reprints: Connecticut Gazette, December 13, 1776; Connecticut Gazette, December 20, 1776; Connecticut Gazette, December 27, 1776.

Connecticut Courant, May 26, 1777.

Deserted from Capt. Woodbridge's company in Col. Swift's regiment, about the 10th of April. one John Hough, 24 years of age, red complexion, sandy hair, grey eyes, 6 feet high, belongs to New-Concord in New-York State. Derick Sliter, 35 years of age, light complexion, light colour'd hair, blue eyes, 6 feet and 1 inch high, lives when at home in Amenia Precinct, in the State of New-York, and is supposed to be about his own house. Peter Johns, an Indian molatto, 28 years of age, 5 feet 10 inches high, black hair, tied in his neck, one white eye, is supposed to be near the State of Rhode-Island, in the east part of Connecticut. Any person that will secure said deserters in any goal so they may be had, or bring them to New-Milford to join their regiment, shall have five dollars reward for each, and all necessary charges paid, by Reuben Calkin, Lt. May 23, 1777.

Connecticut Courant, June 9, 1777.

Deserted from Col. Charles Webb's regiment, on the 17th, 18th and 19th of May, the following fellows, viz. John Wamper an Indian, 5 feet 9 inches high, had on a claret colour'd coat with brown sleves. Isaac Sheet, 5 feet 7 inches high, had on an old brown jacket. John Sanders, 5 feet 7 inches high, pitted with the small-pox, had on a brown coat . . . the above named are all Indians. Whoever shall secure either of said deserters, shall receive 5 dollars reward for each with reasonable charges, by Daniel Eldridge, Lieut. Stanford, May 14, 1777.

Norwich Packet, June 30, 1777.

Deserted from Capt. Abner Bacon's Company, Col. John Durkee's Regiment, one John Jeffords, an Indian, about 5 Feet 5 Inches high, near 30 Years of Age, wore away a checkered Linen Shirt, and an old white Blanket. Whoever will take up said Deserter, and return him to the Regiment, or confine him in any Goal so that the Subscriber may have him again shall have Five Dollars Reward and all necessary Charges paid by Abner Bacon, Captain. Norwich, June 30, 1777.

Reprints: Norwich Packet, July 14, 1777; Norwich Packet, July 21, 1777.

Norwich Packet, July 28, 1777.

Deserted from Capt. John Ellis's Company, Col. Shearburn's Re[gi]ment, one John Wampey, an Indian, who inlisted by the Name of Amos Clain, about 5 Feet 9 Inches high, 30 Years of Age, wore away a striped Woollen Waistcoat, and a striped Woollen Shirt. Whoever will take up said Deserter and secure him to the Regiment or confine him in any Goal, so that the Subscriber may have him again, shall have Five Dollars Reward, and all necessary Charges paid by me, John Ellis, Captain. Norwich, July 21, 1777.

Connecticut Gazette, February 20, 1778.

Deserted from Capt Sheraway's company, Col. Prev[??]e's regiment, one William Hall, a soldier 5 feet 8 inches high, well set, long black hair and black eyes, had on a small round hat, an old short blue coat, leather breeches, & white shirt, he is an indian born but is scarce to be known from a white man. Whoever will take up said deserter and return him to His regiment or confine him & give due notice, so that he may be had, shall receive ten Dollars reward, with necessary charges paid by me Darius Peck, Ensign.

Connecticut Courant, September 11, 1781.

Deserted from Coventry, one Nathan Clap, an Indian fellow, about 5 feet 7 or 8 inches high, hath lately taken up preaching, said Clap inlisted into the Continental army, as a recruit for the town aforesaid—Whoever will take up said deserter, and give information to the subscriber, shall have ten dollars reward and all necessary charges paid, by Thomas Brown. Coventry, August 28, 1781.

Connecticut Journal, January 21, 1784.

Ten Dollars Reward.

Run away from Long Island, in the Spring, 1781, an Indian Boy, named James, about 17 Years of Age, has a Scar on some Part of his Face: Any Person securing said Boy, so that I may have him, shall receive the above Reward from me, George Smith. Stratford, January 16, 1784.

Reprints: Connecticut Journal, January 28, 1784; Connecticut Journal, February 4, 1784; Connecticut Journal, February 11, 1784.

Connecticut Gazette, May 7, 1784.

Broke out of the county Gaol in New-London, on the night following the first inst. the following persons, viz. Amos Green, a native of Preston, in this State, is about five feet 11 inches high, light complexion, had on a dark brown jacket, and tow-cloth trowsers; also, John Reynolds, and John Collins, both old countrymen, each about 5 feet 8 inches high, each had on a dark blue jacket, and old felt hats; also, Anthony Paul, an Indian of the Mohegan tribe, had on an old brown great coat, an old felt hat, and tow cloth trowsers, is about 5 feet 8 inches high. Whoever will take up the above prisoners, and return them to the gaol, shall have Eight Dollars reward or two dollars for either of them, and all necessary charges. Ebenezer Douglas, Gaoler. New-London, May 2, 1784.

Reprints: Connecticut Gazette, May 14, 1784; Connecticut Gazette, May 21, 1784.

Connecticut Gazette, July 28, 1786.

Ran away from the subscriber about that 26th of May last, an Indian boy named George Tikeing Paul, aged 13 years a well-set lusty boy of his age. Had on when he went away, an old cloth coloured woolen jacket a striped flannel jacket, a pair of dark coloured woolen trowsers, and a Scotch knit cap. Carried off with him, two dark coloured linen jackets, a striped linen shirt, and a pair of striped linen trowsers. Any person who will take up said boy, and deliver him to the subscriber in Stonington, shall have Two Dollars reward, and all necessary charges paid, by Jonathan Gray. Stonington, 22d June, 1786.

Connecticut Courant, July 30, 1787.

Last Saturday night the following prisoners made their escape from the goal in this city, viz. Moses Fisk, a thick set fellow, about 35 years of age, committed for forgery. Ezra Holbrook, about 28 years of age, committed for burglary, and Frederick Way, an Indian fellow, committed for a rape. A reasonable reward and necessary charges paid to any person who will take up and return either of said prisoners to the goal from whence they escaped. Ezekiel Williams, Sheriff. Hartford, July 30, 1787.

Reprints: Connecticut Courant, August 6, 1787; Connecticut Courant, August 13, 1787.

Connecticut Gazette, November 30, 1787.

Two Dollars Reward.

Run away from the subscriber on the 6th day of November inst, an apprentice indian boy named Solomon Tewis, about 17 years of age. of a white complexion for an indian, about five feet six inches high; had on when he went away a brown kersey jacket, a thin buff-coloured under jacket, linen shirt and linen trowsers, while yarn stockings, castor hat, the crown broke. Whoever will take up said runaway, and return him to the subscriber, shall receive the above reward, and all necessary charges, George Denison, jun. Stonington, Nov. 20, 1787.

N. B. All masters of vessels and others, are forbid harbouring or carrying off said apprentice, on penalty of the law.

Reprint: Connecticut Gazette, December 7, 1787.

RHODE ISLAND NEWSPAPERS

Rhode-Island Gazette, October 4, 1732.

Newport, October 3, 1732.

Ran away on the 1st of this Instant October from his Mistress Mrs. Elizabeth Cole of South-Kingstown, a Spanish Indian Man named James, about 20 Years of Age, somewhat round shoulder'd, of a short Stature, pale Complection, and speaks very good English: Had on when he went away a Beaver Hat, a Silk Muslin Handkerchief, a light Grey Coat, with long Pockets, and a dark Grey Camblet Jacket, Tow Cloth Breeches and Shirt, and Grey Yarn Stockins.

Whoever takes the said Indian, and conveys him to his said Mistress, shall have Five Pounds Reward, and all necessary Charges paid.

Reprints: Boston News-Letter, October 27, 1732; Boston News-Letter, November 2, 1732.

Newport Mercury, September 23, 1760.

Run away last Thursday Night, from James Hardy, of Newport, Innholder, an Indian Woman, named Vi[c] Hill (formerly belonging to Thomas Atwood) about 25 years of Age, of a middling Stature and well set. Had on, a light striped short Gown, and a black quilted Petticoat. Whoever delivers her to her Master, shall receive Two Dollars Reward, and be paid the necessary Charges. And whoever entertains or conceals her, shall be prosecuted according to Law, by James Hardy.

Newport Mercury, February 9, 1762.

Newport, February 8.

Run away the 31st past, from Ebenezer Wing, of Sandwich, in the Province of the Massachusetts Bay, two Indian Men, one about 23, the other 24 Years of Age, the one is tall, the other short. 'Tis supposed they are gone, and will continue together. They have been us'd to whaling, and have on a whaling Dress. Whoever apprehends said Indians, and secures them in any of his Majesty's Gaols, and gives Notice thereof to said Wing, so that they may be had again, shall receive Four Dollars Reward for each, and all necessary Charges paid. Ebenezer Wing

Newport Mercury, May 11, 1762.

Newport, April 6, 1702 [*sic*].

Deserted from Newport, the 30th of March last, an Indian Man, named John Micha, a Soldier in the Rhode-Island Regiment; he is about 26 Years of Age, tall, lusty, and well-set. Had on, a dark Shag great Coat, Felt Hat cock'd up sharp, red Woollen Cap, and a Pair of [wide] Trowsers. Whoever takes up said [fel]low, and secures him in any of his Majesty's Gaols in this Colony, shall receive as a Reward, Forty Shillings Lawful Money, and all reasonable Charges, paid by Christ. Hargill, Lt. Col.

Newport Mercury, October 26, 1762.

Ran-away from the Subscriber, on the 9th Instant, an Indian Servant Woman, named Eunice, very fat and lusty. Whoever shall entertain or employ her, will be dealt with according to the Law.
   James Roach.

Reprints: Newport Mercury, November 2, 1762; Newport Mercury, November 13, 1762.

Providence Gazette, April 13, 1765.

Attleborough, April 10, 1765.

Ran away, this Day, from me the Subscriber, one Ezekiel Fuller, being a Mulatto, or half English and half Indian Fellow, Seventeen Years old, and about Five Feet Ten Inches high, strait built, has black Eyes, and long small Legs—Carried away with him of Cloathing, one black and blue Bearskin strait-bodied Coat, with Worsted Buttons; one other strait-bodied Coat, made of nearly the same Cloth, but much worn, with yellow Metal Buttons thereon, one strip'd Jacket, one Pair of Breeches, much the same of the last-mentioned Coat, Stockings of the same Colour, and also one Pair of striped Breeches, an old Pair of Shoes and an old Felt Hat;—he wore his own Hair when he went off. Whoever will secure said Fellow, and deliver him to me, his Master, or give me Intelligence, that I may have him again, shall receive a Reward of Six Dollars, and have all necessary Charges paid, by Jacob Cushman.
   N.B. All Persons are hereby cautioned against harboring or carrying off said Fellow. J.C.

Reprints: Providence Gazette, April 20, 1765; Providence Gazette, April 27, 1765; Providence Gazette, May 4, 1765.

Newport Mercury, March 10, 1766.

Ran away from Thomas Ninegrett of Charlestown, an Indian Boy about 14 Years Old, named Sampson Seedux; had on when he went away, a dark colour'd Bearskin great Coat, and a Jacket of the same Cloth, lighter colour'd, a pair of Pumps, with Brass Buckles, a pair of striped Flannel long Trowsers, a blue Cap, with a remarkable large Patch upon it; he also had with him an English felt Sea Hat, bound with Black, two white flannel shirts and a flannel under Waistcoat, a pair of yarn Stockings : He has had a Kick by a Horse in the Face, which broke his upper Jaw and knocked out three of his Teeth. Whoever will secure the said Run-away so that his Master may have him again, shall receive Four Dollars Reward, and all necessary Charges paid by Thomas Ninegrett.

N. B. All Persons are forbid entertaining, concealing, or carrying away the said Lad, as they will avoid the Penalty of the Law.

Reprints: Newport Mercury, March 17, 1766; Newport Mercury, March 24, 1766; Newport Mercury, March 31, 1766; Newport Mercury, April 7, 1766; Newport Mercury, April 14, 1766.

Newport Mercury, March 6, 1769.

Fifty Dollars Reward.

To be paid by the Subscriber,
Unto William Cotton,
Who sailed from New-Haven in April, A.D. 1767, in the Brigantine Minerva, Mr. Adam Babcock, Owner, and William Shearman, Master, who left said Brig in May following, at St. Crox, if he will attend the Hon. Superior Court, to be holden at Norwich, in the County of New-London, on the 4th Tuesday of March next: And also Five Dollars to Samuel Robbins, (an Indian Boy about 18 Years old) who entered on Board said Brig soon after said Cotton left her, and came to New-Haven, upon his attending said Court: And a meet Reward to said Cotton and Robbins, upon their applying to the Subscriber, in Stonington said County, any Time afterwards. Phineas Stanton, jun. Stonington, Feb. 21, 1769. (48)

Reprint: Newport Mercury, March 13, 1769.

Newport Mercury, October 9, 1769.

Ran away from the Subscriber, the 27th of this inst. Sept. From on board the sloop Dolphin, Sampson Ezekiel, a Mustee, indented servant, about 24 years of age, with curled black hair, sometimes tied up, his forehead shaved, a wellset fellow: Had on a dark homespun jacket, no stockings, canvas shoes, and pinchbeck buckles, who plays well on the fiddle: And also one John Saunders, (an Indian) about the same age, a short, wellset fellow, pitted with the small-pox, who was shipped to go a whaling voyage on board said sloop, and received forty-five pounds to perform the same, which two fellows in the night, broke open two chests in said sloop, stole and carried away two checked shirts and one Keg of rum, and stole the boat. Whoever takes up and secures said Sampson, that he may be brought to justice, and the matter receive him again, shall have five dollars reward, and four dollars reward for bringing the said John Saunders to justice, and all necessary charges paid, by me Lillibridge Worth. Newport, Sept. 29, 1769. [78]

Reprint: Newport Mercury, October 16, 1769.

Newport Mercury, December 11, 1769.

Ran away from the Subscriber, at South-Hampton on Long Island, about 3 Weeks past, a light coloured Indian Servant, named Jacob Wooly, of a middle Stature, reads and writes well; whoever will secure said Indian, in any of his Majesty's Jails, and give Notice thereof, or deliver him to the Subscriber, at South Hampton, shall receive Three Dollars Reward, and all necessary Charges, paid by Joseph Jacob. Dec. 11, 1769. (88)

Reprints: Newport Mercury, December 18, 1769; Newport Mercury, December 25, 1769.

Providence Gazette, May 18, 1771.

Run away, on the 12th instant, from the Subscriber, a Spanish Indian Ma[n] Servant, named Peter, about 28 Years of Age, speaks broken English, is well set, about 5 Feet 8 Inches high, one of his Thumbs has a crooked stiff joint, and has a large Scar, occasioned by a Cut, between the Wrist and Elbow of one of his Arms: Had on when he went away, an old Claret coloured Jacket, a striped Flannel Ditto, a Check Flannel Shirt, Buckskin Breeches, and long white Trowsers. Whoever takes up said Runaway, and conveys him to George Gordon, at Volentown, in Connecticut, or commits him to any of his Majesty's Goals, so that his Master may have him again, shall have Ten Dollars Reward, and all necessary Charges, paid by me George Gordon.

N. B. All Masters of Vessels are forbid to take off said Indian Servant, as they will answer the contrary at their Peril. May 18, 1771.

Reprints: Providence Gazette, May 25, 1771; Providence Gazette, June 1, 1771; Providence Gazette, June 8, 1771.

Newport Mercury, September 30, 1771.

Ran away, from me the Subscriber, of Block-Island, the 23d of this Inst. Sept. A Mustee Slave named Timothy, about 18 or 19 Years of Age, about 5 Feet 7 Inches high, a strait, well built Fellow, of a Yellow Complexion; he had on, when he went away, an old dark-coloured Jacket, and Trowsers; said Fellow went away in a Boat in Company with Two indented Servants, One of them a Mulatto, named Charles Mott, about the same Age as the said Timothy, a stout, well built Fellow, of a dark and surly Countenance, wears his own strait, black Hair, the other an Indian, named Solomon Church, much about the same Age as the other Two, but something shorter in Stature, and of a very light Complexion for an Indian; it is uncertain what Clothes these Two last had on: Whoever will apprehend the said Timothy and return him to me, or secure him in any of his Majesty's Gaols, and give Notice thereof to the Subscriber shall have Five Dollars Reward, and all [necessary] Charges paid; and for the apprehending returning or securing the other Two, shall have Three Dollars Reward for each, and all reasonable Charges, paid by me Abel Franklin. Block-Island, Sept. 25, 1771.

N. B. All Masters of Vessels and others are hereby cautioned against harbouring, concealing or carrying off said Servants, as they would avoid the Penalty of the Law. (82)

Newport Mercury, November 18, 1771.

Ran away from the Subscriber, in North-Kingstown, on or about the 6th of October last,

An indented Indian Boy, named John Anthony, about 16 Years old, and about 5 Feet high, with long black Hair, thickset and pretty light colour'd; had on, when he went away, a Linen Shirt and Breeches, old Shoes and Stockings, a double-breasted striped Jacket, an old light-coloured Jacket, an old Felt Hat, bound with white Cloth:—Whoever will apprehend said Runaway, and deliver him to his Master, or confine him in any of his Majesty's Gaols, so that his Master may have him again, shall receive Three Dollars Reward, and necessary Charges, paid by John Northup.

N. B. All Masters of Vessels, and others, are hereby forewarned carrying off or harbouring said Boy, as they would answer the same on their Perril.

Reprint: Newport Mercury, December 2, 1771.

Newport Mercury, September 28, 1772.

Ran away, on the night of the 21st instant, from Colonel Harnet, of Cape-Fear, just as he was to set sail form this place for New-York, a dark Mustee, or Indian servant, named Frank, a short, slim fellow, wearing long black hair, having on a short blue coat, turned up with yellow, speaks pretty good English, and says he was born in the East Indies:—Whoever will apprehend said fellow, and deliver him to the subscriber at Newport, shall receive four dollars reward, and all reasonable charges, paid by John Oldfield. Newport, Sept. 24, 1772.

Reprint: Newport Mercury, October 5, 1772.

Newport Mercury, November 9, 1772.

Ran away from the subscriber, in Dartmouth, on the second instant, an Indian boy, called Nathaniel Johnson, about 5 feet 4 inches high, wears his own hair, and had on a felt hat, a blue duffil outside jacket, a checked flannel shirt, a pair of striped flannel trowsers, old shoes and stockings, and carried with him two white Holland shirts, one pair of newly footed, gray yarn stockings, a white tow and linen pillow case, and a pair of dun-coloured trowsers: Whoever will return said Indian Boy to the subscriber at Dartmouth, or secure him in any of his Majesty's jails and give notice thereof, shall have three dollars reward, and all necessary charges, paid by Philip Sherman.

Newport Mercury, May 24, 1773.

Five Dollars Reward.

Ran away from Joseph Stanton, jun. of Charlestown, in the colony of Rhode-Island, on the 1st day of May, 1773, a middle-sized Indian servant, about 15 years of age, named George Paul, but tis likely he will change his name; he has been used to farming business, his fingers are rather shorter than common:—Whoever will return said servant to his master, or secure him in any of his Majesty's jails, and give notice thereof, shall receive the above reward, and all necessary charges, paid by Joseph Stanton, jun.

Reprints: Newport Mercury, May 31, 1773; Newport Mercury, June 7, 1773.

Providence Gazette, October 30, 1773.

Run away from the Subscriber, in Warwick, an Indian Man, named Buck, 23 Years of Age, five Feet three Inches high; has a Scar just above his Forehead, and another on one of his Feet, two of his upper Teeth are out, has a Roman Nose, and wears long black Hair; he plays tolerably on the Violin: Had on when he went away, a Pair of new Pumps, a new Pair of worsted Stockings, a pair of blue Broadcloth Breeches, blue Shag Trowsers, a white Flannel Shirt, red Jacket, double breasted, an outside homespun double breasted Jacket, patched, a blue Shag Great-Coat, almost new, and a small Felt Hat. Whoever takes up said Indian, and returns him to his Mistress, or secures him in any of his Majesty's Goals, shall receive Ten Dollars Reward, and all necessary Charges, paid by me, Mary Greene.

N. B. All Masters of Vessels and others are forbid carrying off or harbouring said Indian. Warwick, September 29.

Reprint: Providence Gazette, November 6, 1773.

Newport Mercury, March 7, 1774.

Ran away from Ichabod Babcock, of Charlestown, the 16th day of February, 1774, an Indian girl, named Hannah Skesuck, about 15 years of age; she is fat, thick, wellset, of a light complexion, thick lips; had on when she went away a flannel shift, an old flannel quilt, a striped flannel petticoat, dark coloured stockings, a striped flannel short gown, and a striped linen cooler: Whoever will take up said girl, and return her to her said master, or secure her so that he may have her again, shall have two dollars reward, and all necessary charges, paid by Ichabod Babcock.

Reprint: Newport Mercury, March 21, 1774.

Newport Mercury, September 12, 1774.

Four Pounds, New-York Currency, Reward.

Ran away from the subscriber, about the 16th ult. living on Long-Island, two Indian men, one of which named Peter January, upwards of 5 feet high, and has some grey spots on his head; the other named John Honce, about 5 feet 7 inches high, is a little hard of hearing. Whoever takes up the said Indians, and secures them in any of his Majesty's gaols shall have the above reward, or forty shillings for either of them. Richard Floyd.

Reprint: Newport Mercury, September 26, 1774.

Newport Mercury, January 30, 1775.

Ran away, on the 4th day of January, 1775, from Stephen Hassard, of South Kingstown, a Mustee man slave, named Jo; about 20 years old; a thick, short fellow, long hair behind, a little curled, and on the top of his head cut short; his complexion is as light as an Indian, being part Spanish Indian; had on, when he went away, three jackets, his outside jacket and breeches were of a mill'd colour, but something faded, his jacket had pewter, and his breeches brass buttons; his middle jacket a very short one, one fore skirt of it torn off, and has been torn down the back seem by wrestling, his under jacket is an old red duffil, much patched and faded; a good felt hat about half-worn, a pair of white yarn stockings, and an old pair of shoes:—Whoever will take up said fellow, and secure him in any of his Majesty's gaols, so that his master gets him again, or convey him home, shall have Eight Dollars reward, and all necessary charges, paid by Stephen Hassard.

Variant Reprint: Providence Gazette, February 4, 1775.

Newport Mercury, March 6, 1775.

Ran away, on Sunday last, from Robert Congdon, of Charlestown, an indented Indian servant, named Joshua Cheats, alias Joshua Hazard, about 16 years of age; about five feet, and one or two inches high; a pale, bold looking fellow, with black Indian hair, cut short about his neck; had on, when he went off, a redish grey jacket, with a linen one under it, greasy leather breeches, a white flannel shirt, grey worsted stockings, shoes about one half worn, a new felt hat, with a short grey surtout: He took with him some linen shirts.—Whoever will apprehend said Indian Boy, and deliver him to the subscriber, or secures him in any of his Majesty's jails, so that his master may have him again, shall receive a reward of three Spanish mill'd dollars, and all reasonable charges. All masters of vessels, and others, are hereby cautioned against secreting, or carrying said boy off. Robert Congdon. Charleston, March 2, 1775.

Reprint: Newport Mercury, March 20, 1775.

Newport Mercury, July 3, 1775.

Ran away, from the subscriber, an indented Indian servant, named Joseph Hazard, about 5 feet, 7 inches high, is about 17 years of age; had on, when he went away, an old felt hat, flannel shirt, one grey kersey jacket, a pair of breeches about half worn, one pair of grey yarn stockings, one pair of shoes about half worn—commonly ties his hair behind:—The said fellow went away about the 10th day of April last past; whoever will apprehend said Indian, and deliver him to the subscriber, in South Kingstown, or secure him in any of his Majesty's jails, so that his master may have him again, shall receive a reward of Three Dollars, and all reasonable charges, of Timothy Peckham. S. Kingstown, June 29, 1775.

Reprints: Newport Mercury, July 10, 1775; Newport Mercury, July 17, 1775; Newport Mercury, July 24, 1775; Newport Mercury, July 31, 1775; Newport Mercury, August 14, 1775.

Providence Gazette, January 13, 1776.

Deserted from the Continental Navy, the following Persons, viz. Daniel Col[ler], a short, thick Fellow, about 23 or 24 Years of Age, has a red Face, Pock-broken, stutters very much, supposed to be gone to the Eastward.—An Indian Fellow, named Ben. Hazard, about 23 or 24 Years of Age, about 5 Feet 5 or 6 Inches high, supposed to be gone to Hoosuck.—John Young, about 5 Feet 3 Inches high, about 35 Years of Age, born in Newport; had on a light coloured Jacket and Breeches.—Elijah Simmons, 48 Years of Age, 5 Feet 10 Inches high, pitted with the Small-Pox, stoops when he walks, wears his Hair, which is somewhat grey.—Richard Springer, a middle sized Man, of a middle Age, supposed to be gone to the Westward. Whoever will take up and secure either of the said Deserters, and bring them, or give Information to the Subscriber, shall receive Thirty Shillings Lawful Money Reward for either of them, and all necessary Charges, paid by Nicholas Power. Providence, January 5, 1776.

Providence Gazette, April 19, 1777.

Broke from the Prison in Windham, where he was confined, in the Night of the Ninth Inst, an Indian or Mulatto fellow, named William Placey, much pitted with the Small-Pox, is about 5 Feet 5 Inches high: He had on an old mix'd coloured Coat, red Vest, old Leather Breeches &c. Whoever shall secure and deliver him to Capt. Vine Elderkin, of Windham, or the Prison-Keeper at Windham, or if secured in the Neighborhood of Providence, to Major Hezekiah Biffell, at Providence, shall receive Two Dollars Reward, and their reasonable Expences. Windham, April 10, 1777.

Reprints: Providence Gazette, April 26, 1777; Providence Gazette, May 10, 1777.

Providence Gazette, May 10, 1777.

Deserted from Capt. Thomas Allen's Company, in Col. Talman's Regiment, an Indian Man, named Daniel Jeffery, has short black Hair; had on when he went away a dark Pea Jacket, blue Shag Trowsers.

Also an Indian named Josiah Cornet, has long Hair; had on an outside dark Jacket, lined with red and white Flannel, an under short Flannel Jacket, and Cloth Breeches.

Whoever will take up and return said Deserters, shall have Five Dollars Reward for each, and reasonable Charges, paid by Thomas Swan, 2d Lieut.

N. B. The above Deserters said they belonged to Plymouth. Tivertown May 3, 1777.

Reprint: Providence Gazette, May 17, 1777.

Providence Gazette, May 10, 1777.

Deserted the 26th of February last, from Capt. Samuel Phillips's Company, one John Aire, about 40 Years of Age, formerly lived on Block-Island. Also, deserted from said Company, two Indians, viz. John Daniels, about 20 Years of Age, 5 Feet 7 Inches high, long Hair, belongs to Charlestown. Toby Coy, about 17 Years of Age, 5 Feet 6 Inches high, belongs to Charlestown. Whoever will take up said Deserters, and confines them in any Gaol of the United States, shall have Five Dollars Reward, for each, and all necessary Charges, paid by Samuel Phillips, Capt.

Providence Gazette, July 5, 1777.

Deserted from Capt. Hammet's company, in Col. Stanton's regiment, Benjamin Wicket, an Indian, 26 years of age, about 5 feet 10 inches high, long black hair, cut square off at the ear locks: Had on when he went away, an old red broadcloth coat, a red lappel waistcoat, and a pair of leather breeches, white woolen hose, carried with him an old lappelled green jacket. Whoever will secure said deserter, so that he may be returned to his company, at Tiverton, shall have Eight Dollars reward, and all reasonable charges, paid by me, Malachi Hammet, Captain.

N. B. It is supposed that he has gone to Bedford, to go privateering. All masters of vessels are forbid carrying off or harbouring said deferter, at their peril.

Reprint: Providence Gazette, July 12, 1777.

Providence Gazette, August 16, 1777.

Deserted from Capt. Thomas Thompson's Company, Col. Stanton's Regiment, Peter Toby, alias John Toby, an Indian, about 5 Feet 3 Inches high, a thick set Fellow: Had on when he went away, a brown Jacket, long Trowsers, thick Buff Cap. Abraham Simons, alias Solomon Simons, an Indian, about 5 Feet 7 Inches high: Had on when he went away, a brown Great-Coat, and checked Trowsers. 'Tis suspected they are gone to the Northward. Whoever will take up said Deserters, and return them to their Regiment, or secure them in any Gaol of the United States, shall receive Five Dollars Reward for each, and all necessary Charges, paid by Joshua Babcock, Lieut.

Reprint: Providence Gazette, August 23, 1777.

Providence Gazette, September 27, 1777.

Deserted from Capt. Henry Dayton, on the 11th instant, William Cuff, a stout built Indian fellow, of this state, 5 feet 5 inches and a half high, and has a round face. Whoever takes up and secures said fellow, and gives notice thereof to said Dayton, shall have Five Dollars reward. Providence, Sept 13.

Providence Gazette, March 28, 1778.

Deserted from my company, in Col. Crary's regiment, about the middle of February last, James Allen, a likely, well-set Indian fellow, 22 years of age, 5 feet 5 inches high; he belongs to East-Greenwich. Also Bristol Prime, a lusty Negro fellow, 22 years of age, 5 feet 9 inches high; he belongs to Stonington, in Connecticut. Said deserters, it is supposed, went to sea in the Warren frigate. Whoever will secure them, and send them to the subscriber, at Bristol, in the state of Rhode-Island, or give him notice of their being secured, shall have Three Dollars reward for each, and reasonable charges, paid by James Parker, Capt.

Reprints: Providence Gazette, April 4, 1778; Providence Gazette, April 11, 1778; Providence Gazette, April 18, 1778.

Providence Gazette, October 10, 1778.

Absconded from his master's service, James Gardner, an indented Indian servant, about 17 years of age: Had on when he went off, a grey coatee, the sleeves and cape yellow, cloth coloured breeches, and a decent beaver hat; he had no shoes or stockings. 'Tis is supposed he is gone towards Boston. Whoever will return said servant to his master, the subscriber, shall have Ten Dollars reward, and all necessary charges, paid by William Bowen.

N. B. All persons are forbid harbouring or carrying off said servant. Providence, Oct. 8.

Reprint: Providence Gazette, October 17, 1778.

Providence Gazette, February 26, 1780.

Run away from the Subscriber, living in South-Kingstown, an Indian Servant Woman, named Patience, about 30 Years of Age, short and thick, has a Scar on one side of her Face, and is very talkative. Had on, when she went away, a black quilted Petticoat, somewhat worn, a spotted green woollen Cooler, a blue Cloth Bonnet; and took with her a large white Blanket. Said Indian has been known to change her Name. Whoever will take up said Servant, and secure her in any of the Gaols of the United States, so that her Master may have her again, or return her to her Master in South-Kingstown, shall have One Hundred Dollars Reward, and all necessary Charges, paid by Stephen Potter.

N. B. All Persons are forbid to harbour said Servant. Feb. 23, 1780.

Reprints: Providence Gazette, March 4, 1780; Providence Gazette, March 11, 1780.

American Journal and General Advertiser, April 12, 1780.

Deserted from Col. Greene's regiment, an Indian soldier, about 24 years of age, five feet nine inches high, was born at Warwick, in this State; has black hair, had on a red coat faced with white, but as he took with him a light coloured coat he may perhaps change his dress. He is strait built. Whoever will take up said deserter, and send him to the regiment, at Providence, or to the subscriber, or secure him in any gaol, shall receive fifty dollars reward, and all reasonable charges paid by, David Johnson, Lieut. Providence, April 11, 1780.

Variant Reprints: American Journal and General Advertiser, April 19, 1780; American Journal and General Advertiser, April 27, 1780.

American Journal and General Advertiser, March 10, 1781.

Deserted, the following Recruits, inlisted for Col. Christopher Greene's Regiment, viz.—John White, a Native of England, 26 Years of Age, 5 Feet 6 Inches high, of a ruddy Complexion, has dark brown Hair and dark Eyes, and is a Wheelwright by Trade, inlisted for the Town of Tiverton. James

Gordon, a Native of New Hampshire, 41 Years of Age, 5 Feet 8 Inches high, of a ruddy Complexion, and has a full Face, has brown Hair, and light Eyes, and is a Blacksmith by Trade. John Still, a Native of Virginia, 27 Years of Age, 5 Feet 7 Inches high, of a sandy Complexion, has light brown Hair and hazel Eyes, and is a Carpenter by Trade; he is thin favoured and has a Blemish in his right Eye, inlisted for Providence. Stephen Twift, a Native of Massachusetts, 32 Years of Age, 5 Feet 8 Inches high, of a dark Complexion, has brown Hair and blue Eyes, inlisted for Smithfield. John O'Bryant, a Native of Ireland, 26 Years of Age, 5 Feet 6 Inches high, of a fresh Complexion, has dark brown Hair and blue Eyes. William Bennet, a Native of Massachusetts, 30 Years of Age, 5 Feet 7 Inches high, of a light Complexion, has brown Hair and grey Eyes, and is a Carpenter by Trade, inlisted for Scituate. Robert Morris, a Native of Wales, 45 Years of Age, 5 Feet 4. Inches high, of a light Complexion, has brown Hair and light Eyes, and is a ShopJoiner by Trade, inlisted for Johnston, Obadiah Wickett (Indian) a Native of Massachusetts, 27 Years of Age, 5 Feet 6 Inches high, is full faced, inlisted for North Providence. Francis M'Carney, a Native of Ireland, 23 Years of Age, 6 Feet high, of a light Complexion, has dark Hair, and dark Eyes, John Frazier, a Native of New Jersey, 21 Years of Age, 5 Feet 4 Inches high, of a dark Complexion, has brown Hair and dark Eyes, inlisted for Warwick. Michael Power, a Native of Ireland, 40 Years of Age, 5 Feet 3 Inches high, of a ruddy Complexion, has dark Hair and hazel coloured Eyes, and is a Gardiner by Trade. Edward Jacklin (Negro) born in Connecticut, 24 Years of Age, 5 Feet 5 Inches high, is a Tanner by Trade; he is a likely, well made Fellow, and sometimes wears a false Tail. Charles Greene, a Native of Ireland, 21 Years of Age, 5 Feet 6 Inches high, of a fresh Complexion, has black Hair, and light Eyes, and is a Weaver by Trade, and pitted with the Small Pox, inlisted for Coventry. Whoever will apprehend and deliver either of the aforesaid Deserters to me, at Providence, shall receive a Reward of Twenty Dollars, in Silver, or an equivalent Sum in Paper, and the necessary Charges, paid out of the General Treasury, agreeable to an Act of the General Assembly of this State, passed at February Session, 1781. Jeremiah Olney, Lieut. Col. Providence, March 8, 1781.

Reprints: American Journal and General Advertiser, March 10, 1781; Providence Gazette, March 17, 1781; American Journal and General Advertiser, March 21, 1781; Providence Gazette, March 31, 1781.

Providence Gazette, March 17, 1781.

Deserted from Gloucester, on the 13th Instant, one Robert Wire, an Indian, who had inlisted into the Continental Army for three Years: Had on when he deserted an old brown Coat, a flowered Flannel Jacket, red Overalls, white

Yarn Stockings, and new Shoes: He is a short thick Fellow, about 27 Years of Age.—Whoever will take up said Deserter, and commit him to Providence Gaol, shall receive Twenty Silver Dollars Reward, and all necessary Charges, paid by Asa Kimball.

N. B. All Masters of Vessels are forbid to carry off said Deserter. Providence, March 15, 1781.

Reprints: Providence Gazette, March 31, 1781; Providence Gazette, April 14, 1781.

American Journal and General Advertiser, August 29, 1781.

On the Night of the 24th Instant the House of the Subscriber, in Cranston, was broken open, and the following Articles were stolen, viz—One Chintz Gown, one Worsted Ditto, one Holland Apron, one Holland Shift, one Tow and Linen Ditto, one Holland Shirt, one Holland Sheet, one Tow-and-Linen Ditto, one striped Linen Petticoat, two Silk Handkerchiefs, two Lawn Ditto, one Pair of Thread Stockings, Half a Yard of new Cambrick, one Yard of Gold Lace, and several other Articles. The Person who committed this Robbery is supposed to be an Indian Woman, that has been in the Neighbourhood sometime, and called herself Sarah Phillips, therefore, whoever will take and secure the said Indian Woman, so that she may be brought to Justice, and the Goods recovered, shall receive Ten Silver Dollars Reward. Gideon Westcott. Cranston, Aug. 27, 1781.

Providence Gazette, November 23, 1782.

Ran away from the Subscriber, in the Night of the Fifteenth Instant, a Wench, Half Indian and Half Negro, named Phoebe, Twenty-six Years of Age, large and strong, much pitted with the Small-Pox, has a remarkable piercing Eye, some Scars round her Neck and Back, and is very talkative. Took with her one Calico Gown, one striped Linen Ditto, one Drugget Ditto, a black Cloak, &c. Whoever will bring said Wench to the Subscriber, shall have Two Guineas Reward; or whoever will give Information so that she may be had, shall be handsomely paid for their Trouble. James Dagget. Rehoboth, November 22, 1782.

Reprint: Providence Gazette, November 30, 1782.

Newport Mercury, April 24, 1784.

Eight Dollars Reward.

Ran away, from Dr. Benjamin Bourn, an Indian Boy named Nathan Volentine, about 16 Years of Age, near Five Feet Six Inches high or thereabouts; had on when he went away, a brown Coat, a peach-blossom Jacket and Breeches, and carried away with him a Variety of other Clothing. Any Person who will take up said Indian and bring him to his Master, shall receive the above Reward, and all necessary Charges paid by Benjamin Bourn.

    N. B. All Masters of Vessel and others are forbid concealing or carrying off said Indian, as they would avoid the Penalties of the Law. Sandwich, April 20, 1784.

Reprints: Newport Mercury, May 1, 1784; Newport Mercury, May 8, 1784.

Newport Mercury, April 23, 1787.

Run away from the Subscribe [sic], on the 3d Day of April, Inst. an indented Indian Man Servant, about 28 Years Old, about Five Feet Three Inchies [sic] High, well Made, an Active Quick Fellow; he had on a Striped Brown and White Kersey Jacket, Long Overalls of the same, has a Scar on his Right Cheek, made with a Bayonet, is named James Trasher, sometimes calls himself James Sampson, he Stole and carried away with him, a Blanket and Bed-Tick; any Person who will take him up, and deliver him to the Subscriber, or commit him to Prison, so that the Owner receive him, shall have Three Pounds Rhode-Island Money Reward. Jonathan J. Hazard. Charleston, April 5, 1787.

Reprints: Newport Mercury, April 30, 1787; Newport Mercury, May 7, 1787.

Variant Reprints. Newport Mercury, May 14, 1787; Newport Mercury, June 18, 1787; Newport Mercury, July 2, 1787; Newport Mercury, July 9, 1787; Newport Mercury, July 16, 1787; Newport Mercury, July 23, 1787.

Providence Gazette, August 11, 1787.

Ran away, from the Subscriber, an Indian Boy, named Stephen; had on, when he went away, Towcloth Trowsers and Shirt, an old grey Jacket, and an old Felt Hat.—Whoever will take up said Boy, and bring him to his Master, shall have Two Shillings Reward, paid by Job Randall.

    N. B. All Persons are forbid harbouring, or carrying him away, on any Pretence whatever. Pawtuxet, August 7, 1787.

Reprints: Providence Gazette, August 18, 1787; Providence Gazette, August 25, 1787.

Chapter 2

Mid-Atlantic Colonies

NEW YORK NEWSPAPERS

New-York Weekly Journal, November 3, 1740.

Run away the first of October 1740. from John Breese, of the City of New-York, Leather-Dresser, a Mulatto Indian Slave Named Golloway, Aged 21 Years, about five foot four, Inches high, a thin Body and Face, markt with Small-Pox, he was Born, in the Fort at Albany, can speak Duth [sic] and lived many Years with Paul Richards. Esq; some Years Majer of this City; had on when he went away a dark gray homespun Jacket lin'd with the same, a pair of Linnen Breeches, and new Shoes; on the 3 Instant he was seen and challenged at Coll. Philipse's, Mill, and escaped by asserting he was sent in purs[u]it, of a Cuba Man Run away, and took the Road towards New-England, he loves Rum and other strong Liquors, and when Tipsey, is a brave fellow and very abusive; Whoever Secures the said Slave so that his Master or his Attorney may dispose of him shall have Forty Shillings, Reward, and Reasonable Charges paid by. John Breese.

Reprint: New-York Weekly Journal, November 10, 1740.

New-York Weekly Journal, May 25, 1741.

Run away from John Jackson, in Whippeny TownShip, in Morris County, two Negroe Slaves, one is a Man about Forty Years of Age, named Robin a short thick wellset Fellow and a round Fat Face. The other is a Young Fellow about 20 Years of Age, named Caeser, half Spanish Indian, half Negro; a very likely Fellow he has lost a Piece of one of his Ears Bit off by a Horse. Whosoever takes up the said slaves or either of them so that their Master may have them again shall have three Pounds Reward for each slave and all Reasonable Charges paid by me. John Jackson.

New-York Evening Post, June 30, 1746.

Advertisement.

Run away from Sampson Crooker of Oyster-Bay on Long-Island, an indented Indian Servant named Jeffrey, aged about twenty eight' Years, middle size something stooping in his Gate, but very spry and Active, professies himself to be something of a tailor. Had on when he went away a good Kersey Jacket, a Two Short and Breeches, a pair of old shoes and stockings, whosoever takes up said servant, and secures him so that his Master may have him again shall have forty shillings Reward, and reasonable Charges paid by Sampson Crooker.

New-York Gazette, or Weekly Post-Boy, February 23, 1747.

Run away on Sunday the 15th February, from Capt. Abraham Kip, of the City of New-York, an Indian Fellow named Tierce, about 19 Years of Age, Long-Island born, and can speak nothing but English; of a middling Stature, short Hair, and a fair Complexion for an Indian: Had on when he went away, a light colour'd Cloth Coat with slash Sleeves, an indifferent good Hat, and a pair of Trousers. Whoever takes up the said Fellow, and brings him to his Master, or secures him, so that he may he had again, shall have Twenty Shillings Reward, and all reasonable Charges, paid by Abraham Kip.

Reprints: New-York Gazette, or Weekly Post-Boy, March 2, 1747; New-York Gazette, or Weekly Post-Boy, March 9, 1747; New-York Gazette, or Weekly Post-Boy, May 4, 1747; New-York Gazette, or Weekly Post-Boy, May 11, 1747; New-York Gazette, or Weekly Post-Boy, May 18, 1747; New-York Gazette, or Weekly Post-Boy, May 25, 1747.

New-York Gazette, or Weekly Post-Boy, April 27, 1747.

Deserted at sundry Times, from Capt. James Parker's Company, at Albany, the following Men, viz. Daniel Lacy, David Wells, William Mursey, Gersham Store, an Indian, James M''Carty, Alexander M''Carty, Francis Buckelew, Daniel Rice, John Asey, Thomas Nelson, John Bryen, Timothy Conner, Henry Price, George Nichols, Andrew M''Cullom, and Barnet Sutphen. Whoever takes up and Secures either of the said Men, and gives Information thereof to John Deare, Esq; Sheriff of Amboy or the Subscriber in the same Place, shall have Three Pounds Reward and all reasonable Charges paid by Thomas Robinson. Lieut. of the Company.

N.B. If all or either of the said Men, return by the first of May next, and deliver themselves up to the Sheriff of Amboy or to the Lieutenant of the Company, they shall receive Pardon, otherwise not.

Reprint: New-York Gazette, or Weekly Post-Boy, May 4, 1747.

Variant Reprints: New-York Gazette, or Weekly Post-Boy, May 11, 1747; New-York Gazette, or Weekly Post-Boy, May 18, 1747; New-York Gazette, or Weekly Post-Boy, May 25, 1747.

New-York Gazette, or Weekly Post-Boy, May 4, 1747.

Run away on April the 25th, from Capt. Abraham Kip, in New-York, an Indian Man, about Eighteen Years old, and speaks good English: Had on when he went away, a grey Cloth Jacket, an old Pair of Trowsers, and an Iron Ring about his Neck, and one about his Leg, with a Chain from one to the other. Whoever takes up and secures the said Indian so that he may be had again, shall have Twenty Shillings Reward, and all reasonable Charges paid by Abraham Kip.

Reprints: New-York Gazette, or Weekly Post-Boy, May 11, 1747; New-York Gazette, or Weekly Post-Boy, May 18, 1747; New-York Gazette, or Weekly Post-Boy, May 25, 1747.

New-York Gazette, or Weekly Post-Boy, December 5, 1748.

Run-away on the first of November last, from John Tuthill, of the Oyster Ponds, at the East End of Long-Island, a Mulatto Man Slave, named Toney, aged about 19 Years: Had on when he went away, a Felt Hat, a brown Camblet Coat, a red Jacket, and speckled Trowsers. Also run away in Company with him, an Indian Man named Jack, belonging to John Petty of the same Place, aged about 18 Years, and has his Hair cut off: Had on when he went away, an old Beaver Hat, a lightish colour'd close bodied Coat, a red Jacket. Leather Breeches, and speckled Trowsers.

Whoever takes up the said Tony, and sends him to his said Master, or to Obadiah Wells in New-York, shall have Forty Shillings Reward, and Twenty Shillings for doing the same with the said Jack, and all reasonable Charges paid by John Tuthill, John Petty, or Obadiah Wells.

Variant Reprints: New-York Gazette, or Weekly Post-Boy, December 12, 1748; New-York Gazette, or Weekly Post-Boy, December 19, 1748; New-York Evening Post, March 6, 1749; New-York Evening Post, March 13, 1749; New-York Evening Post, March 20, 1749; New-York Evening Post, March 27, 1749.

New-York Gazette, or Weekly Post-Boy, May 1, 1749.

Run away from Samuel Moore and Francis Bloodgood, of Woodbridge, in New-Jersey, two Negro Men; one of which is a lusty young black Fellow, named Mando, aged about 20 Years; the other a yellow Madagascar Fellow, named Tom, about 40 Years old, of a middle Size, well set, and can read: We hear he has got a sort of an Indenture with him, under Pretence of being free. Whoever takes up the said Negroes, or either of them, and secures them, so that his or their masters may have him or them again, shall have Three Pounds Reward for each of them, and all reasonable Charges paid; by us Samuel Moore. Francis Bloodgood.

   N.B. 'Tis thought they are gone towards Albany, and that there is another Fellow in Company with them, belonging to Samuel Nevill, short and well set, half Negro and half Indian, near 30 Years old.

Reprint: New-York Gazette, or Weekly Post-Boy, May 8, 1749.

New-York Evening Post, May 8, 1749.

Run away from Nicholas Bayard, an Indian Man Slave, named James, about 40 Years of Age, well sett, about 5 Foot 10 Inches high, wears his own Hair, and formerly liv'd with Gabrial Legett at West-Chester: Whoever takes him up, and secures, him so that his Master can have him again, shall have Twenty Shillings Reward and all reasonable Charges paid by, Nicholas Bayard.

Reprints: New-York Evening Post, May 15, 1749; New-York Evening Post, May 22, 1749.

New-York Gazette, or Weekly Post-Boy, August 26, 1751.

Run away from Josiah Martin, living on the Edge of Hampstead-Plains, a young Indian Fellow, middle siz'd and well-set; had on when he went away, an Ozenbrigs Shirt, Waistcoat and Trowsers, and a brown Waistcoat over all, also, a Pair of Indian Shoes, and as he has carried away his Bed and Blankets, 'tis thought he may dress himself like an Indian; his Name is Jacob, and last

Year liv'd with the Chief-Justice. His hair is but half grown. Whoever will secure the said Fellow, so that he may be delivered to the said Josiah Martin, or to Mr. David Algee, at Brs. Breese's in New-York, shall have Thirty Shillings Reward, and all reasonable Charges, paid by either of the Persons before-mentioned.

Reprints: New-York Gazette, or Weekly Post-Boy, September 2, 1751; New-York Gazette, or Weekly Post-Boy, September 9, 1751; New-York Gazette, or Weekly Post-Boy, September 16, 1751

New-York Mercury, August 9, 1756.

Run away, on the 18th day of July last, from Joseph Concklin, of Southold, on Long-Island, an indian [sic] boy named Shadrack, is a stout well-made fellow, and about 16 years of age: Had on when he went away, a mixed kersey coat, the under part of the sleeves of a different colour, a flannel shirt, and a pair of deer skin breeches. Whoever takes up said boy, and secures him, so that his master may have him again, shall have Five Dollars reward, and all reasonable charges paid, by me Joseph Concklin.

Reprints: New-York Mercury, August 30, 1756; New-York Mercury, September 6, 1756; New-York Mercury, September 13, 1756

New-York Gazette, or Weekly Post-Boy, January 24, 1757.

Run away from Caleb Ferris of East-Chester, in the Province of New-York, sometime before last Christmas; a lusty likely Man Slave, named Joe, aged about 25 Years: He is of a yellow Complexion, being mixed Indian and Negroe, much of an Indian Countenance, speaks altogether English, he is well set every Way, about five Feet ten Inches high, understands all Sorts of Plantation Work, and is an excellent Hand to make Stone-Wall; he was born of a Slave, and brought up by Martha Clark, of W. Chester, and since her Death he is often running about, he sometimes pretends to be free, and it is supposed that a vile Fellow has given him a Pass: He is a great Fidler, and when he went away he took his Fiddle and a Bundle of Cloaths. Whoever will take up said Servant and secure him, so that his Master may get him again, shall have Three Pounds Reward, and all reasonable Charges paid by me, Caleb Ferris.

All Persons are hereby forewarned from harbouring or carrying off said Servant.

Reprints: New-York Gazette, or Weekly Post-Boy, January 31, 1757; New-York Gazette, or Weekly Post-Boy, February 28, 1757.

Variant Reprints: New-York Gazette, or Weekly Post-Boy, October 3, 1757; New-York Gazette, or Weekly Post-Boy, October 10, 1757; New-York Gazette, or Weekly Post-Boy, October 17, 1757; New-York Gazette, or Weekly Post-Boy, November 7, 1757; New-York Gazette, or Weekly Post-Boy, November 28, 1757.

New-York Mercury, May 30, 1757.

Run away from Frind Lucas, at the Mines, near Second-River, an Indian slave, called Wan, about 30 years of age, a little slim fellow, about 4 feet 4 or 5 inches high, short thick hair, which was cut off last fall: He was seen at Elizabeth-Town, with a blueish great coat, and a rusty beaver hat, and offer'd to list a soldier, and, am inform'd, was since at Amboy, Whoever takes up and secures said Indian, so that his master may have him, shall have forty shillings reward, and reasonable charges paid, by Frind Lucas.

Reprints: New-York Mercury, June 6, 1757; New-York Mercury, June 13, 1757; New-York Mercury, June 20, 1757; New-York Mercury, June 27, 1757; New-York Mercury, July 4, 1757; New-York Mercury, July 11, 1757.

New-York Gazette, or Weekly Post-Boy, August 1, 1757.

Run away from Thomas Wilde, of Philipsborough, on the 24th of July; an Indian Fellow, named Jacob, aged about Twenty Years, of a middle Stature, speaks good English: Had on when he went away, a Felt Hat whipt round with yellow Silk, a brown Coat and Waistcoat, light-blue Breeches and Stockings, one Tow Shirt and one fine, a Pair of single soal'd Shoes; his Hair is off.

    Whoever secures the said Servant, so that his Master may have him again, shall have Forty-shillings Reward, and reasonable Charges paid by Thomas Wilde.

    N.B. All Masters of Vessels, and Others, are forbid to carry off the said Fellow, at their Peril.

Reprints: New-York Gazette, or Weekly Post-Boy, August 1, 1757; New-York Gazette, or Weekly Post-Boy, August 8, 1757; New-York Gazette, or Weekly Post-Boy, August 22, 1757; New-York Gazette, or Weekly Post-Boy, August 29, 1757.

New-York Gazette, or Weekly Post-Boy, October 17, 1757.

Woodbridge, October 8, 1757.
Ran away from Robert Moores, of Woodbridge, an Indian Wench named Patience Rutter, about 19 Years old. Had on when she went away, a red

and yellow check Joseph, with ruffled Sleeves, a Petty-Coat of the same, an Indian Blanket, a Cap, and two Shifts. Whoever takes up and secures the said Wench, so that her Master may have her again, shall have Forty Shillings Reward, paid by Robert Moores.

Reprints: New-York Gazette, or Weekly Post-Boy, October 24, 1757; New-York Gazette, or Weekly Post-Boy, October 31, 1757; New-York Gazette, or Weekly Post-Boy, November 7, 1757; New-York Gazette, or Weekly Post-Boy, November 14, 1757; New-York Gazette, or Weekly Post-Boy, November 21, 1757.

New-York Mercury, June 12, 1758.

Run away, on the 20th of May last, from the Subscriber, living at North-Castle, County of Westchester, and Province of New-York, an Indian Servant Wench named Kate, is about 15 Years of Age, of a middle Size, and her Hair a little curl'd: Had an Iron Collar about her Neck, when she went away, and in all Probability will equip herself in Men's Cloths, and inlist for a Soldier, as she did once before, but was detected. She had a Pass for one Week, to look for a Master. Whoever takes up and secures said Wench, so that her Master may have her again, shall receive Twenty Shillings Reward, paid by Aaron Forman, Jun.

Variant Reprints: New-York Mercury, June 19, 1758; New-York Mercury, June 26, 1758; New-York Mercury, July 3, 1758; New-York Mercury, July 10, 1758.

New-York Gazette, or Weekly Post-Boy, July 17, 1758.

New-York, July 11, 1758.
Deserted from the several undermentioned Companies belonging to the New-York, Regiment the following Persons. viz.

John Evans, of McEver's, 5 Feet 6 Inches high, 25 Years old, brown Complexion, Carpenter by Trade, black Hair, born in England.
------- Jefferies, of Moore's, 5 Feet 11 Inches, 24 Years old, dark Complexion. John Sutton, of ditto, 5 Feet 8 Inches, 26 Years old, fair, born in Virginia. Henry Walton, of ditto, 6 Feet high, 25 Years old, dark Complexion, born in Pennsylvania. Henry Cooly, of ditto, 5 feet 6, 29 Years old, an Indian, born in New-York. John Fitzgerald, of ditto, 5 feet 9, 29 Years old, dark Complexion, born in the Jerseys. John Belcher, of ditto, 5 Feet 8, 30 Years old, dark Complexion born in the Jerseys. John Collin, of ditto, 5 Feet 7, 23 Years old, fair Complexion, born in Ireland. John Gerbus, of ditto, 5 Feet 8, 29 Years old, Fair Complexion, born in Germany. John Conway, of ditto, 5

Feet 7, 28 Years old, fair Complexion, born in Ireland. John McAlster, of ditto, 5 Feet 6, 25 Years old, born in Ireland. Thomas Kernon, of ditto, 5 Feet 8, brown Complexion, and born in Ireland.—All the foregoing enlisted at New-York.

John Miller, sen. of ditto, 5 Feet 6, brown Complexion, born in England, enlisted at Philadelphia. Gabriel Dicker, of Smith's Company. Robert Robertson, of Potter's; Amos Wilcot, of ditto. Thomas Pay, of Steyversant's. Zepheria Cornie, of ditto.

Daniel Mills of Paulmig's, Labourer, 5 Feet 10, aged 51, ruddy Connecticut born. Henry Stevens of Johnston's; Joseph Decker, of Van Veight's; Joseph Duddon, of ditto, Rufford Ridden, of ditto. Abraham Rice, of Yate's.

Andrew Rice, of ditto. Deliverance Conkling, of Verplank's, 5 Feet 1-2, 25 Years old, ruddy, born at Philadelphia; Benjamin Akerly, of ditto, 5 Feet 9, aged 23, ruddy, Long-Island born. John Williams, of ditto, 5 Feet 10, 34 Years old, black Hair, Long-Island born: William Johnson, of ditto, 5 Feet 10, aged 24, red Hair, Long-island born; William Brock, of ditto, 5 Feet 8, aged 34, brown Hair.—Downs, of Lockwood's, Mariner, 5 Feet 4 1-2, aged 23, ruddy Complexion, sandy Hair. Abraham Mezgan, of Bradgsley's, 5 Feet 11, Blacksmith, born in the Jerseys; John Yates, of ditto, 6 Feet high, aged 24, a Sadler, Robert Bessee, of ditto, 5 Feet 10, a Farmer, born in Boston; John Eliot, of ditto, 5 Feet 7, a Farmer born in Connecticut. Henry Miller, of Seely's 5 Feet 4, aged 24, of a red Complexion, born in Germany, enlisted at Ulster County: John Conner, of Hewlet's, 5 Feet 6, 30 Years old, fair Complexion, born in Ireland, enlisted in Queens-County: Hamilton Blackwood, of ditto, 5 Feet 9, aged 29, Mariner, of a brown Complexion, born in Ireland, enlisted at Queens-Country. William Steel, of ditto, 5 Feet 6 Inches high, 25 Years old, dark Complexion, born in England, and enlisted at Queens-Country.

Whoever apprehends any, or either of the aforesaid Deserters, and gives proper Notice thereof to the Commissioners in New-York, shall have forty shillings Reward.

Reprint: New-York Gazette, or Weekly Post-Boy, July 24, 1758.

New-York Mercury, March 10, 1760.

Run away from Stephen Ward, of Eastchester, in Westchester County; an Indian Servant Boy, named Anthony Cockchick, about 15 Years of Age, and speaks good English; Had on when he went away, a Snuff coloured Broadcloth Coat, blue Everlasting Breeches, a Felt Hat, and strait Hair, about half grown. Whoever takes up and secures said Servant, so that his Master may have him again, shall receive Four Dollars Reward and all reasonable Charges paid, by Stephen Ward.

Reprints: New-York Mercury, March 17, 1760; New-York Mercury, March 24, 1760

New-York Mercury, December 1, 1760.

Whereas a Negro Man that went by the Name of Toby Hazard, run-away from his Master, from Charles Town, in the Province of Rhode-Island, in March 1760, and inlisted in the New-York Provincial Service, in Capt. Wright's Company, and passed for a free Man; and as the Campaign is now over, he has received his Pay, and absconded, in order as 'tis supposed to escape by Sea: He is between an Indian and a Negro, his Hair not like a Negro's, but a little longer; about 5 Feet 6 Inches high, and plays on the Violin with his left Hand, is 23 Years old. Whoever takes up and secures the said Fellow, and brings him to the subscriber, at Charles-Town above mentioned, shall receive 20 Dollars, and reasonable Charges paid by John Stanton.

Reprint: New-York Mercury, December 8, 1760.

New-York Mercury, May 31, 1762.

Run away, on Friday last, the 28th Instant, from the Subscriber, an Indian Servant Lad, named—, about twelve Years old, and has a remarkable Scar on his Head: He went off without Shoes, Stockings, Wig, Hat, or Cap, having just come in from Jamaica, and had on only an Oznabrigs Frock and Trowsers: He is supposed to be gone to Long-Island. Whoever takes up and secures the said Lad so that he may be had again, shall have Forty Shillings Reward and all reasonable Charges, paid by Francis Welch.

Reprint: New-York Mercury, June 7, 1762.

New-York Mercury, December 20, 1762.

Run away from Adrian Van Brents, of Eutricht, a Wench about 15 Years old, between the Indian and Negro Breed; Was bought last October from Mr. Jaques De Nise, of Eutricht; her name is Fanny: Had on, a striped Gingham josey, and homespun Pettycoat. Whoever brings her to Mr. Van Brents, shall be well rewarded for their Trouble: Or if any one can give Information of any Person that harbours her, on Proof thereof, shall have Five Pounds Reward.

Reprints: New-York Mercury, December 27, 1762; New-York Mercury, January 3, 1763; New-York Mercury, January 10, 1763; New-York Mercury, January 17, 1763.

Variant Reprints: New-York Gazette, January 17, 1763; New-York Mercury, January 17, 1763; New-York Gazette, January 24, 1763; New-York Gazette, January 31, 1763; New-York Mercury, February 7, 1763.

New-York Mercury, May 7, 1764.

Run away, the 13th of April ultimo, from Simon Fleet, of Huntington, on Long-Island, an indented Indian Apprentice, named Charles; he is Long-Island born, and 18 Years old: Had on a Pair of Tow Trowsers, and a homespun Great Coat, and is supposed to be gone towards New-York. Any Person apprehending and securing said Apprentice, if on Long-Island, shall have 30S. Reward, or if taken in New-York, 40S. and all reasonable Charges, paid by Simon Fleet.

All Masters of Vessels are hereby forbid to carry him off.

New-York Mercury, September 10, 1764.

Run away on Monday the 27th of last Month, August, from Gilbert Smith, of Upper Freehold, in Monmouth County, East New-Jersey, a Slave, named Jacob, but has several Times changed his Name, calling himself James Start, and James Pratt, &c. his Mother was a Negro, and his Father an Indian, but he passes himself for an Indian, and is like one, of a yellowish tawney Colour; is about 23 Years of Age, 5 Feet 4 or 5 Inches high; his Hair cut short on his Crown, but curls round his Neck; has a remarkable Scar on one of his Cheek Bones, occasioned by a Scald or Burn, and speaks good English: He is much addicted to Smoaking and Drinking. He went from his Work at the Plough, was without Shoe or Stocking, and had on no other Clothes but an Oznabrig Shirt and Trowsers, an old ragged brown Waistcoat, and an Old Hat. He came to New York on Wednesday Morning last, with one Aaron Buck, in a Sloop from Barnegat, or Tom's River, and has since been seen in Town. Any Person that will bring the said Run-away to Mr. John Talman, in New York, Butcher, or to Mr. Francis Field, on Golden-Hill, or commit him to any public Goal, giving Notice to one of the said Persons, will receive from either of them, Forty Shillings Reward, and all reasonable Charges. Gilbert Smith.

N.B. All Masters of Vessels are forbid to harbour, conceal, or carry him off, as they will answer it at their Peril.

Reprint: New-York Mercury, September 17, 1764. New-York Mercury, July 21, 1766.

Variant Reprints: New-York Mercury, July 7, 1766; New-York Mercury, July 21, 1766

New-York Gazette, October 1, 1764.

Run away, an Indian Wench a Slave, calls herself Mary she has been about Eight Weeks from Montreal, speaks and reads broken English, 26 Years of Age, short and thick Set; had on when she went away, a Cap with a black Ribbon tied under her Chin, wears her Hair platted, a Calico short Gound, with the colours washed out, a black Pettycoat, bare-footed, with a Rag bound round her Heel, having been hurted. Whoever secures her in any of his Majesty's Goals, or brings her to the Work-House of this City, and delivers her to Mr. Forbes, shall receive Four Dollars Reward, and all reasonable Charges paid.—N.B. All Masters of Vessels are forbid at their Peril to take her off. [October 1.]

Variant Reprint: New-York Gazette, May 6, 1765.

New-York Gazette, April 15, 1765.

Run away from Jost Bush, of Fish-Kill, in Dutchess County, on Monday the 24th of March, an Indian Servant, about 19 Years old, about five feet and an half high, midling slim, full faced, strait black Hair, has a Scar on his Left Arm, and several Marks on his Left Leg and Thigh: Took with him, a Wool Hat, an Homespun Jacket, a red Great Coat and a Leather Britches.—Whoever secures him so that his Master may gave him again, shall have the above Reward and Charges paid by Jost Bush. Ap, 15, 1765.

Reprints: New-York Gazette, April 29, 1765; New-York Gazette, May 20, 1765; New-York Gazette, May 27, 1765.

New-York Mercury, September 15, 1766.

Run away the 3d instant, from the subscriber in New-York a negro boy, named Tom, about 16 years old, part Indian; he has had the small-pox, and has a seal'd head, part of the top of the head bald; Had on when he went away, a white shirt, tow trousers, an old double breasted swanskin jacket, and a sailor's hat. Whoever takes up said run-away, and brings him to the subscriber, shall have Forty Shillings reward, and all reasonable charges, paid by Robert Hallett.

N.B. All masters of vessels are forewarned from carrying him off, at their peril.

New-York Mercury, May 25, 1767.

Run-away from the subscribers, on the 19th inst. May, a Negro man, named Dover; he is about 18 years old, a tall well-built fellow, about 5 feet 9 inches high, country born: Had on when he went away, a blue broad-cloth coat with white-metal buttons, one blue sagathee jacket, one red calimanco, one calico do, with red buttons, one streaked linsey-woolsey do. a red ratteen do. brown broad-cloth breeches, and home-made trowsers, white and check shirts, wears an old Beaver hat; has a sham pass. Also, an Indian Mulatto fellow, about 19 years old, goes by the name of Samuel Siscat; a very slim tall fellow, has a pass signed by Governor Fitch, which he carried to sea a few years past: Had on when he went away, a brown home-made coat, a blue jacket lined with striped cloth, breeches the same with the coat, striped trowsers, blue and grey stockings, a double-breasted home-made jacket, flapt felt hat; about 5 feet 10 inches high. Whoever shall take up and secure said fellows, so that their masters may have them, shall have Five Dollars reward, and all reasonable charges, paid by William Johnson, John Beldin, jun. Norwalk, May 20, 1767.

Reprint: New-York Mercury, June 1, 1767.

New-York Mercury, August 24, 1767.

Run away from the Subscriber, living in Upper Freehold, Monmouth County, near Imlay's-town, on the 22d ult. A Mulattow [sic] Slave, half Indian, named Charles Quite; it's likely he will alter his Name: He is about 28 Years of Age, and about 6 Feet 2 Inches high, well-set, something knock-kneed, large Feet, and of a yellow Complexion, with a scar on one of his Cheeks near his Temple, long Hair, very much curl'd, and thin on the Top of his Head: Had on when he went away, a light-grey home-spun Coat, with streaked Lining, about half-worn, his Jacket is of a more darker colour, and more worn, Tow Shirt and Trowsers, and a Felt Hat: Whoever secures said Slave, so that his Master may have him again, shall have Three Pounds Reward, and reasonable Charges paid, by Richard James.

New-York Journal, October 29, 1767.

Run away on Monday the 21st Instant, from John Thomas, Esq; of Westchester County, in the Province of New-York, an Indian Slave, named Abraham, he may have changed his Name, about 23 Years of Age, about 5 Feet 5 Inches high, yellow Complexion, long black Hair something curl'd; a thick set Fellow, one of his four Teeth in the lower Jaw broke off;—had on when he went away, a white double breasted Vest, made with full'd Homespun Cloth with white Metal Buttons, the over Vest made with yellow brown Homespun Cloth, and Breeches of the same, blue Stockings, Shoes made with the Grain outward, a new Felt Hat:—Whoever takes up said Fellow, and secures him in any of his Majesty's Gaols, or brings him to his said Master, shall have Five Pounds Reward and all reasonable Charges paid, by me John Thomas. Rye, September 21, 1767.

Reprints: New-York Mercury, November 9, 1767; New-York Journal, November 12, 1767; New-York Mercury, November 16, 1767; New-York Journal, November 19, 1767; New-York Gazette, December 7, 1767; New-York Gazette, December 14, 1767.

Variant Reprints: New-York Journal, September 28, 1769; New-York Journal, October 5, 1769; New-York Journal, October 12, 1769; New-York Journal, October 19, 1769.

New-York Gazette, and Weekly Mercury, August 29, 1768.

Run away, from William Mott, of Great-Neck, on Long-Island, on Monday the 15th Instant, a young Indian Servant Fellow, named Stephen, but sometimes Pompey, about 5 Feet 6 Inches high: Had on when he went away, a Tow homespun Shirt and Trowsers, a grey homespun Jacket, a Pair of old Shoes, and an old Felt Hat; is well-set, and has streight black Hair. Whoever takes up and secures the said Fellow, so that his master may have him again, shall, if found on Long-Island, receive Twenty Shillings Reward; and if taken up off the Island, 40S. and all reasonable Charges, paid by William Mott.

N.B. It is supposed he may have a Pass.

Reprints: New-York Gazette, and Weekly Mercury, September 5, 1768; New-York Gazette, and Weekly Mercury, September 12, 1768; New-York Gazette, and Weekly Mercury, September 19, 1768; New-York Gazette, and Weekly Mercury, October 3, 1768.

New-York Gazette, and Weekly Mercury, November 20, 1769.

Five Dollars Reward.

Run away from the subscriber last Wednesday, an Indian man, named John Andress, a stout well made man, about 20 years of age, formerly a servant to Captain Giles, at the North-River; and afterwards a servant to Mr. Palmer, who lives in the country; he was born at Point-Judith, close by Rhode-Island, and was some time ago purchased of Mr. Dobs, keeper of the bridewell; he is well known in this town: Had on when he went away a blue jacket, frock and trousers. Whoever takes up said run-away, and brings him to me the subscriber, shall have the above reward, and all reasonable charges paid, by James Prince.

Reprints: New-York Gazette, and Weekly Mercury, November 27, 1769; New-York Gazette, and Weekly Mercury, December 4, 1769; New-York Gazette, and Weekly Mercury, December 11, 1769; New-York Gazette, and Weekly Mercury, December 18, 1769

New-York Gazette, and Weekly Mercury, December 10, 1770.

Forty Shillings Reward.

Ran away from the Subscriber on Friday the 23d ult. a servant Fellow, part Negro and part Indian, named James; he is about 5 Feet 9 Inches high, well set, has a large bushy Head of Hair, he is Lame with a Sore on his left Heel: Had on when he went away, a light colour'd Vest with blue Lining, a striped under Vest, a new Felt Hat, a wooling Check Shirt, tow and linen Trowsers: Whosoever takes up said Servant and secures him, so that his Master may have him again, shall have the above Reward and all reasonable Charges, paid by me Jacob Balding.

Fish Kills, Dutchess County, Nov. 27, 1770.

Reprints: New-York Gazette, and Weekly Mercury, December 24, 1770; New-York Gazette, and Weekly Mercury, January 14, 1771.

New-York Gazette, and Weekly Mercury, December 24, 1770.

Run away from Zacheus Newcomb, Charlotte precinct, in Dutchess county, an Indian Boy, named Jeffery, of 18 years old, about 5 feet 4 inches high, with black curled hair:—Had on when he went away, a short brown coat, and worsted vest without sleeves, woollen breeches; born on Long-Island, and stole from his master, one new coat and vest, homemade, mix'd colours of a deep and pale blue, plain made, with Philadelphia buttons; one castor hat, and two silk handkerchiefs. Whoever takes up the said servant, and brings him to his said master, or secures him in any of his majesty's goals, so that he may have him again, shall have Three Pounds reward, and all reasonable charges paid by me, Zacheus Newcomb. Dec. 12, 1770.

Reprints: New-York Gazette, and Weekly Mercury, December 31, 1770; New-York Gazette, and Weekly Mercury, January 7, 1771.

New-York Gazette, and Weekly Mercury, March 18, 1771.

Run away on Thursday the 7th of March, from Peter Low, a mulatto slave named Syme, or Symon, (half negro and half indian breed) about 24 years old, is a chimney sweeper: Had on when he went away, an old thickset coat, an old beaver hat, an old watch coat, and other old cloathes; had his utensils for sweeping with him. He is short and well set, walks heavy, speaks slow and thick, both Dutch and English, has short but strait Indian like hair, and is apt to smile when spoken to; as he may perhaps pretend to be a free man, masters of vessels and others, are forewarn'd from carrying him off; and whoever takes up the said slave, and secures him so that his master may have him again, shall have Two Dollars, and if taken out of the city of New-York, Four Dollars reward, with all reasonable charges, paid by Peter Low.

Reprint: New-York Gazette, and Weekly Mercury, March 25, 1771.

Variant Reprints: New-York Journal, March 21, 1771 (Reward increased); New-York Journal, March 28, 1771; New-York Journal, April 11, 1771.

New-York Gazette, and Weekly Mercury, May 13, 1771.

Forty Shillings Reward.

Run away from the Subscriber, two Slaves, one an Indian Boy, about 18 Years of Age, named Jack, with long black Hair, 5 Feet 1 or 2 Inches high: Had on a blue Cloth Coat, with white metal Buttons, white Flannel Jacket, and black Manchester Velvet Breeches: The other lately belonged to Doctor Chovet, named Brutus, near 5 Feet 8 Inches high, about the same Age: Had on a black short Jacket, with an under yellow one, and Buckskin Breeches, with old Shoes and Stockings, can read and write, and probably may forge a Pass. Whoever secures them both, or brings them to the Subscriber, shall have the above Reward, and reasonable Charges, or for either Twenty Shillings, Wm. Brownejohn, jun.

Reprints: New-York Gazette, and Weekly Mercury, May 20, 1771; New-York Gazette, and Weekly Mercury, May 27, 1771.

New-York Gazette, and Weekly Mercury, October 26, 1772.

Run away from the Subscriber, living at Huntington on Long-Island, an Indian Fellow named Peter, better than 5 Feet high, and middling well set, has two white Spots upon the right Side of his Head: Took with him a Felt Hat, a red tight-bodied Coat, a brown Jacket, striped Trowsers, and a Gun: Whoever takes up the said Fellow and secures him, so that he may be had again, or delivers him to his Master, shall have Two Pounds Reward, and all reasonable Charges, paid by Gilbert Fleet.

Reprints: New-York Gazette, and Weekly Mercury, November 2, 1772; New-York Gazette, and Weekly Mercury, November 9, 1772; New-York Gazette, and Weekly Mercury, November 16, 1772; New-York Gazette, and Weekly Mercury, December 7, 1772.

Rivington's New York Gazetteer, July 8, 1773.

Five Dollars Reward,

Run away on Thursday last from on board the Brig Hannah, Capt Henderson, an Indian Fellow, called Jack, about 22 years of age, thick and well set, about 5 feet high, streight black hair, which he generally wears tied behind; had on when he went away a green jacket, oznaburg trousers, a check shirt, a new pair of shoes, a sailor's hat; he has since been seen at the Ferry on Long Island. Whoever apprehends the said Indian, and secures, or returns him, to his master in New-York, shall have the above reward, and all reasonable charges paid by Walter and T. Buchanan, and Co.

N.B. It is requested, that no masters of vessels, or others, will harbour, or carry off said Indian, otherwise they may depend on being prosecuted.

Reprint: Rivington's New York Gazetteer, July 15, 1773.

Rivington's New York Gazetteer, September 30, 1773.

Forty Shillings Reward.

Run away from the subscriber, living at Westchester, on Monday last the 26th instant, an indented Indian fellow, who calls himself John Anderson, a very lusty well set fellow; had on a blue half-thick jacket, tow shirt and trousers, and was bare foot, a new wool hat, had in his pocket a Scotch nightcap of a dull brown colour, it has been painted and it is likely he may wear it, is much pockmarked, has a very full face, short bushy hair. Whoever apprehends said fellow, so, that his Master may have him again, shall be paid the above Reward and all reasonable charges by me Moses Wayman.

Westchester, September, 27th 1773.

It is supposed he may endeavour to go to sea, as he has been bred to it.

Reprints: Rivington's New York Gazetteer, October 7, 1773; Rivington's New York Gazetteer, October 14, 1773.

New-York Journal, February 10, 1774.

Run away Last Night, from the Brig Sparrow, Moses Sawyer, Master, two indented Servants. viz. one Indian Fellow, about 25 Years old, about 5 Feet 6 Inches high, a thick, fat Fellow, with straight, black Hair, something of a down Look. Had on when he ran way, a brown Devonshire Kersey Jacket, lined with red Baise; a red Baise Shirt, and red Duffle Trowsers; and took with him a striped Blanket. The other a Mustee Fellow, with bushy Hair, about 5 Feet 3 or 4 Inches high; had on much the same Clothes as the Other: Took with him a Blanket and sundry other Clothes. Any Person that will secure the said Fellows, in any of his Majesty's Gaols, within one Month from the Date, shall receive Ten Dollars Reward by John Foster.

N.B. All Master's of Vessels, or other Persons, are forbid carrying off, or harbouring, the said Fellows, as it is supposed they are harboured in some Part of this Town.

New York, Feb. 9 1774.

New-York Gazette, and Weekly Mercury, February 28, 1774.

Four Pounds Reward.

Run away from the subscriber, on the morning of the 24th instant, an indented servant man, named Benjamin McDonald, alias Indian Ben; he is half an Indian, a stout well made fellow, better than six feet high, long black hair, wears it tied behind, but may probably cut it off; much addicted to strong drink: Had on, when he went away, an old blue coat and olive colour'd jacket, an old pair of leather breeches, an old beaver hat, a pair of blue yarn stockings and a new ozenbrigs shirt; but 'tis likely he may change his dress, as he had many with him; he went off by water; also, he took with him a large skiff newly trim'd. Whoever takes up said servant, and secures him in any of his Majesty's goals, giving notice to the subscriber at said city, shall be entitled to the above reward, and all reasonable charges, and for the skiff two dollars. All masters of vessels and others are strictly forbid to carry off, conceal or harbour the said servant, as they will answer it at their peril. N.B. He is supposed to be gone for Long-Island. Isaac Bonnel.

Perth-Amboy, Feb, 7, 1774.

Reprints: New-York Gazette, and Weekly Mercury, March 7, 1774; New-York Gazette, and Weekly Mercury, March 14, 1774.

Variant Reprints: Rivington's New York Gazetteer, March 17, 1774; Rivington's New York Gazetteer, March 24, 1774.

New-York Gazette, and Weekly Mercury, August 1, 1774.

Four Pounds Reward.

Run away from the subscriber about the 16th ult. living on Long-Island, two Indian Men, one of which named Peter January, upwards of 5 Feet high, and has some grey Spots in his Head; the other named John Honce, about 5 Feet 7 inches high. Whoever takes up the said Indians, and secures them in any of his Majesty's Goals, shall have the above Reward, or Forty Shillings for either of them. Richard Floyd.

Reprint: New-York Gazette, and Weekly Mercury, August 8, 1774.

New-York Journal, August 25, 1774.

Manor of St. George, August 23, 1774.
Ran away from the subscriber, at the manor of St. George on the south side of Long Island, opposite to Brookhaven, a mulatto slave, half Negro and half Indian, named Dick, about 5 feet 8 inches high, full faced, has thick lips, bushy hair, and is about 23 years of age. He carried with him a bundle of clothes, which cannot be particularly described, except a red cloth jacket among them, and a blue cloth coat.—Also ran away, along with him, from Colonel Nathaniel Woodhull, of the same place, an Indian fellow named Joe, 20 years of age, about 5 feet 6 inches high. Whoever takes up either of the said fellow and secures him or them in any of his Majesty's gaols, or shall bring one or both of them to their masters, shall have twenty shillings reward for each of them, if taken up in this colony, and five pounds for each if taken in any other colony, and all reasonable charges, paid by William Smith.

Reprints: New-York Journal, September 1, 1774; New-York Journal, September 8, 1774; New-York Journal, September 15, 1774.

Note: Smith and Woodhull also advertised for Dick and Joe in the colony of Connecticut.

New-York Journal, March 9, 1775.

Four Pounds Reward.

Run away from the subscriber, living in East Chester, on the 6th instant, a Negro man named Robin, about 5 feet 7 inches high, a well set fellow, of a yellow complexion, part Indian, a great bushy head of hair, somewhat different from a Negro, speaks good English, and can speak Dutch, no particular mark, if he can get liquor is apt to get drunk; it is imagined he has get a pass, being very intimate with a Negro fellow, who can write, had on a felt hat half worn, a blue duffle great coat, a tann coloured over jacket, and an under one, frize, a buck skin pair of breeches, took along with him two pair of black woollen stockings, and two pair of shoes; it is imagined he has

directed his course toward the North River, to get over among the Indians, he lived at the Fish Kill, on Phillips's Manor, and on York Island. Whoever takes up and secures the said Negro fellow, so that his master may have him again (in any of his Majesty's goals) shall have the above reward, if taken in this county (five pounds, if taken in any other county) and seven pounds if taken among the Indians, with all reasonable charges paid by Isaac Ward.
   East Chester, March 7, 1775.

Reprints: New-York Journal, March 16, 1775; New-York Journal, March 23, 1775; New-York Journal, March 30, 1775.

New-York Journal, August 15, 1776.

Five Dollars Reward.

Deserted from my Company and in Col. Cary's regiment at New-Haven, an Indian Man, named Ephraim Frost, about 22 years of age, five feet eight inches high, long hair;—had on when he went away, a claret coloured coat faced up with red, breeches of the same, white stockings, and a straw hat and feather;—he plays on the fife and fiddle; his native place is Rehoboth.— Whoever shall bring said Deserter to the Regiment in New-York, shall receive the above Reward, and all necessary charges, paid by Nathaniel Carpenter, Capt.
   N.B. Said Frost deserted on the 30th of July last.

New-York Gazette, and Weekly Mercury, July 14, 1777.

Five Pounds Reward.

Run away from the subscriber, on Tuesday the 15th of April last, negro man, of a yellow complexion, part Indian, well set, walks with his knees wide apart, flat nose, about five feet eight or ten inches High, forty five years of age, or thereabouts, goes by the name of Abraham: Had on when he went away, a brown homespun jacket, tow shirt, a pair of buckskin breeches, black and white yarn stockings, and a new pair of shoes.
   The said negro [sic] took with him a small mulatto wench, by the name of Moll, which he claims as his wife, and two negro children; one a boy three years old, the other a girl five months old. The above negroes were seen on Long-Island, not long since. Whoever apprehends the said run-aways, and brings them to Thomas Harrow, in New-York, or to the subscriber, or secures them so that the owner may get them again, shall receive the above reward,

or Three Pounds for the negro, and Two Pounds for the wench and children, and all reasonable charges paid by Thomas Pell.
Manor of Pelham, June 12, 1777.

Royal American Gazette, January 28, 1779.

Deserted from the sloop Harlequin, Frank, a middle aged Indian slave: He is about the middle size, squat and broad, has a remarkable broad countenance and short neck, wears his own hair and speaks very bad English, hardly to be understood, is a good seaman but fond of liquors, and like other Indians very ungovernable in his cups. Five dollars reward will be given to any person who will apprehend and deliver him to Henry Mitchell, at No. 33, Maiden-Lane. Commander of privateers and others are warned not to carry him off or harbour him. Henry Mitchell.

New-York Gazette, and Weekly Mercury, May 17, 1779.

Five Dollars Reward.

Run away from Hamilton Young, an Indian boy name Dick, about 5 feet high, well set; had on when he went away, a brown fustian coat, vest and breeches, and white stockings. Whoever will bring him to the Printer, shall receive the above reward and all reasonable charges.

New-York Packet, June 17, 1784.

Five Pounds Reward,

Run away from the subscriber, living nearly opposite West-Point, a Yellow Slave, about quarter Indian, twenty-eight years of age, smart and active, speaks good English, is fond of singing and dancing, about six feet high, a small scar on the side of his nose, a black speck on the white of his eye, about the size of a pin head, a scar on his belly nearly three inches long, occasioned by a burn, a hurt between his toe, which occasions a lump, a little stiff in his right arm. He went off about four years ago, was seen in Danbury, in Colonel Canfield's regiment, called himself Job, his proper name is Sam. He is supposed to be somewhere in Connecticut or Massachusetts Bay. Whoever takes up said Negro, and delivers him to his master or to the Printer hereof, shall be paid the above reward, and reasonable charges. William Davenport.

Reprints: New-York Packet, June 17, 1784; New-York Packet, July 8, 1784; New-York Packet, July 12, 1784.

Independent Journal, August 3, 1785.

Ten Pounds Reward.

Run away from the Subscribers, on Monday evening the 1st instant, a Mulatto Man named Pomp, the property of Benjamin Gitfield. He is about thirty years old, has something of the Indian breed, about five feet ten inches high; straight and well made, smooth skin, large drooping nose, thin visage, and usually wore a false tail. Had on when he went off a dark blue coat and waistcoat, and long trousers. He also carried off with him two pairs of tow cloth and one pair of nankeen trousers, and sundry other wearing apparel.—Also the Wife of said Pomp, the property of Robert Johnston, a Mulatto Woman, about thirty-two years old, named Dinah, something whiter than her husband, low set stature, long black hair, and much pitted with the small pox. Had on when she went away a calico gown, white dimmity petticoat, and gauze cap; took with her a stripped stuff gown, two black callimanco skirts, two white short gowns, and sundry other kinds of apparel. Whoever apprehends and secures them both, so that they may be recovered, shall be entitled to the above Reward, or five pounds for either of them, with all reasonable charges, from Benjamin Gitfield, No. 208, Queen-Street. Robert Johnston, No. 177, Water-Street.

All Masters of Vessels are forbid from harbouring or carrying off the above Negroes, otherwise they will be prosecuted according to law.

New-York, August, 3 1785.

Reprints: Independent Journal, August 6, 1785; Independent Journal, August 10, 1785; New-York Packet, August 11, 1785.

New-York Packet, August 11, 1785.

Ran away from the subscriber, on or about the fifth of May last, a Mulatto Wench, named Nan, about 18 years of age, about four feet four inches high, very lusty: she took with her her mulatto child, about 18 months old, named Bill, they are of the Indian breed.—Likewise a Negro man, named Joe, about 20 years old, a stout well made fellow, very talkative, and a great singer, he went off on the 24th of July, and took with him a check shirt, a plain brown ditto, a waistcoat without sleeves, a pair of striped and one ditto plain trowsers, and a frock. Whoever will take up said Runaways, or secure either of them in any of the gaols, so that they may be had again, shall receive for each of them a reward of Three Pounds, and all reasonable charges, by Abraham Bussing.

N.B. It is expected that they are gone up the North-River. Any person taking them up there, will receive the above reward, by applying to James Stoutenburg, at Cromelbow.

Reprints: New-York Packet, August 15, 1785; New-York Packet, August 22, 1785; New-York Packet, August 25, 1785.

Daily Advertiser, July 17, 1788.

Twenty Shillings Reward.

Ran away, on the 15th inst. an Indian Servant Wench named Margaret, 24 years of age, about five feet high, stout made, much marked with the small pox, black strait short hair tied in a club; had on when she went off, a homespun grey short gown and petticoat, and took with her also one made of callico. She speaks French well, and English tolerably.—Whoever will take her up, or give information so that her master may have her again, shall have the above reward, with reasonable charges. Geo. C. Anthor, Dyes-Street, near Greenwich-Street. July 17.

Reprints: Daily Advertiser, July 18, 1788; Daily Advertiser, July 19, 1788; Daily Advertiser, July 21, 1788; Daily Advertiser, July 22, 1788; Daily Advertiser, July 23, 1788; Daily Advertiser, July 24, 1788; Daily Advertiser, July 25, 1788; Daily Advertiser, July 26, 1788; Daily Advertiser, July 28, 1788; Daily Advertiser, July 29, 1788; Daily Advertiser, July 30, 1788.

Variant Reprints: Daily Advertiser, November 3, 1789; Daily Advertiser, November 4, 1789; Daily Advertiser, November 6, 1789; Daily Advertiser, November 7, 1789; Daily Advertiser, November 10, 1789; Daily Advertiser, November 12, 1789; Daily Advertiser, November 13, 1789; Daily Advertiser, November 18, 1789.

PENNSYLVANIA NEWSPAPERS

American Weekly Mercury, April 14, 1720.

This Day Run away from John M'Comb, Junier, an Indian Woman, about 17 Years of Age, Pitted in the face, of a middle Stature and Indifferent fatt, having on her a Drugat Wastcoat and Kersey Petticoat, of a Light Collour. If any Person or Persons, shall bring the said Girle to her said Masteh [sic], shall be Rewarded for their Trouble to their Content.

Reprints: American Weekly Mercury, April 21, 1720; American Weekly Mercury, March 31, 1720.

American Weekly Mercury, April 21, 1720.

Run away the 17th of March last from James Patterson an Indian Trader, at Pexton on Sulquehanna River, a Servant Lad named John Maccahee or Makee about Eighteen Years of Age, but of a small Stature and very much Marked in the Face with the small Pox and Freckles he hath been seen at one Indian Town called Pehoquellamen on Delaware River, There is also with him an Indian Man belonging to Andrew Radford at Amboy Ferrey, Named Toby, of a middle stature well set Aged about 23 Years he speakes good English, he goes like the Natives. Whosoever shall take up said Servants and bring them to their said Masters or to John Davis in Philadelphia (next door to the Printers) or give Notice thereof so that they may be had again shall have five Pounds as a Reward, with Reasonable Charges, it is supposed they are gone towards Albany or New-England.

Reprints: American Weekly Mercury, April 28, 1720; American Weekly Mercury, May 5, 1720.

American Weekly Mercury, September 28, 1721.

Runaway from Thomas Hill of Salem, on the 18th of this Instant September, An Indian Man named Pompey, of middle Stature, pritty [sic] much pox-broken, aged about Thirty Years, he wears a Yellow Thickset Coat, with Horn Moulds, covered with Block-Tin, an Ozenbrig Shirt and Draws, and a Pair of white Yarn Stockings. He took with him a little black Pacing Horse, banded on the near Side with the Letters H.M. standing thus, EI Whoever takes up the said India, and secures or brings him to his said Master, shall receive reason satisfaction.

Reprint: American Weekly Mercury, October 5, 1721.

American Weekly Mercury, November 23, 1722.

Advertisements.

Run away from Ezekiel Balding of Hempstead on Long-Island, one Indian Man Slave, named Dick, of Middle Stature and of a smiling Countenance. He speaks English pretty well, and no other Language. He can read. He has a big Nose, and has white Scratches on his Arm, and a blue spot on the Inside of one of his Wrists, a little above his Shirt wrist-bands. He run away about the Beginning of September, and had a home-spun Shirt and a dark coloured Drugget Coat. We have been informed, that he intended to get into Indian Habit. Others tell, that he has said he would go towards New-London and Rhode-Island, and so to Sea.

Whoever can take up the said Indian Man, and secure him, and give Notice to his Master so that he can be had again, shall have Three Pounds Reward, besides reasonable Charges.

Reprints: American Weekly Mercury, November 29, 1722; American Weekly Mercury, December 11, 1722.

American Weekly Mercury, July 29, 1725.

Run away from their Masters William Biffell of the City of Philadelphia, Blacksmith, and John Coats of the same place, Brickmaker, two Carolina Indians, a Man and a Woman, the Man's name is Peter, of a short Stature, about 26 Years of Age. He has a striped homespun Tickin Jacket and Breeches, also a Kersey Jacket, two Shirts one fine the other Ozenbrigs, two pair of shoes, and a Felt Hat. The Woman's name is Maria, of a middle Stature, well set, about 40 Years of Age. She hath with her four striped Peticotes and several Jackets and other Cloaths, a new pair of Shoes, she has also a Blanket with her. They both speak good English.

Whosoever shall take up the said Indians, or either of them, and secures them, and gives Notice to their said Masters so that they may have them again, shall have 40 Shillings for each as a Reward, besides all reasonable Charges.

American Weekly Mercury, September 4, 1729.

Run away from Benjamin Acton, of Salem, Two Servant Men, one White, the other an Indian. The White Man's Name is Henry Stack, short of Stature, and has a Scar in his Face, his Hair newly cut off, and is of a tawney Complection; had on a brown Duroy Coat and Vest, the Coat full trimm'd, Oznabriggs Trowsers, thin shoes seam'd round the Quarters, and a Felt Hat almost new.

The Indian is called Isaac Gunnitt, is of a middle Size, has very thick Lips, and speaks good English; had on an old Vest and Breeches, old Stockings and Shoes, and an old Hat. Whoever secures the said Runaways, so that their Master may have them again, shall have Forty Shillings Reward for each, and Reasonable Charges, by Benjamin Acton.

Reprints: American Weekly Mercury, September 11, 1729; American Weekly Mercury, September 18, 1729; American Weekly Mercury, September 25, 1729.

American Weekly Mercury, August 6, 1730.

Run away the 20th Day of July, 1730. from Stephen Onion of Principio Iron-Works, an Indian Man, named Pompey, aged about Thirty Years, formerly belong'd to Sir William Keith, mark'd in his Forehead with the Letter R, in Blue or Gunpowder, had on a short Pea-Jacket of a Light Brown, Leather Breeches, Shoes, Stockings and Hat. Whosoever takes up the said Indian, and secures him, so that he may be had again, shall be paid Fifty Shillings Reward, by me, Stephen Onion.

N B. The said Indian cross'd the River Delaware the 26th Instant, without Breeches, Shoes, or Stockings, at Marcus-Hook.

Reprint: American Weekly Mercury, August 20, 1730.

American Weekly Mercury, August 9, 1733.

Run away, the 3d of July last from Bermuda, in an open boat, Built with Cadar, with two Masts and two Sails, and about 16 Feet Keel. Three Soldiers, one Negro Man and one Indian, viz.

Willian Frary, born in Suffolk, a Smith by Trade, aged about 30 Years, of middle Stature, fair Complexion, wears his own Hair, had on when he departed, a stript Tickin Wastcoat and Breeches, an Ozenbrigs Frock, white yarn Stockings, square-toed Shoes and an old Hat.

John Hunter, born in Lancashire, was bred a Countryman aged about 27 Years, of middle Stature, brown Complexion speaks very Country like, much Freckled, has on his own Hair, has three Jackets, one red, one brown Fustin and one stript Ticken; two pair of Breeches, one brown Fustin, the other stript Ticken; white yarn Stockings, and round too'd Shoes.

Thomas Hawkins, born in Cambridgeshire, short of Stature, fair Complexion, a flat Nose and pretty red, aged about 21 Years, had on a white Canvis Frock, a stript Ticken Jacket and Breeches, white yarn Stockings, and round too'd Shoes, they had thick Felt Hats bound round with Lace.

One Negro Man named Hazard, speaks broken English being born in Guinea, a spare Body and long Vissage, one of his Legs has been broke, had on Ozenbrigs Clothing.

One young Indian named Will, a short well-set Fellow with a very round smooth Face, had on a dark coloured Kersey Jacket, and an Ozenbrigs Shirt and Breeches.

If any Person shall take up any of the said Person and delivers them to Mr. Andrew Bradford, Post-Master of Philadelphia, shall receive as a Reward, for each white Man Two Pistoles, and for each Slave Four Pistoles, and all reasonable Charges.

Reprints: American Weekly Mercury, August 23, 1733; American Weekly Mercury, August 30, 1733.

American Weekly Mercury, October 24, 1734.

Run away, the 26 of June last, from Samuel Leonard of Perth-Amboy in New-Jersey, a thick short Fellow, having but one Eye, he is half Indian half Negro tho' as black as most Negroes; he had on when he went away a blue Coat; his Name is Wan, he plays on the Fiddle, and speaks good English and this Country Indian. Any Person bringing home the said Fellow to his Master, shall have Three Pounds Reward with reasonable Charges, paid by Samuel Leonard.

Reprints: American Weekly Mercury, October 31, 1734; American Weekly Mercury, November 7, 1734.

Pennsylvania Gazette, May 5, 1737.

Philadelphia, April 20, 1737.
Run away on the 3d of July last, from Mary Wilson, in Queen-Ann's County, near Choptank River, a Servant Man named Moses Williams, a Half Indian (his Father being an Indian and his Mother a white Woman) is about 30 Years of Age, of middle Stature, and has a Scar by a Cut over his Eye. He had with him two Felt Hats, one of them old and the other new, two coarse Shirts, a country-made Jacket made half white and half black, one Pair of Trowsers, a Pair of strong Leather Breeches, black and white stockings, two pair of shoes, one pair old the other new.

And on the 13th of this Instant April, ran away from the said Mary Wilson, a West-Country Servant named John Bennet, about 25 Years of Age, short and well set, of dark Complection, hath black Eyes, and is by Trade a Butcher. He had on an old Beaver Hat, an old Kersey Great Coat, a snuff colour'd Broad cloth close-bodied Coat turn'd and patch'd on the Elbows lin'd with blue silk and blue shaloon; a linnen Vest flower'd with yellow silk, lin'd with linnen, dark broad cloth Breeches with Buckles at the Knees, two pair of blush worsted stockings, old shoes with buckles. Took with him a grey Mare branded on the shoulder, and H upon the Buttock, undock'd, trim'd to a rock Mane, black Saddle and Housen, without a Crupper.

Whoever secures the said Servants so that they may be had again, shall have Five Pounds Reward for the first, and Three Pounds for the latter, with reasonable Charges, paid by Mary Wilson, or by Thomas Dunning Innkeeper in Philadelphia.

Variant Reprints: Pennsylvania Gazette, October 3, 1745; Pennsylvania Gazette, October 10, 1745. In these notice for Moses Williams, dated September 26, 1745, Samuel Shiver is identified as the fugitive's master.

Pennsylvania Gazette, October 5, 1738.

Run away from George Dasheil of Somerset County, in Maryland, the 27th of August last, an Indian Man Slave, he is short and well set, speaks broken English, a little inclining to Indian, has the Letter P set in his Forehead with Gun Powder, which he commonly cover'd with a lift or strap. He had on when he went away a coarse Shirt much worn, a pair of corded fustian Breeches, and an old Matchcoat, and with him some Fox-skins, and a Wild-Cat's Skin which he carried at his Back as the Indians usually do.

  Whoever secures the said Slave so that his Master may have him again, shall have him again, shall have Four Pistoles Reward, besides what the Law allows, paid by George Dasheil.

Reprint: Pennsylvania Gazette, October 12, 1738.

Pennsylvania Gazette, October 11, 1739.

Run away on the 20th of Aug. past, from the Subscriber near the Head of Bush River in Baltimore County, Maryland, an Indian Man, named Pompey, aged about 24 Years, of middle Stature, well set, speaks nothing but English, very much scarrified on the Body with whipping in Barbadoes; he had on his Neck when he went away an Iron Collar, but its suppos'd he has got it off: Also a lusty Negro Woman named Pegg, aged about 22 Years, this Country born and speaks plain English; They carried away with them a striped Duffle Blanket, an old Ticken Jacket and Breeches with black Buttonholes, a Felt Hat near new, a coarse linnen Bag, a new white Linsey woolsey Petticoat and other coarse Negro Apparel. Whoever secures the said Indian and Negro so that their Master may have them again, shall have Five Pounds Reward and reasonable Charges paid by Richard Ruff. October 11 1739.

Reprints: Pennsylvania Gazette, October 18, 1739; Pennsylvania Gazette, October 25, 1739; Pennsylvania Gazette, November 1, 1739.

Pennsylvania Gazette, October 2, 1740.

Run away last Night, from on board the Sloop Triton, James Hodges, Master, two Indian Men Servants, viz. One named Jeremiah Robin, of middle Stature, well set, flat Nose, strait short Hair, about 30 Years of Age: Had on an homespun Jacket, cotton check'd shirt, and ozenbrigs Trowsers. The other named Nehemiah Robin, something shorter than the other, short Hair, aged about 24; Had on same sort of Clothing as the other.

Whoever takes up and secures said Indians, so that their Master may have them again, shall have Twenty Shillings Reward, paid by James Hodges.

Variant Reprints: Pennsylvania Gazette, October 9, 1740; Pennsylvania Gazette, October 16, 1740.

Pennsylvania Gazette, July 9, 1741.

Run away from the Snow Lancashire Witch about 14 days ago, a Spanish indian [sic] man about 30 years of age, low stature, a very yellow Complexion, and speaks but few words of English; He is now skulking about Town, and is entertain'd by some persons unknown. Whoever secures him, and brings him to Emerson and Graydon, shall have 20 shillings Reward.

N. B. All persons are forwarn'd from entertaining him. Emerson & Graydon.

Reprints: Pennsylvania Gazette, July 16, 1741; Pennsylvania Gazette, July 23, 1741. This notice included a footer with the following text: "Philadelphia, July 16. 1740."

Pennsylvania Gazette, October 3, 1745.

Philadelphia, Sept. 26. 1745.
Run away on the 15th Instant, from Samuel Shivers, of Greenwich, of Gloucester County, New-Jersey, a Servant Man, named Moses Williams, an Indian Mullato, being half Indian and half Irish, of a swarthy Complexion, no Hair, middle Stature, a bold or rather a surly Look, and speaks good English, being this Country born: Had on when he went away an Ozenbrigs Shirt, Woollen Stockings, Peek-toed Shoes, with Buckles, brown Holland Jacket and Breeches, a striped Cotton Handkerchief, and old Bever Hat, with narrow Brim.

Whoever takes up said Servant, and secures him, so that he may be had again, shall have Twenty Shillings Reward, paid by Samuel Shivers.

N. B. The said Servant, 'tis supposed, has taken with him an old Indenture and Pass, thinking thereby the better to travel.

Reprint: Pennsylvania Gazette, October 10, 1745.

Pennsylvania Gazette, October 1, 1747.

Run away, on the 20th of September last, from Cohansie Bridge, a very big Negroe man, named Sampson, about 50 years of age, has some Indian blood in him, is hip-shot, and goes very lame; he has taken his son with him, a boy about 12 or 14 years of age, named Sam; he was born of an Indian woman, and looks much like an Indian, except in his hair; both belonging to Silas Parvin of Philadelphia, and are both well clothed, only the boy is barefoot; they have taken with them a gun and ammunition, and two rugs; can both talk Indian very well, and it is likely they have dressed themselves in Indian dress, and gone towards Carolina. Whoever secures said slaves, so that their master may have them again, shall have Five Pounds reward, and all reasonable charges, paid by Silas Parvin.

Reprints: Pennsylvania Gazette, October 8, 1747; Pennsylvania Gazette, October 15, 1747.

Variant Reprints: Pennsylvania Journal, or, Weekly Advertiser, October 1, 1747; Pennsylvania Journal, or, Weekly Advertiser, October 8, 1747; Pennsylvania Journal, or, Weekly Advertiser, October 15, 1747; Pennsylvania Journal, or, Weekly Advertiser, October 22, 1747; Pennsylvania Journal, or, Weekly Advertiser, October 30, 1747; Pennsylvania Journal, or, Weekly Advertiser, November 5, 1747; Pennsylvania Journal, or, Weekly Advertiser, November 12, 1747; Pennsylvania Journal, or, Weekly Advertiser, November 19, 1747; Pennsylvania Journal, or, Weekly Advertiser, November 26, 1747; Pennsylvania Journal, or, Weekly Advertiser, December 3, 1747; Pennsylvania Journal, or, Weekly Advertiser, December 10, 1747; Pennsylvania Journal, or, Weekly Advertiser, December 15, 1747; Pennsylvania Journal, or, Weekly Advertiser, December 22, 1747; Pennsylvania Journal, or, Weekly Advertiser, December 29, 1747; Pennsylvania Journal, or, Weekly Advertiser, January 5, 1748; Pennsylvania Journal, or, Weekly Advertiser, January 12, 1748; Pennsylvania Journal, or, Weekly Advertiser, January 19, 1748; Pennsylvania Journal, or, Weekly Advertiser, January 26, 1748; Pennsylvania Journal, or, Weekly Advertiser, February 2, 1748; Pennsylvania Journal, or, Weekly Advertiser, February 2, 1748; Pennsylvania Journal, or, Weekly Advertiser, February 9, 1748; Pennsylvania Journal, or, Weekly Advertiser, March 8, 1748.

Pennsylvania Gazette, January 24, 1749.

Run away, on the 16th instant, from the plantation of Horsham, in Philadelphia county, belonging to Dr. Graeme, a Molattoe man, nam'd Will, about 28 years of age, of a Negroe father, and an Indian mother, born in the country, pretty tall, and well built, somewhat mark'd with the small-pox, his speech soft and mild, but a sensible, cunning, ingenious fellow. Whoever takes up said Molattoe, and secures him in any goal, or brings him to his master, Doctor Graeme aforesaid, shall have Three Pounds reward, and reasonable charges. At the same time all persons, Negroes, as well as others, are forbid to harbour him at their peril.

Reprint: Pennsylvania Gazette, January 31, 1749.

Variant Reprints: Pennsylvania Gazette October 12, 1752; Pennsylvania Gazette, October 19, 1752; Pennsylvania Gazette, October 26, 1752.

Pennsylvania Gazette, May 24, 1750.

Run away from the subscriber, of Cecil County, Maryland, on the 10th of April last, an indented Indian or Molatto servant-man, named John Maycum, about 25 years of age, a tall and well-set fellow, saws with a whip-saw, and plays on the violin: Had on when he went away, a castor hat, and white linnen cap, check shirt, blue drugget jacket, dark brown cloth breeches, with shoes and stockings. Whoever takes up said servant, and secures him, so that his master may have him again, shall have Forty Shillings reward, and reasonable charges (if brought home) paid by John Chick, Junior.
    N.B. The above fellow has been used to the seas.

Reprints: Pennsylvania Gazette, May 31, 1750; Pennsylvania Gazette, June 7, 1750.

Pennsylvania Gazette, November 15, 1753.

Lancaster, October 31, 1753.
This day was committed to the goal of this county, on suspicion of being a runaway servant, Indian Thomas, who says he's a free man, and served his time with Samuel Lippincut, near Mount-holy iron-works, in the Jerseys. And on the day following Abigail Allen, who says she's a freewoman, and served her time with John Rowls, in Chester, These are to desire their masters to

come or send for them, otherwise they will be sold to pay their cost, by John Clark, Goal-keeper.

Reprint: Pennsylvania Gazette, December 6, 1753.

Pennsylvania Gazette, December 27, 1753.

Broke goal, and made their escape from the sheriff of Monmouth, in East New-Jersey, on the 8th of this [inst], the following persons, viz. An Irishman, named E[?]yan Dorne, of middle stature, fair complexion, blue eyes, lightish brown hair: Had on when he went away, a lightish colour'd d[r]ugget coat, a brown drugget jacket, leather breeches, lightish blue stockings, and a felt hat. Also a lad named James Wolling, about 16 or 17 years old, swarthy complexion, down look, in a a very poor apparel. Likewise an Indian fellow, named William Pumsher, small size, talks good English, can read and write: Had on when he went away, A dark kersey jacket, check linen breeches, woollen spatterdashes, and ozenbrigs shirt. Also a servant girl, named Catherine Car[?]e, belonging to Thomas Leonard, small of stature, down [l]ook: Had on, and carried with her, A striped linen and woollen gown, dark striped cotton gown, new Leghorn hat, worsted quilt, and sundry other clothes. Any person that takes up the said persons, and secures them, so as they may be had again, shall have Six Pounds reward, or for either Thirty Shillings, and all reasonable charges, paid by John Taylor, sheriff, or Thomas Leonard.

Pennsylvania Gazette, October 23, 1760.

Run away from Gilbert Smith, in Mansfield, West-Jersey, on the 17th of this instant October, a Mulattoe [sic] Fellow, named Jacob, about 5 Feet 6 Inches high, has a remarkable Scar on one Side his Face, thought to be on the Left Side, occasioned by a Scald or Burn: Had on, when he went away, a black and white homespun fly Coat, with flat white Metal Buttons, homespun Tow Shirt, and Crocus Trowsers, old Shoes, and Worsted Stockings. He had an Indian Father, pretends to be free, and will be very likely to change his Name and Apparel, as he was committed to Philadelphia Goal some time ago by the name of James Start. Whoever takes up and secures said Mulattoe, so that his Master may have him again, shall have Forty Shillings Reward, and reasonable Charges, paid by Gilbert Smith.

N.B. All Masters of Vessels are forbid to carry him off at their Peril.

Reprints: Pennsylvania Gazette, October 30, 1760; Pennsylvania Gazette, November 6, 1760.

Pennsylvania Journal, or, Weekly Advertiser, November 26, 1761.

Run away last Sunday night, from Capt. Robert Whyte, of this City, a Spanish Indian slave, a tailor, speaks Spanish and French and very little English, named Lewis, is a thick short fellow, with black Hair; had on a blue Jacket and short Trowsers. Whoever takes up said Indian and secures him so that he may be had again, shal have Three Pounds reward, and reasonable charges paid by Robert Whyte.

Pennsylvania Gazette, March 14, 1765.

Ten Pistoles Reward.

Run away from the Subscriber, living near the Great Falls of Potowmack, in Frederick County, Maryland, a Mulattoe Man Slave; he has been gone upwards of two-Years, and last January was twelvemonth he was seen near Reading Town, and have since heard he was at Hacket's Iron-works, in West-Jersey; he is about five Feet eight or ten Inches high, he resembles an Indian, as his Father was one, walks very upright, something bow-legged, had very black Hair, which he takes great Care of, and curls, has little or no Beard, broad across his Eyes, a Scar on one Side of his Nose, and several on his Head, one very large; went by the Name of Daniel, but may have changed his Name, very apt to get drunk, and then is bold and saucy; he understands Farming Business, about Forty-three Years of Age. Any Person that will secure him in any Goal, and gives Notice to the Subscriber, shall have the above Reward, paid by Thomas Davis, Tavern-keeper.

Reprints: Pennsylvania Gazette, May 2, 1765; Pennsylvania Gazette, May 16, 1765; Pennsylvania Gazette, May 23, 1765; Pennsylvania Gazette, May 30, 1765; Pennsylvania Gazette, June 20, 1765.

Pennsylvania Gazette, July 2, 1767.

Run away from the Subscriber, on the 10th of this inst. June, a Musqueto Shore Indian Slave, named Jack, about 5 Feet 6 or 7 Inches high, thick set, about 21 Years old, with long black Hair, which he generally wears tied behind; took with him a Fiddle, plays badly on it, and had a halfworn Felt

Hat, a lightish coloured Stuff Coat, a blue Broadcloth Waistcoat, Ozenbrigs Shirt and Trowsers, a Pair of old Shoes, with Brass Buckles; he took a fine Shirt with him. Whoever takes up said Slave, and secures him in any Goal on the Continent, so that he may be had again, or brings him to the Subscriber, at Whitehill, in Burlington County, West Jersey, shall have Three Pounds Reward, and reasonable Charges, paid by Robert Field.

N.B. All Persons are forewarned harbouring him, and all Masters of Vessels taking him off at their Peril.

Reprints: Pennsylvania Gazette, July 9, 1767; Pennsylvania Gazette, July 23, 1767.

Variant Reprints: The Indian Slave Jack absconded with a Negro slave named Richard or Dick. Field had that notice printed in the Pennsylvania Chronicle, August 24, 1767; Pennsylvania Chronicle, August 31, 1767; Pennsylvania Gazette, September 3, 1767; Pennsylvania Chronicle, September 7, 1767; Pennsylvania Chronicle, September 14, 1767; Pennsylvania Gazette, September 17, 1767; Pennsylvania Gazette, October 15, 1767.

Pennsylvania Gazette, August 6, 1767.

Run away from the subscriber, living in Upper Freehold, Monmouth county, near Imley's town, on the 22d of last month, a servant Negroe [sic] man, half Indian, named Charles, but probably will alter his name, about 28 years of age, about 6 feet two inches high, well set, something knock kneed, large feet, a scar on one of his cheeks, near his temple, a yellow complexion, long hair, very much curled, and thin on the top of his head; had on, when he went away, a light grey hom[e]spun coat, streaked lining, about half-worn, his jacket of a darker colour, and more worn, tow shirt and trowsers, and felt hat, and it is likely he may change his clothes. Whoever secures said servant, so that his master may have him again, shall have Three Pounds reward, and reasonable charges, paid by Richard James.

Reprints: Pennsylvania Gazette, August 20, 1767; Pennsylvania Gazette, September 3, 1767.

Pennsylvania Gazette, October 6, 1768.

Eight Dollars Reward.

Run away from his Bail, on the 28th of September, a native Indian Man, who goes by the Name of William Joshua, has been brought up among the

English, and has but little of his own Language; he is about 21 Years of Age, 5 Feet 9 or 10 Inches high, smooth faced, and has strait black Hair: Had on when he went away, a light coloured Cloth Coat, Russia Sheeting Shirt, old Trowsers, a Leather Apron, and new Shoes, with Buckles; is a Chair-maker by Trade. He has fresh Scars over his left Eye, and it is probable he will change his Clothes, and get an Indian Match-coat. Whoever takes up said Indian, and secures him in any of his Majesty's Goals, so as the Subscriber may have him again, shall have the above Reward, paid by William Kerlin, living in Birmingham Township, Chester Country.

Reprints: Pennsylvania Gazette, October 13, 1768; Pennsylvania Gazette, October 20, 1768.

Pennsylvania Gazette, December 20, 1770.

Five Pounds Reward.

Run away on the 22d of April last, from the subscriber, living in Kent county, on Delaware, a Mulattoe slave, named Joe, a slim Indian made fellow, has had 5 fingers on each hand, which is visible to be seen; had on, and took with him, a jacket and breeches of mixed Negroe cloth, a snuff coloured broadcloth coat, a blue and yellow damask jacket, tow trowsers, good shoes, and stockings. Whoever takes up said slave, and secures him, so that his master may have him again, shall have the above reward, paid by Henry Stevens.

Reprint: Pennsylvania Gazette, December 27, 1770.

Pennsylvania Gazette, January 20, 1773.

Christiana Ferry, New-Castle County, January 8, 1773.
Run away, last night, from the subscriber, a lusty yellow fellow, part Indian and part Negroe, about 5 feet 11 inches high, calls himself Jerry Clark, is a thick strong made fellow, a great liar, fond of strong liquor, and boasts much of his having been at sea; had on a pair of trowsers and a jacket, both made of a blue duffil, tow shirt, coarse white yarn stockings, good shoes, old hat; has a cut on one side of his head, which is sore at this time, and has several scars, one in partcular on his left hand. Whoever apprehends said fellow, and secures him in any of his Majesty's goals, so that his master may get him again, shall be entitled to a reward of Four Dollars, paid by Morton Morton.

Pennsylvania Packet, August 29, 1774.

Twenty-Five Pounds Reward.

Ran away from the subscriber, living near Mr. Samuel Worthington's, about sixteen miles from Baltimore Town, three servant men, viz. Henry Boswell, an half East-Indian, about 6 feet high, very well made, has high cheek-bones, a long sharp nose, a wide mouth, short black hair and dark eyes, with a cast in them, his arms and fingers are rather shorter than common, he hath had a scald between his shoulders near his neck, he chews tobacco, and talks in the west of England dialect: had on when he went away, an oznabrigs shirt, crocus trowsers, and an iron collar round his neck. Timothy Shane, a stone mason and bricklayer, about 25 years of age, and an Irishman, he is about 5 feet 5 or 6 inches high, a trunchey well set fellow, has a fair complexion, (but much sun-burnt), short light brown hair, and grey eyes, his arms hang in a particular manner, and he is thicker through the jole than common: had on and took with him a good felt hat, an old brown coat much tarr'd, a brown jacket with white yarn stocking sleeves, two old white linen shirts, two check ditto, patched on the shoulders with coarse white linen, two pair of new oznabrigs trowsers, one pair of Welsh cotton drawers, and sundry other cloaths not known. William Easun, an Englishman, about 35 years old, a house joiner by trade, is about 5 feet 3 inches high, of a dark complexion with black eyes, and a large hanging under lip, he is left handed but works at the bench with his right hand: had on and took with him an old brown cloth coat tarr'd, two nankeen jackets, one of them with sleeves, two pair of new oznabrigs trowsers, one pair of Welsh cotton drawers, one check shirt patched on the belly and in other places with white coarse linen, one striped linen ditto, patched in the same manner, with new striped linen of a different kind, one pair of speckled worsted stockings, with black leather shoes, and plain steel buckles, a pretty good castor hat, a short dark bob wig, and blue studs in his sleeves, his breath smells very offensive; hath taken with him some files, and is supposed will get off Henry Boswell's collar; he and the other mason can both write very good hands, and very probably will forge passes.. Whoever shall secure the two servants, Timothy Shane, and William Easun, so that I may get them again, shall receive the reward of Ten Pounds for each of them, and for the other, Henry Boswell, the reward of Five Pounds.

Benjamin Nicholson.

N.B. 'Tis judged they will make for Philadelphia, by the way of York town, and Lancaster.

Pennsylvania Packet, July 4, 1780.

One Hundred Dollars Reward.

Ran away about the 1st of June last, an Indian apprentice Boy, about twelve years of age, had on when he went away, an old plane coat the sleeves torn off, a Russia sheeting shirt, oznabrig trowsers, a small wool hat and a pair of shoes; has frequently ran away and loitered about town until brought home. Whoever takes up said boy, and secures him so that his master may have him again, shall receive the above reward and reasonable charges, paid by Robert Elliot, two doors from Mr. Dunlap's Printing-Office.

Reprint: Pennsylvania Packet, July 11, 1780.

Freeman's Journal; or, the North-American Intelligencer, July 3, 1782.

Five Pounds Reward.

Ran away the 13th of June, 1782, from the subscriber, living in Little Creek hundred, in the state of Delaware, a mulatto man shewing of the indian blood, named Lott, about forty years old, five feet nine or ten inches high, thin visaged, shews some gray hairs in his beard, he is apt to get drunk, and very abusive when he is so, the forepart of his hair lately trim'd, and bushy behind, had on when he went away, a small round hat half worn, strip'd linen trousers, an under jacket, the fore parts white, the back gray, short blue and white strip'd coatee, a white home spun linen shirt, shoes almost new: took with him two pair of tow trousers, and a greyish coat half worn. Whoever apprehends and secures the said servant, so that his master may have him, shall receive the above reward and reasonable charges, by me, J Wheilton.

Reprint: Freeman's Journal; or, the North-American Intelligencer, July 17, 1782.

Variant Reprint: Pennsylvania Packet, July 6, 1782.

NEW JERSEY NEWSPAPERS

New-Jersey Gazette April 23, 1778

200 Dollars Reward.

Was stolen by her mother, a Negro Girl about 9 or 10 years old, named Dianah—Her mother's name is Cash, and was married to an Indian named Lewis Wolis near 6 feet high, about 35 years of age—They have a male child with them between three and four years old. Any person that takes up the said Negroes and Indian and secures them, to that the subscriber may get them, shall have the above reward and all reasonable charges.

Any person that understands distilling rye spirits, may find encouragement by applying to the subscriber at his own house. Kenneth Hankison.

Penelapon, East-Jersey, April 15, 1778.

Reprints: New-Jersey Gazette, May 13, 1778; New-Jersey Gazette, Mary 27, 1778; New-Jersey Gazette, June 17, 1778.

Chapter 3

Southern Colonies

VIRGINIA NEWSPAPERS

Virginia Gazette, April 21, 1768.

Isaac, an Indian slave, aged about 40 years, run away from my plantation on George's creek, in Buckingham, last Easter was twelve months. He was both and lived many years on the Brodk Chickahominy, and has some connections in Goochland, where he may probably be at present. He wore long curled hair before his elopement, but his countenance and disposition are altogether Indian. His height is about 5 feet 8 inches. He is outlawed. I will give Forty shillings to whoever will bring him to me. Robert Bolling, jun.

Virginia Gazette, May 2, 1771.

Run away from the subscriber, a dark mulatto man slave named Bob Col[?]mand, 25 years old, tall, slim, and well made, wears his own hair pretty long, his foretop combed very high, a blacksmith by trade, claims his freedom under pretence of being of an Indian extraction. Whoever brings me the said slave shall have Five Pounds reward. John Hardaway.

Virginia Gazette, November 11, 1773.

Run away from the subscriber, last month, a Negro man of the name of Tom, about 5 feet 6 inches high, of a yellowish complexion, much the appearance of an Indian, has one of his teeth out before, and one of his feet has been much burnt, as also one of his arms, and, as well as I can recollect, on the fame side of the foot. His hair is of a different kind from that of a Negro's, rather more of the Indian's, but partaking of both, which, though short, he frequently ties behind; had on a Russia sheeting coat and breeches, a red cloth jacket, rather the worse for wear, and a white linen shirt. The said slave is by trade a cooper and shoemaker, is remarkably fond of drink, and if indulged, will certainly get drunk, and when so, is apt to be very talkative, is a very artful fellow, and will, I imagine, attempt to pass for at freeman. His connections are mostly in Halifax and Charlotte counties, and, I presume, he will make that way. Whoever will convey the said runaway to me, in Amelia county, living near Rocky Run church, or so secure him that I may get him again, shall have it reward of Five Pounds, besides what the laws allows, if taken in Virginia, and if brought from another colony, Ten Pounds. Dorothy Jones.

Reprint: Virginia Gazette, November 18, 1773.

Virginia Gazette, March 18, 1775.

Run away from the Subscriber, about the first of January last, a very bright Mulatto Man named Stephen, 5 Feet 6 or 7 Inches high, about 22 Years of Age, well set, has a remarkable broad Face, with a Mole on the side of his Nose, and a Scar upon one of his Legs. He was clothed in Negro Cotton Waistcoat and Breeches, Osnabrug Shirt, and a Pair of blue Gambadoes; his Hair is cut close off the Top of his Head, and the Front Part combed back. His Wife Phebe went away with him, a remarkable white Indian Woman, about the same Age, and was with Child; she has long black Hair, which is generally clubbed, and carried off with her a blue Negro Cotton Waistcoat and Petticoat, a Virginia Cloth Waistcoat and Petticoat, and a Virginia Cloth Bonnet. She can spin well, and I imagine they will both endeavour to pass as free. Whoever apprehends the said Slaves, and brings them to me, in Dinwiddie, near the Courthouse, or secures them in Gaol, so that I get then again, shall have 10l. Reward from Henry Hardaway.

Reprint: Virginia Gazette, March 25, 1775.

Virginia Gazette, April 29, 1775.

Bute County, North Carolina, March 20, 1775.
Run away from the Subscriber, a Slave of the Indian Breed, a tall slim made Fellow, with long straight black Hair, about 23 Years of Age, had on, when he went away, a blue Dussil Waistcoat, old Check Shirt, &c. but changed his

Dress. He is branded on both Cheeks, with the letter R on the right, and the letter T on the left. It is supposed he will make for Prince George County in Virginia, or to some seaport Town on James River. Whoever secures him in any of his Majesty's Gaols, so that I may get him again, shall have 40s. Reward, to be paid to the Gaoler. The Brands on his Cheeks were fresh given him by the Person of whom I bought him, and were not cured when he left me, William Tabb.

All Persons are forewarned employing or harbouring the said Slave, at their Peril.

Reprints: Virginia Gazette, May 6, 1775; Virginia Gazette, May 13, 1775.

Variant Reprints: Virginia Gazette, December 9, 1775; Virginia Gazette, December 9, 1775; Virginia Gazette, December 16, 1775.

Virginia Gazette, January 6, 1776.

Fourteen Pounds Reward.

Run away from the subscriber, the 26th of November last, 4 negro men, viz. Harry, Virginia born, 5. feet 8 or 9 inches high, 30 years of age, a dark mulatto, with long bushy hair; he is of the Indian breed, straight and well made, dresses neat, and has a variety of clothes with him, amongst others, blue fearnought great coat. He has worked several years at the carpenter's and wheelwright's trade, and can glaize and paint. Lewis, an outlandish, short, thick fellow, remarkably bow-legged, an excellent wheelwright and waggon maker, and a very good blacksmith. He carried with him, amongst other clothes, a blue suit. Aaron, a likely Virginia born fellow, of the midde size, .stoops a little, has a hoarse voice, and had on the usual clotheing of negroes. Matthew, Virginia born, dark mulatto, 18 years of age, 5 feet 8 or 9 inches high, stampers a little, and speaks quick, when surprized, and is close-kneed. There 4 went off in a yawl with two others, who have been since committed to the public gaol. As one of them was taken in the yawl without the cape, I conclude the other 4 are in lord Dunmore's service. I will give Five Pounds each for securing the two first, and Forty Shillings each for the other two, besides what the law allows. They are all outlawed. Edmund Ruffin. Prince George, December 23. 1775.

Reprints: Virginia Gazette, January 10, 1776; Virginia Gazette, January 13, 1776.

Virginia Gazette, July 19, 1776.

Prince William, June 1, 1776.

Ten Dollars Reward.

Run away from the subscriber, on his journey from Williamsburg, on the 11th of May, near King William courthouse, a mulatto servant man, named John Newton, about 20 years of age, an Indian by birth, about 5 feet 6 inches high, slender made, has a thin visage, four look, remarkable projected lips, and wears his own black hair tied behind, with long curling locks at his ears: had on a light brown frieze postilion coat lappelled, and waistcoat of the same, with common plate buttons, a beaver hat much worn, leather breeches, coarse yarn stockings, and old shoes, with a pair of large single rimmed pinchbeck buckles. He was left behind on the road with a pretty large well made bay horse (which had tired) a good saddle with a blue fringed housing and bridle, with instructions to follow his master slowly, but has never since made his appearance at home, or been heard off. Whoever takes up the said servant, with the horse and saddle, &c. and brings them to the rev. mr. [sic] Scott's, in Prince William, or secures them so that the owner may get them again, shall have the above reward, or 30s. for either, with reasonable charges paid by W. Browne.

He shaves and dresses well, but is much addicted to liquor.

Reprints: Virginia Gazette, July 26, 1776; Virginia Gazette, August 2, 1776.

Variant Reprints: Virginia Gazette, July 20, 1776; Virginia Gazette, July 27, 1776; Virginia Gazette, July 29, 1776; Virginia Gazette, September 7, 1776; Virginia Gazette, September 14, 1776; Virginia Gazette, September 27, 1776.

Virginia Gazette, August 8, 1777.

Run away from the Subscriber, in Amelia County, the 19th of last June, a large young Mulatto Fellow named Sam, of the Indian Breed. I expect he is in James City County, as he has a Mother who lives there with one Mr. Francis Riddleburst. I will give Three Pounds to any person who will take up the said Slave, and confine him so that I get him again. (2| |) Daniel Hardaway.

Reprint: Virginia Gazette, August 15, 1777.

Virginia Gazette, October 18, 1780.

Run away from the subscribers in Goochland, a negro man named Joe, about 5 feet 6 inches high, 50 years old. He is of the Indian breed, with long black hair tied behind, took off with him, a negro woman named Nan, about 5 feet 3 inches high, of a yellow complexion, about 28 years old. The fellow has the first joint his middle finger on his left hand cut which occasions it to stand crooked; he took with him a set of shoemakers tools. I expect they will endeavour to pass for free man and woman, for the follow is very sensible. If any person will take up the said slaves, and bring them to us, shall receive 200 dollars, besides what the law allows, if taken out of the county, or 100 dollars to secure them in any jail so that we get them again.
 William Woodson. John Brumfield.

Virginia Gazette, December 18, 1779.

Run away about June last, a negro fellow named Caesar (commonly called Indian Caesar) and his wife Kate. They were formerly the property of Robert Ruffin, decease, and sold to Col. William Johnson of North Carolina, but now the property of the subscriber, living near Brunswick court house, who will give handsome reward to any person that will apprehend the said negroes, or give such intelligence that I may get them. James M'Invaill.

Virginia Gazette and Weekly Advertiser, May 21, 1785.

Five Pounds Reward,

Run away from the subscriber on the first of March last, a negro man slave named Tom, about fifty five years of age, of a yellow complexion, mixed with the Indian, which occasions his hair to be rather longer than common; he is about five feet seven or eight inches high, a remarkable large mouth, with very thick lips, and has lost the greatest part of his teeth; is a subtle artful fellow, very fond of strong drink, and then very talkative; on his right or left foot has a fear, and the sinew appears very large on the top of his foot, and on the same side on his arm between the elbow and the shoulder is a large scar, occasioned by a burn. Had on when he went away a Virginia cloth suit, single wove, mixed with blue. Whoever apprehends and contrives the said slave to me in Amelia county, or secures him so that I get him again, shall receive the above reward. Amelia, April 18. P . John Jones.

Virginia Journal and Alexandria Advertiser, September 15, 1785.

Thirty Dollars Reward.

Broke Gaol, on the night of the 4th of August last, a Mulatto Man, named Thomas Valentine, about 5 feet 10 or 11 inches high, a very down, Indian look; had on when he made his escape, an Irish linen shirt, 2 short brown jacket, striped holland trousers, London made shoes, silver buckles, and a tolerable good hat; but he may change his cloaths, as he has many. I have heard that he was taken up in Alexandria since he broke gaol, but made his escape. . . . Whoever will take up said fellow, and secure him in any gaol, or deliver him to the Subscriber, shall receive The above Reward, and reasonable charges, paid by Samuel Abell, Sheriff of Saint Mary's. County, Maryland. September 14, 1786.

Reprints: Virginia Journal and Alexandria Advertiser, September 22, 1785; Virginia Journal and Alexandria Advertiser, September 29, 1785; Virginia Journal and Alexandria Advertiser, October 6, 1785; Virginia Journal and Alexandria Advertiser, October 13, 1785.

MARYLAND NEWSPAPERS

Maryland Journal, February 25, 1785.

A Runaway dark Mulatto Slave.
Five Pounds Reward.

Ran away, from the subscriber's plantation, in Montgomery Township, Franklin County, Pennsylvania, (commonly called Conegocheague) on the 14th of February, instant, a dark Mulatto Fellow, named Tony, who calls himself an Indian, is about 18 or 19 years of age, 5 feet 3 or 4 inches high, has short black Indian like hair; he had on, when he went away, a new thick white homspun cloth coat, a pair of light blue breeches, a pair of blue yarn stockings, and a pair of linsey leggings, middling good shoes, with pewter buckles, and an old fur hat.—Whoever apprehends and secures the said Runaway, so that his master gets him again, shall have the above Reward, with reasonable charges paid, by James Huston.

N. B. All masters of vessels are forbid harbouring, concealing, or carrying off the said Slave, as they will answer it at their peril. Montgomery Township, Feb. 21, 1785.

Reprints: Maryland Journal, February 25, 1785; Maryland Journal, March 1, 1785.

Maryland Journal, September 2, 1785.

Stop the Runaways!
Ten Pounds Reward.

Two Fellows went from me on Saturday evening, the 2d of July—Bill, a miller, about 5 feet 7 or 8 inches high, of a swarthy complexion, down look, with short black hair, and thick lips; he is well made, and neat about his feet and legs, his eyes are large, and seldom looks at the person he converses with. He some years since lost the the [sic] last joint of a finger of his right hand, and his left arm having been broke below the elbow, is a little crooked. He is extremely ingenious, well acquainted with farming, and mows with uncommon ease and dexterity; was bred a miller, and understands that business in all its various branches, is handy with carpenters', turners, and shoemakers' tools, a good fiddler, fond of company and spiritous liquors; drinking freely tends to make him stupid rather than enliven him; when afraid, or his passions in any manner agitated, his face becomes remarkably dark-coloured; he called himself the additional name of Mullen.

George, about 5 feet 10 or 11 inches high, of a slender make, fairer complexion and sour look, with short dark-coloured hair; he lately had the small-pox by inoculation, and since much troubled with eruptions; his eyes are generally sore, is a careless slovenly fellow, was bred upon a farm, has occasionally attended a merchant-mill, waited upon a single person, and drove a waggon, and when angry, will beat his horses unmercifully; his address rough, addicted to swearing, fond of spiritous liquors, and seldom misses an opportunity to be drunk, and of consequence, talkative and noisy; he is an indifferent performer, and fond of the fiddle.

These Fellows are about 24 years old, twins, and natives of this place, descended, by the mother's family, from an Indian female slave, their grandmother, and by bastardy, not to be distinguished from white persons. They were promised freedom for servitude to November, 1791, and sooner in case of good behaviour. They have little complaisance, and as they talk on the Scotch-Irish dialect, may pass for Irishmen. Each had a jacket, or a short coat, of a dark grey imported cloth, and other cloathing. Bill had the best and greatest variety. It is probable they may change their names, cloathes, and professions, and may continue together, or near each other. They are specious, artful and knowing. Frequent occasions to make excuses, has habituated them not to be ignorant of the art of deception; their stories will be plausible, and if taken, will, with infinite dexterity, attempt or effect their escape.—Whoever will take and secure, or put them in a gaol, so that I may get them again, shall have Five Pounds for each; if taken many miles distant and brought home, reasonable travelling expences shall be paid, and a liberal Reward for extraordinary trouble. Michael Wallace.

N.B. Masters of vessels are cautioned not to take them away.

Maryland, Cecil County, Little Elk, July 6, 1785.

Reprints: Maryland Journal, September 2, 1785; Maryland Journal, September 6, 1785; Maryland Journal, September 20, 1785.

Appendix A
Advertisements for Mustees

In the colonial vernacular, the term "mustee" characterized a person of mixed ancestry. In many instances, the word "mustee" had been used interchangeably with the word "mulatto" to denote a person of African ancestry. In other instances, however, the word had been used to indicate a person of Native American heritage. In both cases, "mustee" and "mulatto" signified that the individual had been a person of mixed racial background. While the inclusion of a surname and a reference to the person's hair texture might underscore the possibility that the individual may be a person of mixed ancestry, the exact nature of their race is inconclusive. In the absence of additional references, I leave it to the reader to make their own determination as to the background of the "mustees" enumerated in the advertisements below.

NEW ENGLAND COLONIES

Boston Gazette, September 25, 1744.

Ran away from her Master George Tibbits of North Kingstown, a Mustee Servant Woman named Phelice, of a short Stature, fat of Body, very crooked Legs, about 30 Years of Age; she hath taken away with her two Gowns, one a striped Cotton, the other a striped black and white Drugget, a quilted Coat, and a striped Flannel Coat, three Shifts two old Tow and one a Flannel; she went away the 13th of this Instant in the Night in Company with a Mustee Man named Benjamin: They have taken sundry Things from said Tibbits. Whoever shall take up said Servant Woman, shall have Three Pounds old Tenor and five Pounds for both of said Runaways, and all necessary Charges paid, they conveying them or either of them to said Tibbits, or securing them so that said Runaways may be had again. Septemb. 14th 1744. George Tibbits.

Boston Post-Boy, July 6, 1752.

Run away the 11th Instant from his Master Jeremiah Brown of South-Kingstown, in this Colony, a Mustee Fellow, named Simon, aged about 20 Years, something short of Stature, and round favoured. Had on when he went away, an old blue Coat, striped Flannel Jacket, pretty good Hat, black Wig, Linen Trowsers, white Yarn Stockings, and an old Pair of mended Shoes. Whoever shall take up said Run-away, and deliver him to his said master, or secure him, so that he may be had again, shall have Twenty Pounds, old Tenor Reward, and all necessary Charges paid by Jeremiah Brown.

Reprints: Boston Post-Boy, July 13, 1752; Boston Post-Boy, July 20, 1752.

Boston Evening-Post, July 27, 1752.

Run away last Night from Thomas Brownell, of Portsmouth, a Mustee Fellow named Jack, about 23 Years of Age, is a short thick Fellow, and had on when he went away, a half worn Bever Hat, a Linen Cap, a dark coloured Fly Coat, chequer'd like Diamonds, with Metal Buttons, a striped Flannel Jacket, a white Tow Shirt, striped Tow Trowsers, a pair of dark colour'd Yarn, and a pair pale blue Worsted Stockings, and a pair of Pumps. Whoever takes up the said Fellow, and delivers him to his Master, or secures him, so that he may be had again, shall have Thirty Pounds, old Tenor, Reward, and all necessary Charges paid, by Thomas Brownell. All Masters of Vessels and others, are hereby forbid carrying of or concealing said Fellow, as they would avoid the Penalty of the Law.

Reprint: Boston Evening-Post, August 3, 1752.

Boston Post-Boy, June 18, 1753.

Ran away the 19th Instant from Isaac Fowler, of North Kingstown, a dark Mustee Fellow, named Caesar about 21 Years of Age, well-set, has a thick short neck, and a down Look. Had on when he went away, an old Felt Hat, striped Flannel Jacket, and a Full-cloath dark grey Jacket, Check Shirt, Leather Breeches, white Thread Stockings, and old Shoes; took with him a Frock and Trowsers. Whoever takes up and secures said Fellow, so that his Master may have again, shall have Twenty Pounds Reward, and all necessary Charges, paid by, Isaac Fowler.

Appendix A

Reprint: Boston Post-Boy, June 25, 1753.

Boston Post-Boy, October 14, 1754.

Run away the 3d Instant from his Master Joseph Dennis of Portsmouth, on Rhode-Island, a Mustee or Molatto Man Servant, named Pero, about 27 Years of Age, very large of Stature; hath a Scar on each Thumb, which causes them to stand crooked, and a round large Scar on the outside of the Calf of his left Leg, resembling the Scar of a Burn. Had on when he went away a Homespun full-cloth grey-coloured double breasted Jacket, with large flat Brass Buttons, notch'd or scollop'd round the Edges, a Pair of Tow Trowsers, and a Tow Shirt. Whoever takes up said Molatto, or secures him, so that his Master may have him again, shall have Ten Pounds old Tenor Reward, and all necessary Charges, paid by me, Joseph Dennis.

Reprint: Boston Post-Boy, October 21, 1754.

Boston Evening-Post, April 7, 1755.

Ran away from Jeremiah Niles of South-Kingston, on the 30th past, a pale Negro or Mustee Man called Toney, with bushy hair. Had on a light Mill coloured Kersey Fly Coat, a white and grey Kersey Wastcoat, a pair of white Kersey Breeches, and an old Felt Hat, pair of thick double soled Shoes, with Nails in the Soles, and white y[arn] Stockings. He is a short Fellow. Whoever takes him up and returns him to said Niles, shall have Ten Pounds, old Tenor, Reward, and all necessary Charges paid by Jeremiah Niles.
    South Kingston, April 1st, 1755.

New-London Summary, February 4, 1763.

Twelve Dollars Reward.

Ran away from Epenetus Smith of Smith-Town Long-Island, a Mustee Slave named Cesar, thin Visage, tall and slim, Indian hair, discovers guilt in his Look, has lost all his Toes of one foot, I think the right. Whoever takes up said Slave and brings him to his said Master or Benjamin Giles of Groton Connecticut, shall have the aforesaid Reward and all Necessary Charges.

Reprints: New-London Summary, February 11, 1763; New-London Summary, February 18, 1763.

The Newport Mercury, May 9, 1763.

Run away from Jonathan Haszard of South-Kingstown, on the Eleventh of this Instant April, a Mustee Boy, about thirteen Years of Age, a thick sett

Fellow, his Countenance something hard, with a large Scar on the Top of one of his Feet: He had on a blue Broad Cloth Jacket and Breeches, a pretty good Beaver Hat. Whoever will apprehend said Fellow, and bring him to his said Master, or put him in any of the Goals in said Colony, shall have Thirty Pounds Old Tenor Reward paid by me. Jonathan Haszard.

The Newport Mercury, September 9, 1765.

Ran away from his Master, Jonathan Haszard, Esq; of Boston-Neck, in South-Kingstown, on the 16th Instant, a Mustee-Man-Slave, named Ben, twenty Years of Age; he has a remarkable gray Spot of Hair on the back Part of his Head, and several Scars about his Wrist; he is about five Feet eight Inches high; had on when he went away, a Thunder and Lightning Woollen Coat, a double breasted striped flannel Jacket, a Tow Shirt, and Worsted Stockings: He carried off, two Pair of Shoes, one Fair new, and the other old.—He likewise carried off a Bundle of Cloaths, consisting of Tow Shirts, and a Check Shirt, with other Things unknown.—Whoever will apprehend and secure said Mustee Man Slave, so that his Master may have him again, shall receive Four Dollars Reward, and all necessary Charges paid by Jonathan Haszard. South-Kingstown, August 17, 1765.

Reprint: The Newport Mercury, October 7, 1765.

The Newport Mercury, Monday, May 11, to Monday, May 18, 1767.

Ran away from the Subscriber, in South-Kingstown, on the 20th of this Instant, April, a Mustee Fellow, a Slave, named Harry, about five Feet ten Inches high, has a bushy Head of Hair; had on when he went away, two Check Flannel Shirts, a Pair of striped Kersey Trowsers, the Stripes running round the Legs. Whoever will secure said Fellow in any of his Majesty's Gaols, or bring him to me, shall Five Dollars Reward, and all necessary Charges paid. S. Kingstown, April 23, 1767. Enoch Haszard.

The Newport Mercury, January 23–30, 1769.

Eight Dollars Reward.

Ran away from the Subscriber in South-Kingstown, on the 7th Instant, a light-coloured Mustee Indented Servant, named Cudjo, but commonly called Hunk, a lusty stout Fellow, about Nineteen Years of Age, near Six Feet high, having a large bushy Head of Hair; had on a white Wollen Jacket, and white Breeches and Stockings: Whoever will apprehend said Fellow, and deliver him to Capt. Robert Lillibridge, jun. at Newport, or send him to any of his Majesty's Jails in this Colony, and give Notice thereof to said Lillibridge, or to the Subscriber, shall have the above Reward, and all necessary Charges, paid by said Lillibridge, or by William Hull. South Kingstown, January 12, 1769

The Providence Gazette, January 26 to February 2, 1771.

Run away from the Subscriber, on the 14th Instant, a Mustee Apprentice Boy, named David Jenings, About 16 Years of Age, tall and slim, has a large Head of black Hair, which he wears tyed behind; has a small Scar on his Nose; took with him a good Felt Hat, a fulled Cap, two Pair of Shoes, three Pair of Stockings, two Pair of Breeches, two Pair of Trowsers, two Flannel Shirts, four Jackets, a blue Great-Coat, a strait-bodied brown Coat, and a black Silk Handkerchief. Whoever takes up the said Fellow, and brings him to the Subscriber, shall have a handsome Reward, and all necessary Charges, paid by Hannah Thomas.

Reprints: The Providence Gazette, February 2–9, 1771; Providence Gazette, February 23 to March 2, 1771.

The Newport Mercury, December 6, 1773.

Ran away from John Earle, in Dartmouth, on Sunday, the 15th of November inst. a Mustee slave, about 5 feet 4 inches high, thick and well set, 25 years old, having a remarkable scar on one of his cheeks, and another on his right arm, a very fine set of teeth, and true Negro hair; had on a cloth colour'd double-breasted jacket, and a pair of new leather breeches, and fustian breeches with him, with sundry other articles. Whoever will apprehend said run-away, and return him to said Earle, or confine him in any of his Majesty's jails, and give notice thereof, shall receive Six Dollars reward, and all necessary charges, paid by John Earle, Nov. 29.

Reprint: The Newport Mercury, December 13, 1773.

Connecticut Courant, June 17, 1776.

(Twenty Dollars Reward)

Runaway from the subscriber, a Mustee Fellow named Sy, about 5 Feet 5 Inches high, about 25 Years of Age, has short cul'd Hair nearly resembling a Negroes, well built, had on when he went off, a thick Jacket of a mix'd Colour, black and white, striped trowsers, Buckles in his shoes, a striped flannel under jacket, a check linen shirt blue and white, a white Holland shirt, a felt hat, has a fiddle with him, his upper lip very short, and has altered his name to Joseph Symonds. Whoever takes up said Negro, secures him, or returns him to his Master, shall have Twenty Dollars Reward, and all necessary Charges paid by James Rogers, late of New London, Great-neck. New-London; March 8, 1776.

The Providence Gazette, September 4, 1779.

Ran away from the Subscriber, on the 20th Day of June last, a Mulatto Man Servant, called Primus, about 25 Years of Age, a likely well made Fellow, speaks good English; had on, and took with him, when he went away, a Pair of Leather Breeches, almost new, two Pair of Linen Trowsers, two Linen and two Woollen Shirts, three Flannel Waistcoats, two Pair of Hose, one Pair of good Shoes, a new Beaveret Hat, one Irish Linen Shirt, a Suit of green Cloaths, not much worn, and an old Great-Coat; also took with him a considerable Sum of Money. Also ran away the last Evening, a Mustee Apprentice Boy, called Primas Watt, alias Toby, aged about 14 Years; had on when he went away a Linen Shirt, Flannel Waistcoat, a thick homespun Jacket over it, a Pair of Shoes, and a small old Hat, lopped, and pieced round the Brim. If either of them will return to their Master, before taken up, they shall be forgiven their Crimes; but whoever shall take up said Servant, and convey him to his Master at Warwick Neck, in the County of Kent, shall have Twenty Dollars Reward; and whoever shall take up said Apprentice, and return him to said Master, shall have Ten Dollars Reward, and all reasonable Charges, paid by Benjamin Greene. N.B. All Masters of Vessels, and others, are cautioned against harbouring or concealing said Servant or Apprentice, as they would avoid the Penalty of the Law, in such Cases provided. Warwick-Neck, September 2, 1779.

Reprints: The Providence Gazette, September 11, 1779; The Providence Gazette, September 18, 1779.

The Providence Gazette, September 20, 1783.

Ran away from his Master, the Subscriber, on Monday last, a Mulatto or Mustee Servant Boy, named Pero, about ten Years of Age, cross-eyed, and has black curled Hair resembling that of a Negro; had on, when he went away, a Shirt and Trowsers of Linen. Whoever will take up said Boy, and return him to his Master, shall be handsomely rewarded, and have all necessary Charges paid, by Amos Atwell. Providence, Sept. 19, 1783.

Appendix A

The Newport Mercury, July 3, 1784.

Four Dollars Reward.

Ran away, from the Subscriber, on Monday the 21st instant, a Mustee Boy, named Jonathan White, about 15 Years of Age, is a short, thick, well set Fellow, has a Scar on his left Thumb; had on when he went away, white Tow and Linen Shirt and Trowsers, with a Stock round his Neck, two grey Jackets, one with Sleves, the other without, a Felt Hat bound, and a Pair of Shoes, one or both cap'd at the Toe. Whoever will apprehend said Boy, and return him to the Subscriber shall receive the above Reward, and all reasonable Charges paid, by Thomas Tripp. Dartmouth, June 24, 1784.

MID-ATLANTIC COLONIES

Pennsylvania Journal, or, Weekly Advertiser, March 27, 1753.

Run away the 29th of December, from William Burk of Lancaster, an apprentice Boy, named William Bishop, he is a mustee, and a Plasterer by trade, 5 feet 9 Inches high; had on when he went away, a bearskin coat with metal buttons, leather breeches, yarn stockings, blue and white spotted cap, and a blue and white spotted silk handkerchief, but it is like he may change his cloaths. Whoever take up said apprentice and secures him so that he may be had again, shall have Twenty Shillings Reward if taken in Town, and if out of Town, Forty Shillings, and reasonable charges paid by William Burk.

N.B. All Persons are forbid entertaining him, and all Masters of Vessels from carrying him off.

Reprint: Pennsylvania Journal, or, Weekly Advertiser, April 3, 1753.

Pennsylvania Journal, or, Weekly Advertiser, December 11, 1784.

Sixteen Dollars Reward.
Ran away, the 15th of August last, from the subscriber, living in Franklin county, Canecocheague,

A Mustee fellow, commonly calls himself Paddy, or Patrick Hunley, about 19 years of age, near six feet high, slim made, stoop shouldered, a simple looking fellow, his hair straight and of a light colour; appears much like a white man, and will strive to pass as such: Had on a dark lead coloured coat, with steel buttons, and a new wool hat, his other cloths uncertain; also took with him a riffle gun, brass mounted, maker's name D. Dickey, cut on the barrel and lock, also the name of William McKee cut on the brass box. Whoever takes up said fellow, and secures him and the gun, shall have the above reward, paid by me James Poe. Nov. 9, 1784.

N.B. I have been informed that he has been sold out of Chester gaol for his fees, to a certain Mr. Samuel Lindsey, and has run away from him, and was seen passing into Philadelphia about two weeks ago.

SOUTHERN COLONIES

Georgia Gazette, October 25, 1769.

Run away from Augusta, a Mustee Fellow, named Harry. He is middle aged, and has a halt in his walk from a rheumatick complaint he is subject to. He has carried off with him his wife, named Cassandra, a tall slim young black wench. The fellow is very artful and plausible, and both he and his wife are well known about Savannah, though it is supposed they may endeavor to get to the Indian nation. or to Mobille, where the wench's parents and other relations live. Whoever will apprehend them, and deliver them to me at Augusta, or to the Warden of the Work-house at Savannah, shall receive 20 sterling reward for each, besides all reasonable charges; and if any persons harbour them they may expect to be prosecuted. Andrew Johnston.

Reprint: Georgia Gazette, November 1, 1769.

Virginia Gazette, June 7, 1770.

Run away from the subscriber, living in Northampton county, North Carolina, on the 10th of April 1769, a mustee woman slave named Annis, about 22 years of age, near 5 feet high, thick and well set, straight hair, scarred on the back part of her neck by cupping, has a scar on the elbow joint of her right arm, branded on the right cheek E, and on the left R, is very cunning, and will endeavour to make her escape. Whoever apprehends the said slave, and secures her so that I get her again, if taken in this province shall have 5 l. reward, if out thereof 7 l. 10 s. Edward Rutland.

Virginia Gazette, April 18, 1777.

Run away from mr. Lodowick Jones, late of Middlesex county, deceased, a mustee complexioned man slave named Sam, about 5 feet 5 or 6 inches high, well made, has a smooth tongue, but snuffles a little. Nature has furnished him with a covering for his head, which when grown out is thick and bushy. It is needless to describe the clothes he went off in. He is, it is supposed, lurking about col. Corbin's quarters in King & Queen county. Ten dollars will be given to any person who secures the said slave in some jail of this state, and gives notice thereof to Le Roy Peachey, exec. I will sell the said slave for 80 1. as he runs.

State Gazette of South-Carolina, November 3, 1785.

Run away.
From the subscriber, about three weeks ago,

A Mustee or Mulatto Man, with a bushy head of hair, and Samuel, hard of hearing, a Shoemaker by trade, well set, about 5 feet 6 or 6 inches high, about 45 years of age, had on when he went away, a great coat and striped jacket. Whoever will deliver the said slave to the subscriber in Charleston, shall receive a Reward of Five Guineas. Patrick Hinds.

Charleston, Nov. 1, 1785.

N.B. The said Mulatto was away for two years, at Lynch's creek, with Captain Watts, he is well known in that neighbourhood.

Reprints: State Gazette of South-Carolina, November 7, 1785; State Gazette of South-Carolina, November 10, 1785; State Gazette of South-Carolina, November 14, 1785; State Gazette of South-Carolina, November 17, 1785.

State Gazette of South-Carolina, August 17, 1786.

Two Guineas Reward.

Absented himself about 5 weeks ago, a Mustee Fellow, about 5 feet 10 inches high, has a very bushy head of hair, and with a scar on the right cheek. Whoever will deliver the said fellow to the Warden of the Work-House, or to the subscriber on James Island, shall have the above reward, and all reasonable charges paid by Joseph Rivers.

James Island, August 7, 1786.

Reprint: State Gazette of South-Carolina, September 7, 1786.

Norfolk Herald, June 23, 1798.

Thirty Dollars Reward.

Ran away from Norfolk, about the 20th March a Mustee Man named Jack Page has long black hair, slender made about 5 feet 10 inches high, carries his head a little to one side, 25 years old, thick lips, can read, write, and figure a little. Has been used to mind horses and wait on a Gentleman. The above Reward will be paid on delivery of the said slave to me in Williamsburg, or securing him in any jail so that I get him again. James Wright. Williamsburg, June 23.

Appendix B

As the Law Directs: Social Death in Julian's Massachusetts

The acts and statutes enumerated below are but a few in which free persons in Massachusetts defined and curtailed the status of unfree and enslaved persons in the Bay Colony. In addition to illustrating social death, they document the ways the power broker in eighteenth-century New England shaped the public imagination of all of the residents in the colony. Although these acts and statutes listed below are not a complete listing of all of the laws the assembly in Massachusetts passed between 1633 and 1740, it is nonetheless representative of the legal, social, and cultural dimensions in which the English colonists considered Native Americans strangers in their Promised Lands.

1633

Servants are discouraged from absenting themselves of their Masters' service. In the event that they elect to run away, the Magistrate or Constable is empowered to pursue the said runaway and return them to their owner.

1637

No person shall "sell, give or Barter, directly or indirectly, any Gun or Guns, Powder, Bullets, Shot, Lead to any Indian . . . upon penalty" of the Law.

1640

"To propagate the true Religion unto the Indians, and that dives of them are become subject to the English, and have engaged themselves to be willing and ready to understand the Law of God"; the Laws shall be published "to reduce them to civility of life."

1641

Lawful "Captives taken in just Wars, as willingly sell themselves or are sold to us" are subject to "any Bondslavery, Villenage or Captivity amongst us."

1642

"If any man Commit Fornication with any single Woman, they shall be punished, either by enjoyning Marriage, or Fine, or Corporal punishment, or all."

1646

"All Servants and Workmen imbezling the goods of their Masters . . . be lyable to all Laws and penalties."

1647

"Servants, do behave themselves disobediently and disorderly toward their. . . . Masters and Governours" shall be punished in accordance with the Law.

1648

Indians are instructed to fence their "Corn Fields or Ground."
    Indians are forewarned against hurting "the English, in their Cattle."

1655

"No person shall under any pretence sell or any way dispose any Horse, Mare or Colts to any Indians, upon the penalty of" of the Law.

Appendix B

1656

"No person or persons Inhabiting with this Jurisdiction, shall directly or indirectly any wayes give, sell, barter or otherwise dispose of any Boat, Skiffle, or any greater Vessel" under penalty of the Law.

1657

It is unlawful for foreigners, "the French and Dutch" to "trade with any Indian or Indians within the Limits of our Jurisdiction, directly or indirectly by themselves or others, under penalty of Confiscation of all such Goods."

"No Person or Persons, directly or indirectly, shall Trade with the Indians for any sort of Peltry, excepting only such as are Authorized by" the Law.

"For the preventing of Drunkenness amongst the Indians," the sell of "Rum, strong Waters, Wines, strong Beer, Bandy, Cyder, Perry, or any other strong Liquors, going under any other name whatsoever" is prohibited under penalty of Law.

1658

Indians "jointly shall have the power of a County Court, to hear and determine all causes arising among them, the English Magistrate appointing the time and place of the Court." Indians, "especially those Natick and Punquepaog," must live "according to our Laws." They shall "be Authorized to constitute and appoint Indians Commissioners in their several Plantations." No Indian "at any time, *Powaw* or perform outward worship to the false Gods, or the Devil, in any part of our Jurisdiction."

1662

"All persons within this Jurisdiction, whether the Children, or Servants that are under government in Families, that shall wear any Apparel exceeding the quality and condition of their Persons or Estate, or that is apparently contrary to the ends of Apparel."

1666

To discourage the increasing sin of "Drunkenness amongst the Indian," no "strong Liquors, Wine or strong Drink" shall be sold or given to Indians under penalty of the Law.

1668

"The Country to Trade Peltry or Skins with the Indians" shall be regulated in accordance to the Law.

1675

"Those Indians that are desirous to Approve themselves Faithfull to the English, be confined to their several Plantations." Indians, "Strangers not of our Nation," prohibited from being in Boston. "Considering the great Abuse and Scandal that hath arisen by the License of Trading-Houses with the Indians, whereby Drunkenness and other Crimes have been as it were sold unto them. It is Ordered . . . such houses . . . cease." No "said Indians shall presume to go off said Islands voluntarily upon pain of Death; And it shall be lawful for the English to destroy those that they shall finde [sic] stragling [sic] off from the said place of their Confinement."

1676

"Trade with any Indian, or Indians, directly, or Indirectly, by themselves or others; Any Commodity whatsoever upon Penalty" is prohibited.

1677

"Indian Children or Youths are settled or disposed by order of Authority, or with their Parents or Relations consent to any of the English Inhabitants within their Jurisdiction, shall remain with them as Servants; and to be taught and instructed in the Christian Religion, until each of them attain to the age of twenty four years."

The Law to kill any Indians "found without the limits appointed are hereby repealed and declared void."

"All Neighbour Indians" are prohibited from traveling into the woods with guns "without a Certificate."

1679

Servants who engage in Sabbath breaking, "absenting themselves from the publick Worship of God on the Lords dayes," irreligion, "Atheism amongst us," and other forms of debauchery shall be punished as "the Law directs."

Appendix B

1680

"All Persons are strictly :inhibiting . . . from Giving, Selling, Bartering directly or indirectly, Guns, Powder, Shot, Lead, Arms or Ammunition to any Indian whatsoever."

"All Indians that belong to this Jurisdiction except Apprentices or Covenant Servants for years, are to live among, & under Government of the Indian Rulers of Natick, Punkquepaog, Wamesit, which are places allowed by this Court."

No "Master or Skipper of said Ship, Ketch, Sloop or Vessels" shall transport any "Servant or Negro, without the Permit of the Governour."

1683

Any "Person or Persons shall be taken . . . or shall deliver up themselves to any one or more of their Creditors in way of Service for satisfaction of any Debt or Debts . . . with the knowledge and approbation of the Court of that County where such Debtor or Creditor dwell."

1692–1693

"If any man commit fornication with any single woman . . . they shall be fined unto their majesties not exceeding the sum of five pounds, or be corporally punished by whipping, not exceeding ten stripes apiece, at the discretion of the sessions of the peace."

No servant "shall travel on [the Lord' Day], or any part thereof."

1693–1694

"No person who is or shall be licensed to be an inholder, taverner, common victualler, or retailer, shall suffer any apprentice, servant, or negro to sit drinking in his or her house. . . . Nor shall sell any wine, liquors, or other strong drink, to any apprentices, servants, Indians or negros."

No "persons shall presume, either openly or privately, to receive, or buy, of or from any Indian servant, or negro or molatto servant, or slave. . . . And such Indian, negro or molatto servant, or slave, shall be openly whipped, not exceeding twenty lashes."

Appendix B

1694–1695

No "apprentice, or covenant servant . . . without licence and consent of . . . his master, in writing" shall absent themselves from their "parent's or master's service."

AN ACT FOR REGULATING OF TRADE WITH THE INDIANS.

AN ACT FOR ENCOURAGING THE PROSECUTION OF THE INDIAN ENEMY & REBELS, AND PRESERVING SUCH AS ARE FRIENDS.

1695–1696

"No person or persons inhabiting or residing in Trading with any of the towns or precincts within the county of Hampshire, shall presume, directly or indirectly, to give, sell, trade, deal, truck or barter any goods, wares, merchandizes, ammunition, or any sort of strong liquors, unto or with any Indian or Indians whatsoever, or receive any peltry from them."

"All Indians who shall be found within five miles of Indians found Connecticut River, on the easterly side thereof, or within twenty miles on the westerly side of the same, shall be deemed and accounted to be east side or enemies, and treated as such, and the same reward and allowance shall be made and given to any of his majestie's subjects that shall kill, or take and bring in prisoners any Indian or Indians found within the said limits."

1696–1697

"All Indian, molatto and negro servants [are] to be estimated as . . . personal estate."

1697

AN ACT FOR ENCOURAGEMENT OF THE PROSECUTION OF THE INDIAN ENEMY & REBELS.

1698

If any servant "unlawfully cut or take away any grass, com or grain growing, or rob any orchard or garden, or break or cut, pull down or remove any hedge, pale, rail or fence, or that shall hurt, or digg, or pull up, or take away any grafts or fruit trees . . . cut or carry off any manner of wood, underwood, timber, poles or trees standing, lying or growing on the land of any others, or off or from the commons of any town," they will be punished as the Law directs.

"Every person whomsoever which shall presume, either openly or privately, to buy or receive of or from any Indian, molatto, or negro servant or slave . . . goods, wares, merchandizes or provision" shall be punished in accordance to the Law.

1699–1700

AN ACT FOR GIVING NECESSARY SUPPLIES TO THE EASTERN INDIANS, AND FOR REGULATING OF TRADE WITH THEM.

1700–1701

AN ACT FOR PREVENTING ABUSES TO THE INDIANS.

1701–1702

AN ACT TO PREVENT AND MAKE VOID CLANDESTINE AND ILLEGAL PURCHASES OF LANDS FROM THE INDIANS.

1703

AN ACT TO ENCOURAGE THE PROSECUTION OF THE INDIAN ENEMY AND REBELS.

1703–1704

AN ACT FOR DISCONTINUING THE SUPERIOUR COURT OF JUDICATURE, TO BE HOLDEN WITHIN THE RESPECTIVE COUNTIES OF HAMPSHIRE AND YORK, DURING THE PRESENT TROUBLES WITH THE INDIANS.

"No Indian, negro or molatto servant, or slave, may presume to be absent from the families whereto they respectively belong, or be found abroad in the night time, after nine a clock, unless it be upon some errand for their respective masters or owner."

1706

AN ACT TO ENCOURAGE THE PROSECUTION OF THE INDIAN ENEMY AND REBELS.

1706–1707

AN ACT FOR THE FURTHER CONTINUING OF, AND IN ADDITION TO THE "ACT TO ENCOURAGE THE PROSECUTION OF THE INDIAN ENEMY AND REBELS."

1708–1709

AN ACT TO ENCOURAGE THE IMPORTATION OF WHITE SERVANTS.

1709–1710

AN ACT AGAINST INDIANS BEING SUED FOR DEBT.

1712

AN ACT PROHIBITING THE IMPORTATION OR BRINGING INTO THIS PROVINCE ANY INDIAN SERVANTS OR SLAVE.

1713–1714

AN ACT FOR REGULATING THE TRADE WITH THE EASTERN INDIANS.

1718–1719

AN ACT IN ADDITION TO THE ACT FOR PREVENTING ABUSES TO THE INDIANS, MADE IN THE TWELFTH YEAR OF KING WILLIAM.

All Indian, negro and mollatto servants for life, to be estimated as other personal estate; viz., each male servant for life, above fourteen years of age, at fifteen pounds value; each female servant for life, above fourteen years of age, at ten pounds value. . . . And all Indian, negro and molatto male servants for a term of years shall be numbred and rated as other polls, and not as personal estate; and every steer or ox at the age of four years old and upwards, at forty shillings value; and every cow or heif[f]er at the age of three years old and upwards, at thirty shillings; and every horse or mare at three years old and upwards, at forty shillings; and every swine of one year old and upwards, at eight shillings; and every sheep or goat of one year old and upwards, at three shillings; and all decked vessel[l]s at thirty shillings per ton, and all other vessel[l]s at twenty shillings per ton; trading stock at one-quarter part of the true value thereof.

1721–1722

AN ACT TO PROHIBIT TRADE AND COMMERCE WITH THE EASTERN INDIANS.

1722

AN ACT TO ENCOURAGE THE PROSECUTION OF THE INDIAN ENEMY AND REBELS.

1725–1726

AN ACT IN ADDITION TO THE SEVERAL ACTS OR LAWS OF THIS PROVINCE, FOR THE REGULATION OF THE CIVILIZED INDIANS INHABITING THIS PROVINCE, AND PREVENTING OPPRESSION OR ABUSES TO THEM.

An Act For The Allowing Necessary Suppl[ie][y]s To The Eastern Indians, And For Regvlating Trade With Them, And For The Repealing An Act Entituled "AN ACT TO PROHIBIT TRADE AND COMMERCE WITH THE EASTERN INDIANS," MADE AND PASS'D IN THE EIGHTH YEAR OF HIS PRESENT MAJEST[Y][IE]'S REIGN.

1727–1728

AN ACT TO OBLIGE AND REQUIRE, THE FORTY PETITIONERS FOR A TRACT OF LAND AT HASSANAMISCO, TOGETHER WITH THE ENGLISH PROPRIETORS OF OTHER LANDS THERE, TO PAY THE CHARGE OF ERECTING A MEETING-HOUSE AND SCHOOLHOUSE,

AND OF SUPPORTING AN ORTHODOX MINISTER AND SCHOOL-MASTER IN THE SAID PLACE.

"Whereas the solemnizing of funerals on the Lord's day ofttimes occasions great prophanation thereon, by servants and children gathering in the streets, and walking up and down to and from the funerals, and is the means of many disorders and irregularities then committed; for remedy whereof" servants are prohibited from participation without license.

1729

AN ACT IN ADDITION TO THE ACT ENTIT[U]LED "AN ACT FOR ALLOWING NECESSARY SUPPL[IE][Y]'S TO THE EASTERN INDIANS," &c.

1731–1732

AN ACT FOR [THE] ALLOWING NECESSARY SUPPLIES TO THE EASTERN AND WESTERN INDIANS, AND FOR REGULATING TRADE WITH THEM.

1732–1733

AN ACT FOR ALLOWING NECESSARY SUPPL[IE][Y]S TO THE EASTERN AND WESTERN INDIANS, AND FOR REGULATING TRADE WITH THEM.

1734

"The assessors of the several towns within this province . . . shall be chosen" and will determine "a true and faithful list or account, according to their best skill and understanding . . . of all rateable [sic] estates . . . including all Indian, negro[e] and molatto servant, as well for term of years as for life together with all farms and other lands lying adjacent thereunto, with the inhabitants thereon."

Appendix B

1735

AN ACT FOR THE MORE EFFECTUAL REGULATING THE PRIVATE TRADE WITH THE EASTERN AND WESTERN INDIANS, AND THE PREVENTING ABUSES THEREIN.

1737–1738

AN ACT FOR ALLOWING NECESSARY SUPPLIES TO THE EASTERN AND WESTERN INDIANS, AND FOR REGULATING TRADE WITH THEM.

1740

AN ACT FOR THE MORE EFFECTUAL REGULATING THE PRIVATE TRADE WITH THE EASTERN AND WESTERN INDIANS, AND THE PREVENTING ABUSES THEREIN.

Sources

The Colonial Laws of Massachusetts. Reprinted from the Edition of 1672, with the Supplements through 1686. Boston, 1887.

The Acts and Resolves, Public and Private of the Province of the Massachusetts Bay: To which are Prefixed the Charters of the Province with Historical and Explanatory Notes, and an Appendix. Volume 2 (1715–1741). Boston: Wright & Potter, 1874.

Appendix C
Julian's Story as Broadsides Ephemera

Julian's story was memorialized in three broadsides that were circulated throughout New England. Each leaflet used the incident involving the Indian and John Rogers as a cautionary tale to instruct servants, children, and young boys. Each single sheet included woodcuts as a header. Each illustration depicted some aspect that highlighted the finality of death. In first broadside, example, Julian is shown at the gallows. He has a rope around his neck. The esteemed members of the town's clergy are depicted attending the execution. Beneath the illustration, Thomas Fleet reprinted verbatim the Indian man's life story that appeared in his *Weekly Rehearsal* newspaper. In the second broadside, also authorized by Julian, the woodcut depicted the final moments following the bounty hunter's death. In that woodcut, Julian is shown with the Jack-Knife in his hand. Rogers lies dead at his feet. Under the illustration, Fleet printed a rendition of the Native American man's life as a neoclassic poem. Compared to Fleet's previous broadside, this poster included additional details. Several lines, for example, make derogatory references to the bondservant's race. Another line indicates that Julian was sold and adopted at the tender age of three. The third broadside included an illustration of death's face at the top of the sheet. Underneath the header of this unauthorized broadside, Julian's story is recount in verse again. This neoclassic limerick also discloses additional information. In addition to being drunkard, for example, the Indian man is characterized as being a thief and a liar. He is also described as a rogue who fell in with a "wicked Crew." More than this, the poem depicted Julian as a blasphemer and possibly as a fornicator and adulterer. Because these characterizations were not verified by the Indian man who told his own story, it is likely that these portrayals are hyperbole. Incidentally, the printer misspelled the Native American man's name. Instead of Julian, the printer spelled his name Julleyoun.

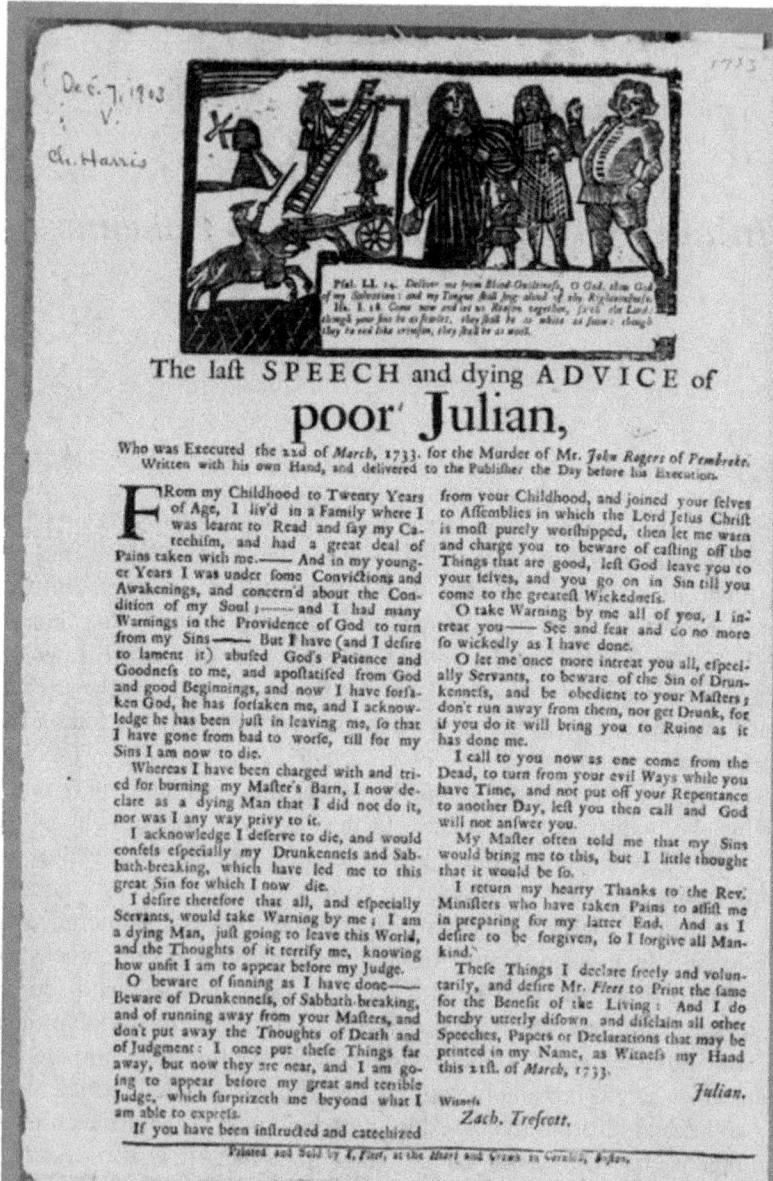

Figure AC.1 Julian. *The last Speech and dying Advice of poor Julian, Who was Executed the 22d of March, 1733. for the Murder of Mr. John Rogers of Pembroke*. Boston: Thomas Fleet, 1733. American Antiquarian Society.

Advice from the Dead to the Living;
OR, A
Solemn Warning to the World.

Occasioned by the untimely Death of

poor Julian,

Who was Executed on *Boston* Neck, on *Thursday* the 22d. of *March*, 1733. for the Murder of Mr. *John Rogers* of *Pembroke*, the 12th of *September*, 1732.

Very proper to be Read by all Persons, but especially young People, and Servants of all Sorts.

THIS Day take warning young and old,
By a sad Sight we here behold,
Of one whom Vengeance in his Chase
Hath taken in his sinful Race.

Here we behold amidst the Throng,
Condemned *Julian* guarded strong,
To Gallows bound with heavy Heart,
To suffer as his just Desert.

Where we for Warning may observe
What cruel Murder doth deserve,
Also the sad procuring Cause
Why Sinners die amidst their Days.

Here now we have a lively View,
Of *Cain's* vile Action fresh and new,
That old Revenge is by Permit
Prevailing in our Natures yet.

Revenge is sweet, we often hear,
How bitter now doth it appear?
It leads to Ruine, Death and Fate,
And bitter Mourning when too late.

We often hear Men to complain,
Their Punishment like guilty *Cain*,
Which justly falleth to their Share,
Is great, and more than they can bear.

The Prisoner owns the bloody Act,
And saith the Sentence on his Fact,
Was pass'd on him impartially,
And therefore doth deserve to die.

By his Account he first was sold,
When he was not quite three Years old;
And by his Master in his Youth,
Instructed in the Ways of Truth.

Was also taught to Write and Read,
And learn'd his Catechise and Creed,
And what was proper (as he saith)
Relating to the Christian Faith.

His pious Master did with care,
By Counsels warn him to beware
Of wicked Courses, that would tend
To his Destruction in the End.

When Twenty Years were gone and past,
By his Account he took at last

To Drinking and ill Company,
Which prov'd his fatal Destiny:

No timely Warnings would he hear,
From kind Reproofs he turn'd his Ear,
Provoked God for to depart,
And leave him to an harden'd Heart.

Since he despis'd the Ways of Truth,
And good Instruction in his Youth,
God then withdrew restraining Grace,
And let him run his wicked Race.

From Sin to Sin advancing thus,
By sad Degrees from bad to worse,
He did at length commit the Crime,
For which he dies before his Time.

He prays his sad untimely Fall,
May be a Warning unto all,
That they no such like Steps do tread,
Nor lead such Life as he has led.

That Children and all Servants they
Would in their Stations all obey,
Parents and Masters every one,
And not to do as he has done.

Obey them with a willing Mind,
Be always honest, just and kind,
And pray to God to give them Grace,
To do their Duty in their Place.

He thanks good Preachers heartily,
For all their Helps of Piety,
Which to his Soul they did extend,
To fit him for his latter End.

So here we leave his pitious Case,
In tender Arms of sov'reign Grace,
Altho' his Crimes are great and sore,
Grace can abound and pardon more.

Now may the Congregation hear,
This awful Voice, and stand in fear,
And being timely warn'd thereby,
may do no more so wickedly.

FINIS.

BOSTON: Printed and Sold at the *Heart* and *Crown* in *Cornhill*.

Note. There being a foolish Paper printed, called Julian's Advice to Children and Servants, said to be published at his Desire; this may certify, that the said Paper is false and spurious, and disowned by the said Julian in the Presence of three Persons.

Figure AC.2 Julian and Thomas Fleet. Advice from the Dead to the Living; OR A Solemn Warning to the World. Occasioned by the untimely Death of poor Julian. Boston: Thomas Fleet, 1733. Boston Public Library.

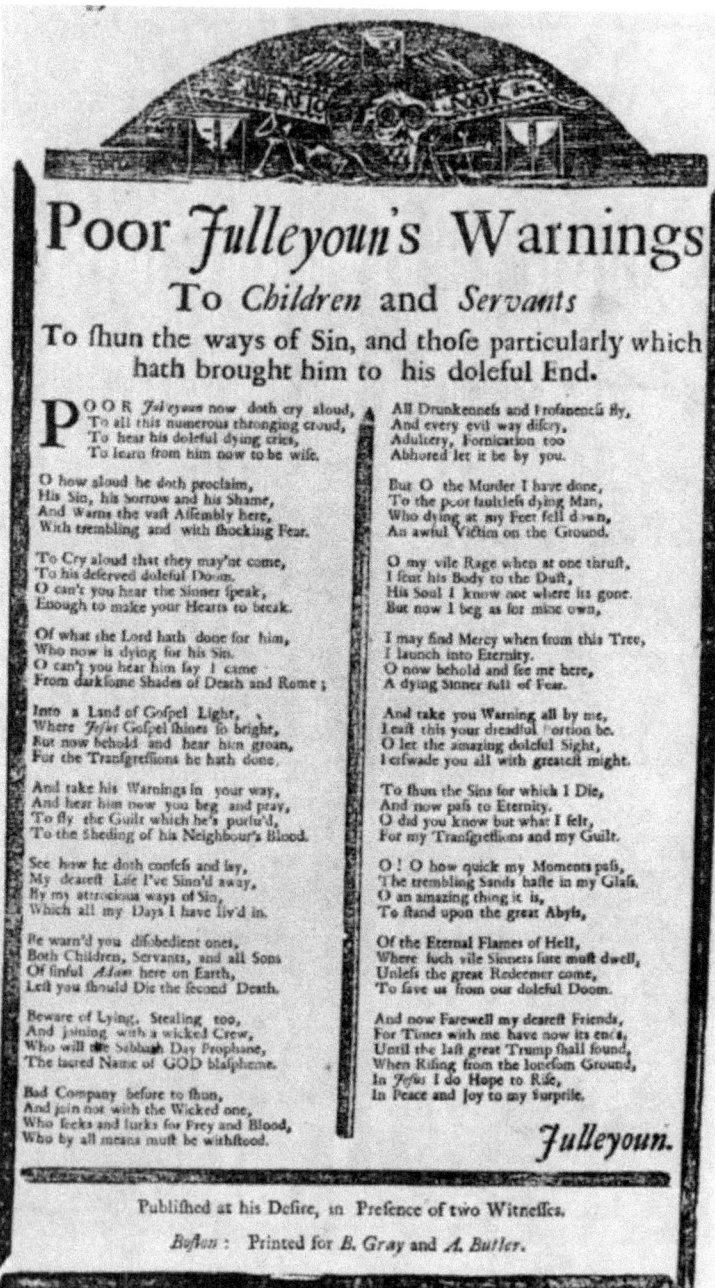

Figure AC.3 Poor Julleyoun's Warning To Children and Servants to Shun the ways of Sin, and those particularly which hath brought him to his doleful End. Boston: B. Gray and A Butler, 1733. Boston Public Library.

Appendix D
Julian's Story Memorialized

These subsequent notices appeared in several New England newspapers between 1732 and 1733. Each of them reveals additional information about Julian the Indian. The notices are enumerated in chronological order.

New-England Weekly Journal, September 18, 1732.

Boston. On Wednesday Evening last an Indian Fellow belonging to Mr. Howard of Bridgewater, was committed to our Goal barbarously murdering one Mr. Rogers of Pembrook, by stabbing him with a Knife in his Breast, the day before, of which Would he dy'd in a few Minutes. Mr. Rogers had taken up the said Indian as a Runaway from his Master, and conveying him home, when the horrid Fact was committed. Mr. Rogers was a Widower, and has left three Children.

Weekly Rehearsal, September 18, 1732.

The following Tragical [sic] Account we have from Brantry, viz. That on Tuesday last, an Indian Fellow belonging to Mr. Howard of Bridgewater (formerly Major John Quincy's of Brantrey) having run away, one Rogers of Pembrook, being then at Weymouth, hearing thereof, went to look said Indian, and after some Time found him on Monday Evening; and lodging that Night at Brantrey, the Indian get away again, which said Roger understanding, on Tuesday Morning offer'd Ten Shillings to a Man to find him again, who went accordingly and soon brought him back. Mr. Rogers, with the Indian, set out on their Journey homewards, and when they had got about five Miles, they went into the House of one Scot, and call'd for a Dram, but they had none; and while the said Rogers and Scot talked together in the House the Indian went and stood without the Door; and Mr. Scot seeing him pass by the Window, told Mr. Rogers the Indian would get away; upon which he went out, and seeing him at a little Distance from the House, ran after him; the Indian looking back, and seeing him coming, took a Jack Knife and opened it, (as Mr. Scot tho't by the Motion of his Arms) and when Mr. Rogers came near, the Indian turn'd about and made up to him, and then stabb'd the Knife into his left Breast, as 'tis thought' up to Haft, the Wound being very deep and open. Mr. Scot and a Negro in the House seeing Mr. Rogers assaulted, ran up to assist him, and finding the Indian with the Knife in his Hand, which Mr. Rogers had then hold of and let go, they with much Difficulty, after bending the Knife double, got it from him: Mr. Scot seeing them both bloody, ask'd Mr. Rogers whether it was his or the Indian's Blood, three times before he made any Answer, and then only said, I am either stabb'd or wounded, and fell down and dy'd immediately. While they were looking after Mr. Rogers, the Indian got away again; but the Negro pursu'd and soon catch'd him, and held him till Mr. Scot got more Help, who then secur'd him. Mr. Rogers was a Widower, about 43 Years old, and has left Three Children. The Coroners Inquest charges the said Indian with the Murder of the deceased, and he was brought to Town last Wednesday Night under a Guard, and committed to Prison.

American Weekly Mercury, October 12, 1732.

Boston, Sept. 14. We have the following melancholy Account of a barbarous Murder committed at Brantrey on Thursday last, about Noon, as related by some that were upon the Jury of Inquest, viz. An Indian Fellow bel to one Mr. Howard of Bridgewater, (formerly to Maj. Quincy of Brantrey having Runaway, Advertisements were issued out after him, and a Reward to take him up, and bring him home, one Mr. Rogers of Pembrook, being at Weymouth, on his way home happen'd to see one of the Advertisements, took it, and returned back to look for the said Indian, and on Monday Evening last, after some enquiry, found him; and lodging that Night at Brantrey, the Indian got away again on Morning Mr. Rogers, finding the Indian was gone, he offered Ten Shillings to a Man to find him again, who accordingly went, and soon brought him back: Mr. Rogers, having the Indian with him, set out on his Journey homewards, and when they had got about Five Miles, Mr. Rogers stopt and went into the House of one Mr. Scot with the Indian, and call'd for a Dram, but they had none; and while they were talking together in the House, the Indian went and stood outside by the Door; and Mr. Scot seeing him pass by the Window, told Mr. Rogers, the Indian wou'd get away; upon which he went out, and seeing him at a little Distance from the House, going towards a Corn-Field, he ran after him; the Indian looking back, and seeing him coming, took a Jack-Knife and open'd it, as Mr. Scot tho't by the Motion of his Arms, and when Mr. Rogers had got near, the Indian suddenly turn'd about, and made up to him, and then stab'd the Knife into his left Breast, as 'tis thought, up to the Haft, the Wound being very deep and open: Mr. Scot and a Negro in the House seeing Mr. Rogers assaulted ran up to assist him, and finding the Indian with the Knife in his Hand, which Mr. Rogers had then hold of and let go, they with much difficulty, after bending the Knife double, got it from him: Mr. Scot seeing them both bloody, ask'd Mr Rogers whether it was his, or the Indians blood, three Times before he made any Answer, and then only said, I am either stab'd, or wounded, and fell down and dy'd immediately. The Indian got away again, while they were looking after Mr. Rogers, but the Negro pursu'd him, and soon catch'd him and held him, till Mr. Scot went and brought others, and then secur'd him. Mr. Rogers was a Widower, of about 43 Years of Age, and has left three Children. The Coroner's Inquest charges the said Indian with the Murder, and he was Yesterday towards Evening brought to Town, and committed to Goal.

New-England Weekly Journal, February 12, 1733.

Boston: This Week the Superiour Court sit here, at which will come on the Tryal of the Indian Fellow belonging to Mr. Howard of Bridgewater, who was committed to our Goal in September last on suspicion of barbarously murdering Mr. Rogers of Pembroke by stabbing him with a Knife on the 12th of said Month.

Boston News-Letter, February 22, 1733.

On Tuesday last in the Forenoon, at the Superiour Court, holden here for the County of Suffolk, came on the Trial of Julian, an Indian Man, who was Indicted at the said Court, for the Murder of Mr. John Rogers, of Pembrook, on Sept. 12th last, by stabing him with a Jack Knife in the Breast at Brantry; a particular and authentick Account of which Fact was inserted in our Number 1494, Sept. 14. The said Trail last about Two Hours and a half, when it was committed to the Jury, who in the After brought in their Verdict, Guilty.

Note: This notice references the original account printed on September 14, 1732.

Boston Gazette, February 26, 1733.

Last Week at the Superiour Court here, Julian, an Indian Man was by Verdict found Guilty of the murder of Mr. John Rogers of Pembrook, by stabbing him with a Knife in the Breast at Brantry, and on Friday last received Sentence of Death. It was observed he behav'd with undaunted Courage till the close of the Judgment, when he fell down in a fainting Fitt. The time for Execution we have not yet heard.

New-England Weekly Journal, February 26, 1733.

On Tuesday last in the Forenoon, at the Superior Court, holden [sic] here, came on the Trail of the Indian Man, who was Indicted for the Murder of Mr. John Rogers of Pembrooke, on Sept. 12. Last. The Trail lasted about two Hours and half, when it was committed to the Jury, who in the Afternoon brought in their Verdict, Guilty, and on Friday last he received Sentence of Death; and tho' he deny'd the Fact upon his Trail, we hear he has since confess'd it, and now appears very penitent, and was yesterday at the New Meeting House in Harvard-Street. This same Indian was Try'd for his Life about a Year ago at Plymouth on suspicion of burning his Master's Barn, but was acquitted.

Weekly Rehearsal, February 26, 1733.

On Tuesday last in the Forenoon, at the Court of Assize and general Goal delivery then held for the County of Suffolk, came on the Trail of the Indian mentioned in our last (whose Name is Julian) for the Murder of Mr. John Rogers of Pembrook. He pleaded not Guilty, and made some Defence, pretending that his Knife being open in his Jacket Pocket, and said Rogers throwing him down and falling upon him, the Knife ran into his Breast and killed him: But after the fair and legal Trial of above Two Hours, it was committed to the Jury, who in the Afternoon brought in their Verdict Guilty. After he was returned to the Prison, he confessed the whole Matter, which agreed exactly with what the Witnesses had deposed against him. On Friday Morning he was brought to Court again to receive his Sentence, at the pronouncing of which he fainted away, but after some Time recovered and was carried back to Prison. According to his Desire, he went Yesterday in the Afternoon to hear the Rev. Mr. Byles Preach, who entertain'd the numerous Audience with an excellent Discourse, prepared and adapted to the miserable Circumstances of the Criminal, from Psalm LI.14. Deliver me from Blood-guiltiness, &c. We are informed he has desired to hear the Rev. Mr. Chickley the next Lord's Day. The Time for his Execution is not yet appointed.

Appendix D

Rhode-Island Gazette, March 1, 1733.

On Tuesday last in the Forenoon, at the Superior Court holden here, came on the Trial of the Indian Man, who was Indicted for the Murder of Mr. John Rogers of Pembrooks, on Sept. 12. Last. The Trail lasted about two Hours and an half, when it was committed to the Jury, who in the Afternoon brought in their Verdict, Guilty, and on Friday last received Sentence of Death, and tho' he has since confess'd it, and now appears very penitent, and was yesterday at the New Meeting House at Harvard Street. This same Indian was Try'd for his Life about a Year ago at Plymouth on suspicion of burning his Masters Barn, but was acquitted.

New-England Weekly, March 5, 1773.

Extract of a Letter from the Island of Nantuckey, Dates the 13th of February, 1732, 3.

We hear that Julian the Indian under Condemnation here, is to be Executed on Thursday the 22d Instant. He appears very penitent, and was yesterday at Mr. Checkley's Meeting House.

Weekly Rehearsal, March 5, 1773.

Extract of a Letter from the Island of Nantuckey, Dates the 13th of February, 1732, 3.

The Time appointed for the Execution of Julian the Indian, now under Sentence of Death in our Goal, is Thursday the 22d Instant. He went Yesterday to hear the Rev. Mr. Checkley, who preach'd in the Forenoon from Gen. 4.10 and the Afternoon from Isa 1.18.

Boston News-Letter, March 8, 1733.

The Time appointed for the Execution of Julian the Indian, now under Sentence of Death In our Goal, is Thursday 22d Instant.

Weekly Rehearsal, March 12, 1733.

Yesterday Julian the condemned Indian went to the Church in Brattle Street; the Rev. Mr. Cooper preach'd in the Forenoon and the Rev. Dr. Coleman Afternoon. He has desired to hear the Rev. Mr. Coleman is to preach the Lecture the Day of his Execution, from Luke XXIII. 43. To Day shalt thou be with me in Paradise.

Boston News-Letter, March 22, 1733.

This Afternoon is the Time appointed for the Execution of Julian, the Indian Man, who received Sentence of Death, at the Superiour Court last held here for the County of Suffolk, for the Murder of Mr. Rogers of Pembrooke, as formerly mentioned.

New-England Weekly Journal, March 26, 1733.

On Thursday last Julian the Indian, who received Sentence of Death at the last Superiour Court held here, for the Murder or Mr. Rogers of Pembrooke [sic] on Sept. 12. Past, was Executed pursuant to the said Sentence. From the time of his Condemnation to Monday last, little impression seem'd to be made upon him by all the unwearied Pains taken with him by the Reverend Ministers of the Town; and 'tis suppos'd till then he had hopes of a Reprieve for a Fortnight longer; but when those hopes fail'd, and he was assur'd he must dye on Thursday following, he seem'd to be in great Consternation, and terribly surprsiz'd at his approaching Death; and express'd his Fears that he shou'd never behav'd: Great Pains were still taken with him to bring him to a sense of Sin and his great need of Christ to be a Saviour to him. On the Day of his Execution the Rev. Dr. Coleman preach'd the Lecture in his hearing and (at his desire) adapted his Sermon peculiarly to his Case, from Luk 23.39 to 44. He desir'd the Rev. Mr. Bylres to instruct him and pray with him at the Place of Execution, who gratify'd hint herein. When he came to the Gallows he acquainted Mr. Byles with the impression Dr. Coleman's Sermon made upon him, and that he had been all along from the Prison to that Place putting up that Petition in the Text, Lord remember me from thy Kingdom. He beg'd the Spectators to be warn'd by his untimely End, bewail'd and caution'd against the Sins of Drunkenness, Sabbath-breaking, rash Anger and Passion &c. warn'd Servants against absconding from their Masters Service, and keeping bad Hours &c. After which Mr. Byles, pray'd with him, and then movingly dispenc'd the Counsels of God to him, which he receiv'd with all the signs of penitency and affection, and retuned him many thanks for the pains he had then and all along taken with him. He own'd the Crime for which he dy'd, and the Justice of the Sentence past upon him for the same. After Mr. Byles left him he pray'd himself, and behav'd very penitently till he was turned off into an awful Eternity.

Weekly Rehearsal, March 26, 1733.

On Thursday last, about Four o' Clock in the Afternoon, Julian the Indian was executed here for the Murder of Mr. John Rogers of Pembroke: And notwithstanding the Severity of the Weather, occasioned by an hard Wind at North[-state] and Snow, the Rev. Mr. Byles accompanied him to the Place of Execution, and pray'd with him there. He made a [little Speech] to the People before he was turn'd off, the same in Substance with what he had delivered the Day before to the Printer of this Paper, written with his own Hand, which he desired might be printed for the Benefit of the Living, and is as follows, viz.

From my Childhood to Twenty Years of Age, I liv'd in a Family where I was learnt to Read and say my Catechism, and had a great deal of Pains taken with me.—And in my younger Years I was under some Convictions and Awakenings, and concern'd about the Condition of my Soul;—and I had many Warnings in the Providence of God to turn from my Sins—But I have (and I desire to lament it) abused God's Patience and Goddness to me, and apostatised from God and good Beginnings, and now I have forsaken God, he has forsaken me, and I acknowledge he has been just in leaving me, so that I have gone from bad to worse, till for my Sins I am now to die.

Whereas I hav been charged with and tried for burning my Master's Barn, I now declare as a dying Man that I did not do it, nor was I any way privy to it.

I acknowledge I deserve to die, and would confess especially my Drunkeness and Sabbath-breaking, which have led me to this great Sin, for which I now die.

I desire therefore that all, and especially Servants, would take Warning by me; I am a dying Man, just going to leave this World, and the Thoughts of it terrify me, knowing how unfit I am to appear before my Judge.

O beware of sinning as I have done.—Beware of Drunkenness, of Sabbath-breaking, and if running away from your Masters, and don't put away the Thoughts of Death and Judgment: I once put these Things far away, but now they are near. And I am going to appear before my great and terrible Judge, which surprizeth me beyond what I am able to express.

If you have been Instructed and catechized from your Childhood, and joined your selves to Assemblies in which the Lord Jesus Christ is most purely worshipped, then let me warn and charge you to beware of casting off the Things that are good, lest God leave you to your selves, and you go in Sin till you come to the greatest Wickedness.

O take Warning by me all of you, I intreat you—See and fear and do no more so wickedly as I have done.

O let me once more intreat you all, especially Servants, as beware of the Sin of Drunkenness, and be obedient to your Masters; don't run away from them, nor get Drunk, for if you do it will bring you to Harme as it has done me.

I call to you now as one come from the Dead, to turn from your evil Ways while you have time, and not put off your Repentance to another Day, lest you then call and Good will not answer you.

My Master often told me that my Sins would bring me tom this, but I little thought that it would be so.

I return my hearty Thanks to the Rev. Ministers who have taken Pains to assist me in preparing for my latter End. And as I desire to be forgiven, so I forgive all Mankind.

These Things declare freely and voluntarily, and desire Mr. Fleet to Print the same for the Benefit of the Living: And I do hereby utterly disown and disclaim all other Speeches, Papers or Declarations that may be printed in my Name, as Witness my Hand this 21st of March, 1733. Julian.

The Physicians of the Town having obtained his Body to Anatomize, have been busily employed all Friday and Saturday last dissecting it, which will be great Advantage to the young Students in Physick and natural Philosophy. 'Tis remarkable, that altho he had lain in Prison above Six Months, yet (to the Praise of his Keeper be is spoken) he cut at least two Inches thick of Fat on the Breast, and much thicker on the Belly.

Weekly Rehearsal, March 26, 1733.

Just published, and sold by T. Fleet, the last Speech and dying Advice of poor Julian, an Indian, who was executed on Boston Neck the 22d Instant, for the Murder of Mr. John Rogers of Pembroke: Written with his own Hand, and delivered to the printer of this Paper the Day before his Execution, in the Presence of several Persons. Also an excellent Poem upon the melancholy Occasion; both adorned with curious Cuts.

Note: This notice appeared in the column next to Julian's account about his life.

Boston News-Letter, March 30, 1733.

The Body of Julian the Indian Man, who was Executed here last Week, having been granted to several young Students in Physick, Surgery, &c. at their Request; The same has for several Days past been dissecting in their presence, in a most accurate manner; and 'tis hoped their critical Inspection, will prove of singular Advantage. The Bones are preserv'd, in order to be fram'd into a Skeleton.

Appendix E

A Timeline of Julian's Story

CIRCA 1700

Julian is born in an Indian village near the town of Boston.

CIRCA 1703

Julian is either sold or adopted by a New England family who begins to instruct the Native American in the Christian faith.

CIRCA 1710

Between the ages of three and twenty, Julian learns to how to read, to say the Church's catechism, and how to write. By his own account, he proved an unruly subject for his fictive New England family.

Before he would become a fugitive, he becomes a drunkard, a Sabbath breaker, and a rogue who falls into bad company.

NOVEMBER 5, 1730–1731

A Plymouth court tries Julian for the act of burning his master's Barn. He is acquitted.

SEPTEMBER 7, 1732

Julian runs away from "one Mr. Howard of Bridgewater."

SEPTEMBER 7–10, 1732

Howard posts several advertisements for the apprehension of his fugitive man. One of the notices attracted the attention of John Rogers, who at the time, is in the town of Weymouth.

SEPTEMBER 10–11, 1732

After making inquiries, Rogers discovers Julian's whereabouts. He finds him in Braintrey [sic]. That evening, the bounty hunter secures the fugitive. They two stay overnight in an ordinary in Braintrey [sic] before returning to Howard's place in Bridgewater—seventeen miles away.

SEPTEMBER 12, 1732

In the "Morning," Julian "got away again." Finding him gone, Rogers offers "a Man" ten shillings to help him reclaim the runaway. The man "soon brought him back," and Rogers and Julian men resumes their journey.

"About Five Miles" into the trip, "about Noon" time, Rogers "stopt and went into the House one Mr. Scot with the Indian." He orders drink. Scot did not have any. As the two men talk, Julian tries to escape again.

In the process of trying to secure his freedom, Julian the Indian stabs and kills John Rogers. As Rogers falls to his death, the Native American resumes his flight. However, a Negro runs him down. Shortly thereafter, the Indian is taken into custody.

SEPTEMBER 13, 1732

Julian is committed to jail for the murder of John Rogers of Pembrook.

SEPTEMBER 14, 1732

Thomas Fleet prints the "melancholy Account of a barbarous Murder committed at Brantrey" in his *Boston News-Letter*. The advertisement details the incident in which Julian kills Rogers.

Appendix E 159

FEBRUARY 17, 1733

"In the Forenoon," the Superior Court of Suffolk County "tryed the Indian Julian" for the crime of murder. The Trail lasts two hours and a half. In the afternoon, the jury finds the Indian guilty.

Later, Julian confesses.

FEBRUARY 20, 1733

The jury sentences the Indian to death. Upon hearing his sentence, the Native American faints.

FEBRUARY 25, 1733

A "very penitent" Julian is seen in the "Afternoon" at the "New Meeting House in Harvard-Street." There, he listens to a sermon preached by "Rev. Mr. Byles." The minister uses a verse from Psalms as the focus of his lesson.

MARCH 4, 1733

Julian attends the service at Rev. Mr. Chickley's Meeting House. The minister preaches from Genesis in the forenoon; the Book of Isaiah in the afternoon.

MARCH 5, 1733

A notice appears in the *New England Weekly* in which the day of Julian's execution has been set: Thursday, March 22.

MARCH 11, 1733

Julian goes to the church in Brattle Street. Rev. Mr. Copper preaches in the forenoon; Dr. Coleman in the afternoon.

MARCH 21, 1773

Julian's composes his life story in a Suffolk County jail cell as he awaits his execution.

MARCH 22, 1733

With Julian's consent, Thomas Fleet publishes two broadsides about the Native American's tragic story.

Around the same time, a third broadside is published without Julian's consent.

MARCH 22, 1733

Julian the Indian at "about Four o' Clock in the Afternoon," is "executed [for] ... the Murder of Mr. John Rogers of Pembroke."

MARCH 23–29, 1733

Doctors are granted permission to claim the Native American's body. They dissect and preserve the bones for the "young Students in Physick, Surgery, &c."

After the autopsy, the remains of Julian's body are discarded.

Appendix F
Julian the Indian in Court Records

In addition to the references that appeared in the newspapers about Julian, extant court records reveal additional information about the Native American man. These records, for example, demonstrate that the matter of Julian's status is inconclusive. In some of the documents, he is described as a slave. In other records, he is described as a servant. One extant court account also identifies the Native American man as a "Spanish Indian." That reference raises a number of questions about Julian's background before his life in Massachusetts. Another document, however, described the Native American as a Negro. Whether he was a Negro or an Indian or a man of mixed ancestry, these documents not only divulge additional details regarding Julian's story, but they also suggest that the Native American man's life before he killed Rogers is unclear.

All of the court documents below have been arranged in chronological order as they appear in Supreme Judicial Court Suffolk files and record books.

Case of Julian (an Indian) and Jeffery (a Negro) slave. Burning a Barn. November 5, 1730.

[Plymo. SS.] to the Keeper of his Majesty's Goal, in Plymouth Greeting.
    Whereas Julian an Indian Servant belonging to Thomas Haywood of Bridgewater was this Day brought before me Nathan'l Thomas Esq. one of his Majesty's Justices of the peace for the County of Plymo. on description of a hand in burning in a Barn of his said Master on ye third day of November instant in the Night and upon his Examination is apparent to me there is great Reason to Suspect that he was Confederate with Jeffery a Negro slave belong to Captain John Field of Bridgewater in burning his sd Master's Barn they are

therefore in his Majesty's to require us to take into ye Custody ye sd Julian and him safely keep in ye said Goal until he shall be those deliverd by due or by Law here of ye may not fail dated plymo. ye 5th day Novem' in the fourth year of his Majesty George Annon Domini 1730. Nath'l Thomas.

A true Copying Examination for John Winslow.

Source:

Supreme Judicial Court, Suffolk Files, Volume 225: 533, Case No. 30449. Massachusetts Supreme Judicial Court Archives, Massachusetts Archives. Boston, Massachusetts.

Case of Julian and Jeffery, negro servants. April 1731.

Plymouth SS to the Sheriff or Marshall of the sd County of Plymouth or Either of their Deputies or Constables of the two of Bridgewater within the sd County or to any or Either of them Greeting.

Whereas Complaint is made to me Joseph Edison Esq. one of his Majesty's Justices of the Peace within and for the County of Plymouth of this fourth Day of Novem' 1730 by Haywood the third of Bridgewater he haveing one Barn Burnt on the 18th of October last and another Barn Burnt on the 3d of Novembr Instant in the Evening and yt he vemently [sic] suspects his Indian man servant Julian or Capt. John Fields, Negro man Jefrey one or Both of them to have fired one or Both of the above sd Barne these are to Require you in his majesty's Name on sight hereof to apprend the above sd Indian and Jefrey or Either of them if they may be found in your Precinct and forthwith Bring them or either of them before me the subscriber hereof or someone of his Majesty's Justices of the Peace for the County of Plymouth to be Examind and to be proceeded against as the Law Directs hereof first not and make few Returns of Your doing herein dated att Bridgewater aforesd this 4th Day of Novemr in fourth year of his Majesty's Reign Att Ammo Domini 1730. Joseph Edson.

Source:

Supreme Judicial Court, Suffolk Files, Volume 231: 35, Case No. 31330. Massachusetts Supreme Judicial Court Archives, Massachusetts Archives. Boston, Massachusetts.

Justice Edson's warrant to Apprehend Julian servant to Thomas Howard.

Plimo. SS At his Majesty's Superior Court of Jurisdiction Court of Assize & Genl Goal delivery held at plimouth ye aforesd County of plimouth on ye last Tuesday of April as ye fourth Year of ye Reign of our sovereign ye Lord King of Great Brittain, France, & Ireland, King Defender of ye Faith in Anno Dom 1731.

The Jurors of our sd Lord & King upon their Oath present that Julian Indian man servant of Thomas Hayward ye third of Brigwater in ye Court aforesd & Jeffry Negro man servant of John Field of Brigwater aforesd Court on ye eighteenth of October last at Brigwater aforesd did with fire and Arms set fire to and burn up a barn of the sd Thomas Hayward and on the third of November last with fire & Arms set fire to Another barn of ye sd Thomas Hayward & burn up ye same against ye Law ye Case provided & against ye peace of Our ye Lord ye King his Crown & Dignity Etc.

Jn Read for [Tuesday]

Witness

Ignoramus
John Atwood Foreman

Source:
Supreme Judicial Court, Suffolk Files, Volume 231: 36, Case No. 31330. Massachusetts Supreme Judicial Court Archives, Massachusetts Archives. Boston, Massachusetts.

Bill of Answer of Julian e at.

Being desired to give a Short Account in Writing of my Discourse with ye Indian suspected. Viz as follows as to the substance of it.

Wn he first came to me with Mr. Johnson he denied ye fact, and said he was abusd & so fore to own it, but after some serious applications to him, with Encouragements that if he would own the Truth we woul'd Interceed for him. He told us that he and Captain Field Negro Jeffrey went over to his Master's Barn after some Discourse, and both Together Blew up a fire in the [illegible word] from said Jeffey's pipe.—At another Time, a few hours after he said to me, that Jeffery had no hand in it, but that, he had a pipe in his Pockett at my house which he got fire in & did it himself alone nobody being privy to it. This is the substance of what I had an Anwswer of from him. Daniel Perkins.

Source:
Supreme Judicial Court, Suffolk Files, Volume 231: 37, Case No. 31330. Massachusetts Supreme Judicial Court Archives, Massachusetts Archives. Boston, Massachusetts.

Bill of Answer of Julian e at.

Plim. SS The Examination of Julian an Indian servant of Thomas Hayward Relating to his burning his Master's Barn.

Q. Where was you that night that ye Master's Barn was burnt?
A. I was at Elisha Howards.
Q. What time of the night was it when His barn was burnt?
A. It was after [dark no one] about
Q. What made you Go from home at that time of the night?
A. I was at Mr. Porksons and carried my fiddle & Mr. Porkons told me I might play there a little while & sometime after Jeffey Capt [Field's] Negro came in & had his pipe & [illegible text] with him & we tarried there about a hour & more. Jeffey & I went to His house his pipe being litt & [illegible text] down to the gate & Jeffery asked me whether I was going & I told him I was going on ye to Elisha Howards to carry [illegible text] a fiddle & Jeffery said to me stay for he was going my way to. I asked him where he was going he said he was going to look for a Cow & he went up towards our & I stayed by the bridge & [illegible text] Jeffery go towards our house & he turned up towards the Barn & I heard [illegible text] & Jeffery tarried sometime & then came to me I I asked him how far he had gone whether he had found the Cow & he said he had not found the Cow. I asked him what he had been doing. He said he had been in the barn & I [illegible text] what he had been doing for he had his pipe & [illegible text] litt when he went from me.
Q. What made you [illegible text] him of Doing any wicked thing?
A. Because his went into the barn with his [illegible text] still in his hand & his pipe in his mouth & I asked him what he had been doing and he gave me no answer at first but afterward he told me he had gone in the barn with his [illegible text] and left it behind & by what he said I did think he did [illegible text] to burn the barn & he went home & I went on ye Elisha Howard & tarried there about two hours & played on my fiddle until the was about fire.
Q. When you were at Elisha Howard & saw a house on fire what made you say it is not Masters House it is up higher?
A. I was in hopes it was not Master's house.
Q. Why did you not go & tell ye Master Jeffry told you that he had left fire in his barn.
A. I thought if he had put fire in barn it would have burnt up [illegible text].

November ye 9th 1730 Taken before me. Nath'll Thomas, Justice of Peace.

Source:

Supreme Judicial Court, Suffolk Files, Volume 231: 38–39, Case No. 31330. Massachusetts Supreme Judicial Court Archives, Massachusetts Archives. Boston, Massachusetts.

Inquisition on the Body of John Rogers. September 13, 1732.

Appendix F

Suffolk ss

An Inquisition Indented taken at Brantree within said County of Suffolk the Thirteenth Day of September in the Sixth year of the reign of Our Sovereign Lord George the Second by the Grace of God of Great Britain, France, Ireland, King Defender of the Faith before Benj Lincoln Gent: one of the coroners of Our said Lord the King within the County of Suffolk aforesaid upon the view of the Body of John Rogers—then and there being dead by the oaths of John Hurst, John Hadens, Ephraim Jones, Arthur Powell, Thos Copeland, John Thayer, Thos French, David Holbrock, Daniel Hunt, Benjn Haywood, Nathl Belcher, Willm Copland, Ebenz Niles, Tho. French, Good and Lawful men of Brantree aforesaid within the County aforesaid; who being charged and sworn to Enquire for our said Lord the King when and by what means and how the said John Rogers came to his death: upon their oaths Say that on the twelfth of September Currant at or near to a Dwelling house belonging to Howard Quincy, Esqr. where liveth on John Scot in the South of Brantree aforesd.

The sd John Rogers endeavoring to apprehend and [Take] one Julian an Endian [*sic*] man who was run away from his master Thos. Howard of Bridgewater was by ye Indian stab'd in his Brest [*sic*] with a Jack knife by means whereof he died immediately and the jurors the aforsd on their Oath say it [illegible text].

In witness whereof as well as the Coroner aforesd as the Jurors aforesd on their Oath say it the aforesd [illegible text] this Inquisition have [Interchangeably] put to our hand seals ye Day & year abovsd.

[David] Holbrook	(seal)	John Hunt	(seal)
Daniel Hunt	(seal)	John [Haywood]	(seal)
Benjamin [Haywood]	(seal)	[Ephraim] Jones	(seal)
Nathaniel [Rockham]	(seal)	Arthur Powell	(seal)
[William] Copleand	(seal)	Thomas Copland	(seal)
[Ebenezer illegible]	(seal)	John Thayer	(seal)
Thomas French	(seal)	Thomas [French]	(seal)

Source:

Supreme Judicial Court, Suffolk Files, Volume 244: 556, Case No. 34229. Massachusetts Supreme Judicial Court Archives, Massachusetts Archives. Boston, Massachusetts.

Case of Julian (an Indian), February 1732–1733.
February 1732/1733
Suffolk SS

April 18. Majesty's Superior Court of Jurisdiction Court of [Assize and General Goal] Delivery on the Tryall of one Julian an Indian man; for killing one John Rogers—

The Constable Bill of Cost

Jurymen to Summoning ye Jury of impost 18 anon	0-18=00
[Item for] boarding on ye jury at ye [legible text]-------------	0=12=00
[Item for] Keeping ye prisoner 12 hours -----------------------	0-12--00
[Item for] my time & for my assistants in Carrying the prisoner to Goals being 4 men & my self	1-00-00
[Item for] what I expended on ye Road & at Boston for my Self & my assistants & our horses	1-00-00

[Item for] sending Cost
  Samuel Arnold
  Constable

Source:
Supreme Judicial Court, Suffolk Files, Volume 247: 111, Case No. 34703. Massachusetts Supreme Judicial Court Archives, Massachusetts Archives. Boston, Massachusetts.

Case of Julian (an Indian). February 1732–1733.

Suffolke SS Att his Majesty's Court of Assize and General Goal Deliver begune held att Boston in for ye County of Suffolke on ye Tuesday of February ye Sixth year of ye reign of our Sovereign Lord George ye Lord of Great Brittain, France, & Ireland, King Defender of ye Faith in Anno Domini 1731.

The Jurors for our sd Sovereign Lord ye King upon oath [present] That Julian an Indian of Bridwater and County of Plymouth, Labourer & Servant of Thomas Howard of Bridgwater aforesd att Brantrey in the County of Suffolke aforesd on or about the twelfth of September last without a having a fear of God before his Eyes but being Stirred up & Instigated thereto by ye Devil att Braintree in ye County of Suffolk aforeds ye sd twelfth of September with force & arms an assault upon ye body of one John Rogers [peace] of God & ye king ye [bring] with a with a Jack knife of ye value of twelve pence which ye sd Julian then & there [hold drawn] in his hand and did commit. [Illegible] the sd Jurors upon oath further say That ye said Julian Did then & there visit att Braintrey in ye County of Suffolke aforesd [with force assault feloniously] voluntarily and of his malice forethought with such Jack knife, which he then & there [illegible text] in his right hand strike, stab & wound the said John Rogers and that the said Julian att Did then & there att Braintree aforeds in the County of Suffolke aforesd with such Jack knife which he then & there he had drawn in his right hand strike & stab & wound the sd John Rogers. There with and there with give John Roger one mortal stroke or wound or wound upon his breast which wound so Given was of the Depth of three Inches & ye [breadth] of one Inch and by which mortal wound ye sd John Rogers languished for ye space of some few minutes & then dyed by means aforesd so ye sd Jurors upon oath say that ye sd Julian att Braintree in ye County of Suffolke aforedsd on ye sd 12th day of September Did feloniously voluntarily & of his malice forethought kill & murder ye sd John Rogers contrary to ye peace Crown & Dignity of our sd Lord & King as aforesd to ye Law in ye Case made [and provided]

Bill Vera: Robt [illegible text] foreman

Source:
Supreme Judicial Court, Suffolk Files, Volume 247: 423, Case No. 34703.
Massachusetts Supreme Judicial Court Archives, Massachusetts Archives. Boston, Massachusetts.

Case of Julian (Indian slave of Thomas Howard). March 1732–1733.

Know all men by [thee] present ye Sam'l Clark of plymo in the County of plymo Keeper of his Majesty goal an holden and stand firmly bound and obliged unto Thos Howard the third of Bridewater in the County of plymo. aforesaid [illegible text] in the [full] and Just sum of forty pounds Currant and [illegible text] in ye province of ye Massachusetts Bay to [be pd] unto ye said Thomas Howard, [his Certain] attorn. heirs [Ex &] admin or assign to ye said payment well and truly to be made [I bind] my self my heirs [Ex & admin] firmly by these presently sealed with my seal and dated this Sixth Day of aprile in the fifth year of ye reign of His Majesty Reign Anno Dom. 1732–

The Conditions of the above Obligation is [surely &]. Whereas above named Thomas Howard's Spanish Indian Slave Named Julian about ye fifth of Novemb 1730 Was [illegible text] from Nathiel Thomas Esq. Committed to the sd Sam'l Clerk keeper of his Majesty's Goal in Plymo affordsd upon suspicion of burning his said Master's Barn as ye [illegible text] may appear at ye Last Sup. Court being aquitted as to sd. Fact was again remitted to sd. Goal until ye Judgm't of last Super' Court be satisfied ye and there held as [illegible text] until ye [illegible text] of man Last as wth time [illegible text] prison'd made Escape he hath'd one at sundry times sure from and Goal whereby a Controversy ariseth by and between ye sd person Howard & Clark [illegible text] the Charges & Expense ye said Clark hath been after regaining the sd Julian, Or Otherwise the Damage the sd. Howard hath been at by his loss of time News of the above bounde in Sam'l Clark his heirs excut. and admit. on their parts and behalf [illegible text] all things well and truly stand to Obey, abide fulfilled and keep the Reward Order Arbitrate finale End [illegible text] of said Sam'l Spraque of Rochester, Daniel Johns of

Bridgewater and Eleaz. [illegible text] of Plymo. All in the County of Plymo. Arbitrator indifferently Elected and Chosen, as well on the part & behalf of the said Howard as of ye Above nam'd Clark to arbitrate award order Judge and Determine offered Covering all means of Causes or Causes of action or actions, suit or Suits, in any ways respecting the aforesaid Controversy and all or any or Whatsoover provided always that said Award [illegible text] and published by said Arbitrator or any two them, in Wittness under their Hands on or before the 27th Day of April instant at ye House of Mr. Wetherelle Jr. Plymouth that these the Above Obligations to be null and void or else to abide and remain in full force and virtue—

Signd, Seal & Deliver'd Sam'l Clark (Seal)
In presence of us
James Shurttesse
Quinton Grymble
A true Case Examined for John Winslow (Seal)
Plymo march Court first Tuesday 1732

Thee Within Named Quinton Grymble appeared and made Oath that he Saw Sam'll Clark Within Named Sign, Seal & Deliver the Within Writton bond as his act and Good Copy Examin'd for John Winslow (Seal) Copy Examd for John Winslow (Seal)

Source:

Supreme Judicial Court, Suffolk Files, Volume 247: 566, Case No. 34703.
   Massachusetts Supreme Judicial Court Archives, Massachusetts Archives. Boston, Massachusetts.

This document appeared in a different collection of Court records. See source cited below the transcription.

Indians Presentment & Sentence, March 1732.

The Jurors for our Sovreign Lord the King upon Oath present That Julian an Indian of Bridgwater [sic] in the County of Plymouth Labourer & Servant of Thomas Howard of Bridgwater aforesd at Brantry in the County of Suffolk aforesd on or about the twelfth of September last not having the fear of God before his Eyes but being Stirrd up and Instigated thereto by the Devil at Brantrey in the County of Suffolk aforesd on the sd twelfth of Sept with force and arms an assault upon the Body of one John Rogers in the peace of God and the King there being with a Jack Knife of the value of twelve pence which the sd Julian then & there held drawn in his hand, did commit; and the sd Jurors upon Oath further say that the sd Julian did then & there viz at Brantrey in the County of Suffolk aforesd with force as foresd Feloniously

& voluntarily and of his malice forethought, with such Jack Knife, which he then and there held drawn in his right hand did strike, stab & wound the sd John Rogers, and that the sd Julian did then and there at Brantrey aforesd in the County aforesd with such Jack Knife which he then & there held drawn in his right hand Feloniously and of his malice forethought strike & stab the sd John Rogers therewith, and did therewith give unto the sd John Rogers one mortal stroke, or wound upon his breast, which wound so given was of the depth of three inches of the breadth of one inch, & by which mortal wound the sd John Rogers languished for the space of some few minutes and then and there dyed by means thereof; And so the sd Jurors upon Oath say that the sd Julian at Brantrey in the County of Suffolk aforesd on the sd 12th day of September did feloniously voluntarily & of his Malice forethought kill and murder the sd John Rogers contrary to the peace Crown and Dignity of our sd Lord the King as also to the Law in that Case made and provided.—Upon which Indictment the said Julian being arraigned at the Bar pleaded not Guilty & ye Jury were Sworn to try this aforesd between our Sovereign Lord the King & the Prisoner at the Bar, and after a full hearing of the Evidences for the King & the prisoners defence [sic] went out to Consider thereof and returned their verdict therein upon Oath by Mr. Rowland Houghton their Foreman that is to say that the said Julian is Guilty. It's therefore considered and ordered by the Court that this Julian shall suffer the Pain of death.

N.B. A warrant By order of Court, issued out requiring the Sheriff to Cause the sd Julian to be hang on March 22d 1732.

Source:
Supreme Judicial Court, Record books, Volume 1730–1733: 267–268, Case Name: Julian's Presentment & Sentence. Massachusetts Supreme Judicial Court Archives, Massachusetts Archives. Boston, Massachusetts.

Appendix G

Graphic Representation of Advertisements for Native American Fugitives

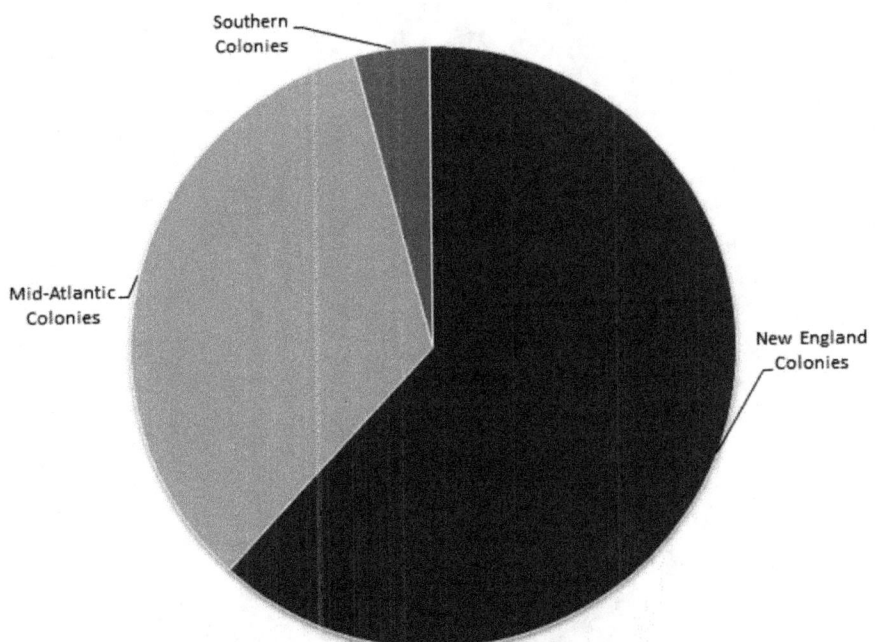

Figure AG.1 Advertisements for Natives Measured by Region of Publication.
Source: Created by author.

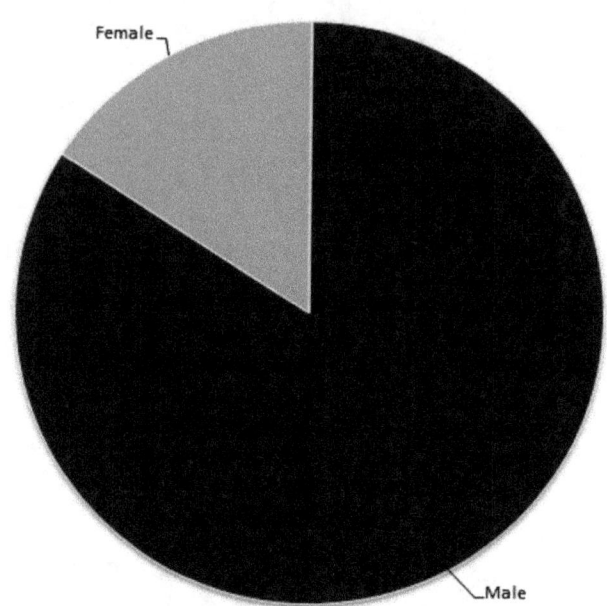

Figure AG.2 Advertisements for Natives Measured by Sex. *Source*: Created by author.

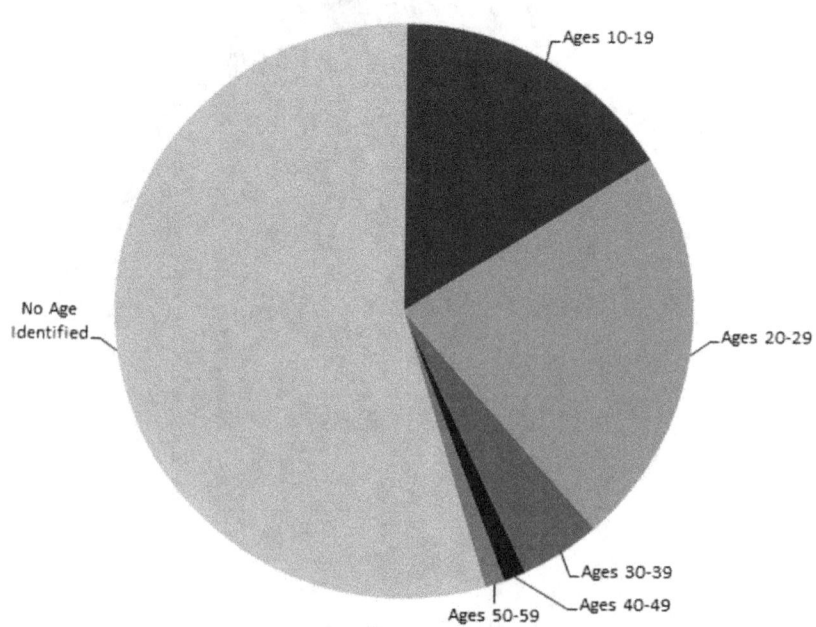

Figure AG.3 Advertisements for Natives Measured by Age. *Source*: Created by author.

Appendix H

Public Days in Julian's Massachusetts: Advertising Native American Slavery, Servitude, and Social Death in Eighteenth-Century America

Public days were important occasions in the eighteenth century. Indeed, on those occasions, throughout British North America, newspapers were routinely read aloud. At select times of the day, designated readers read the assortment of articles typeset in columns, participating in the creation of colorful, entwining scenes that were perhaps one of the most vital aspects of early American life. For during most of those public days, colonial Americans (that included the varied Native groups) corralled together and listened attentively to the newspaper being read. In churches and in courthouses across the eastern seaboard, they discovered the transatlantic comings and goings of their community leaders and of other persons of import whose travels were covered in articles printed in the paper. In taverns and ordinaries, they considered the price of properties offered for let by their neighbors who relied on the newspaper to publish their inventories. Through those public forums, colonial Americans learned not only about foreign and local affairs, but also of the passage of ordinances that impacted their day-to-day lives. On more than one occasion, they engaged in gossip with one another, as the infidelities of wayward husbands and wives became the subject of many newspaper notices. More often than not, however, most of these customary readings of the paper included stories that concerned strayed horses, missing pigs, once an absconded squirrel, and, of course, the bold actions of bound and enslaved persons who stole themselves away from their masters. Consequently, within these assorted settings, if not in the alleyways or on the street, Julian's story, and likewise other like his, were told.

But in addition to revealing Julian's story, newspaper articles divulged the life stories of other Native Americans who did not protest their condition with their feet. Besides hundreds of notices for runaway Native American slaves, servants, apprentices, spouses, and deserters, numerous "To Be

Sold" notices for Natives Americans reveal the another side of life for indigenous people who resided in the land of the forefathers as socially dead persons. Like fugitive slave or servant ads, "To Be Sold" advertisements further illustrate the precariousness of being the subject of the property of another. Relegated to the status of chattel, whether in full or in parts, indeed in most instances their names did not even warrant mentioning, Native Americans who were the subject of "To Be Sold" advertisements were brought and sold like a domesticated animal, like a cow, horse, or a pig. That truth had been particularly evident in Julian's New England where slavery and servitude seemed to have grown up together with the emergence of the colonial press. To be sure, more Indian-for-sale notices appeared in New England newspapers than in any other group of colonies. Before the expiration of their term of years with their masters, quite a few Native American servants likely discovered in certain public spaces that their contracts were the subject of advertisements for sale. While not as numerous as their enslaved African American or bound European counterparts who were also sold away in this manner, the "To Be Sold" notices below capture nonetheless another dimension of Native American slavery and bondage in early America.

NEW ENGLAND "TO BE SOLD" NOTICES

Boston News-Letter, April 29, 1706.

A Surranam Indian Woman, and Child about 5 years old, to be Sold, Inquire of John Campbell Post-master of Boston and know further.

Boston News-Letter, March 31, 1701.

A Pretty Carolina Indian Boy aged about 12 years, to be Sold; Enquire of John Campbell Post-master of Boston and know further.

Boston News-Letter, May 24, 1708.

An Indian Woman, aged about 25 years to be Sold: Inquire at the Post-Office in Boston, and know fuather [sic].

Boston News-Letter, October 11, 1708.

An Indian Woman, aged about 30 years to be Sold: Inquire at rhw Post-Office in Cornhill, Boston, and know further.

Boston News-Letter, April 30, 1711.

An Indian Boy aged about 15 years that can Read and Write English to be Sold: Inquire at the Post-Office in Boston and know further.

Reprint: Boston News-Letter, May 7, 1711.

Boston News-Letter, June 18, 1711.

An Indian Boy aged about 16 years to be Sold: Inquire at the Post-Office in Boston.

Boston News-Letter, August 27, 1711.

A Carolina Indian Woman Aged about 25 years, to be Sold, by Mrs. Grace Rankin; and to be seen at her House in Mackerill Land Boston.

Reprint: Boston News-Letter, September 3, 1711.

Boston News-Letter, November 12, 1711.

A Carolina Indian Boy about Ten years, to be Sold, Inquire at the Post Office.

Boston News-Letter, January 19, 1712.

A Carolina Indian Woman aged about 24 Years a very good Servant to be Sold by Capt William Clark, and to be seen at his House in Clark's-Square, near the North Meeting House in Boston.

Boston News-Letter, June 30, 1712.

Two very good Stills, one that holds near three Barrels, the other better than half a Barrel, to be Sold on reasonable Terms. And an Indian Girl aged about 16 years to be Sold; Inquire at the Post Office.

Boston News-Letter, July 21, 1712.

A Carolina Indian Woman aged about Twenty years; To be Sold by Capt. James Grant, and to be seen at his House in Prince-Street Boston.

Reprint: Boston News-Letter, August 4, 1712.

Boston News-Letter, September 8, 1712.

A Indian Boy about 12 years old Speaks English perfectly well, is very healthy & season'd to the Country, to be Sold by Capt. Wentworth Paxton, and seen a his House in Battery March, Boston.

Boston News-Letter, December 29, 1712.

A very, good Indian Servant Man to be Sold by Mr. John Buchanan Baker, and to be seen at his House in Wood-Lane | near the Sign of the Red-Lyon, Boston.

Boston News-Letter, March 9, 1713.

A Carolina Indian Man Age about 22 years, a very Ingenious Fellow, to be Sold, inquire at the Post Office in Boston.

Boston News-Letter, May 18, 1713.

An Indian Man aged about 20 years that speaks good English, to be Sold and seen at the House of Mr. John Dixwell in Union Street Boston.

Boston News-Letter, May 18, 1713.

An Indian Girl aged about fourteen years, to be sold and to be seen at the House of Capt. Thomas Mathews in Salem-Street at the North End in Boston.

Boston News-Letter, June 1, 1713.

A Carolina Indian Boy eleven years old, to be Sold, Inquire at the Post Office in Boston.

Boston News-Letter, August, 24, 1713.

A Very likely Indian Woman aged about 38 years, to be Sold by Capt. John Steven, and to be seen at his House on the Corner of Love-Street, Boston.

Boston News-Letter, October 12, 1713.

A Spanish Indian Girl aged about 15 years that has been five in the Country, who speaks good English, and can do any sort of Household work, to be Sold, inquire at the Post Office in Boston and know further.

Appendix H 177

Boston News-Letter, April 19, 1714.

An Indian Boy Aged about Sixteen Years very fit for either Sea or Land Service; to be Sold, Inquire at the Post Office in Boston.

Boston News-Letter, May 10, 1714.

An Indian Boy about sixteen Years, and a Negro Man aged about twenty, both of them very likely, and fit for any Service; the speak very good English to be Sold; Enquire at the Post Office in Boston.

Boston News-Letter, March 28, 1715.

An Indian Lad aged about Eighteen years, a Cooper by Trade, to be Sold and seen at the Shop of Joseph Sevell Cooper in King-Street near the Crown Coffee-House in Boston.

Boston News-Letter, July 4, 1715.

An Very likely Indian Woman fit for all sorts of Household Work aged about Twenty one years, to be Sold by Mr. Benjamin Bronsden Merchant, and to be seen at his House in Ship=Street Boston.

Boston News-Letter, July 4, 1715.

A Very likely Indian Girl aged about Nine years, to be Sold by Mr. Benjamin Walker, and to be seen at his House in Corn-hill Boston.

Boston News-Letter, February 20, 1716.

An Indian Woman aged Sixteen years, that speaks good English, to be Sold, Inquire at the Post-Office in Boston.

Reprint: Boston News-Letter, February 27, 1716.

Boston News-Letter, September 3, 1716.

A Spanish Indian Man Servant, about 20 Years of Age, us'd to, and fit for Husbandry Work, who speaks good English, To be Sold, Inquire at Mr. Henry Bridgham's Taner, living in Milk-Street in Boston, and know further.

Boston News-Letter, October 8, 1716.

An Indian Woman of about Twenty Three Years of Age, that can do any Household Work, to be Sold by Simeon Stoddard Esq; at his House in Sudbury-Street, Boston.

Boston News-Letter, April 1, 1717.

A Lusty Indian Man Servant, aged about 20 Years, that speaks very good English, and fit for any Service in Town or Country, to be Sold on reasonable Terms, by Jonathan Williams over against the Post-Office in Cornhill Boston.

Reprint: Boston News-Letter, April 8, 1717.

Boston News-Letter, April 8, 1717.

A Carolina Indian Man, Strong & Healthy, having been Nine Years in the Country, and hardened to our Climate and Diet; between Nineteen & Twenty Year Old, speak & reads English well, and is fit for any Service within Doors or without, and desirous of Husbandry Work; to be Sold on Reasonable Terms: Inquire of the Reverend Mr. Benjamin Coleman in Boston.

Boston News-Letter, September 16, 1717.

A very ingenious Carolina Indian Boy, aged about eleven years that has been right in the Country, to be Sold by William Hutchinson Esq. at his House in Dock Square Boston.

Variant Reprint: Boston News-Letter, March 24, 1718.

Boston News-Letter, February 24, 1718.

To be Sold by Joseph Crosby of Brantry, an Indian Boy aged about 16 Years, Inquire of Mr. George Shoars, in Queen-Street, Boston.

Reprint: Boston News-Letter, March 3, 1718.

Boston News-Letter, March 24, 1718.

To be Sold by Peter Thomas in Wings Lane, Boston, a Carolina Indian Girl aged about 14 Years.

Boston News-Letter, March 24, 1718.

An Ingenious likely Indian Boy, aged about thirteen years to be Sold by William Hutchinson Esq; and to be seen at his House in Dock Square Boston.

Boston News-Letter, December 15, 1718.

A very likely Indian Woman aged about 25 Years, has been Five Years in the Country, to be Sold Inquire of Mr. Anthony Blount, or Mr. John Clough in Orange-Street, Boston.

Boston News-Letter, December 29, 1718.

A Spanish Indian Woman that can do all sorts of Household Work, with her Boy, about half a Year old: To be Sold, Inquire of Mr. William Man Brasier in Dock-square, Boston.

Reprint: Boston News-Letter, January 19, 1719.

Boston Gazette, August 21, 1721.

To be Sold by Publick Vendue September the 7th 1721, at the Sun Tavern on Dock Square Boston at Three of the Clock in the Afternoon, the Late Shop Goods of Mr. John Kilby's & Sundry Household Goods, a Negro Man, and an Indian Woman. The Dwelling House & Land belonging thereunto. The Creditors are allowed to buy & Discount Nine Shillings in the Pound of their just Debts. The Goods to be seen at the Warehouse of Thomas Palmer Esq; & Company, three Days before the Sale, viz. from 9 of the Clock to 12 in the Forenoon, & from 3 to 6 in the Afternoon. Catalogues to be had of the several Allotments at the place of Sale.

Reprints: Boston News-Letter, August 21, 1721; Boston Gazette, August 28, 1721. Boston News-Letter, August 22, 1723; Boston News-Letter, September 4, 1721.

Variant Reprint: Boston Gazette, September 4, 1721.

Boston News-Letter, August 8, 1723.

An Indian Girl, a Clock and sundry Utensils, belonging to a Bake-House; being Part of the Estate of James Scolly Deceased: To be Sold, by Mrs. Bethia Scolly, & Mr. James Scolly, Administrators, to the said Estate, & to be seen at the House of the said Scolly, Boston.

Reprints: Boston News-Letter, August 15, 1723; Boston News-Letter, August 22, 1723.

Variant Reprint: Boston News-Letter, May 7, 1722.

Boston Gazette, March 11, 1723.

To be Sold an Indian Woman, Eighteen Years of Age, has been in New-England 13 Years, she can do all Household work, as Sew, Knit, Brew, Bake, Wash and Iron Cloaths: Inquire at the Post Office.
 N.B. She has had the Small-pox and measles.

Boston News-Letter, July 2, 1724.

A surranam Indian Man Servant, about 25 Years of Age, that can speak good English, hath been in the Country 13 Years, fit for Service either in Town or Country, can Mow well, To be Sold, inquire of the Printer hereof, and know further.

Boston News-Letter, October 5, 1727.

A Likely Indian Woman about Twenty one Years if Age, fit for Service either in Town or Country, her Time for Four Years to be Sold. Inquire of the Printer hereof.

Reprint: Boston News-Letter, October 12, 1727.

Boston Gazette, July 8, 1728.

A Young Indian Woman to be Sold by John Brewster, at the End of Cross-Street Boston.

Reprint: Boston Gazette, July 15, 1728.

New-England Weekly Journal, February 24, 1729.

An Indian Womans time for about 2 Years, who can do all sorts of Household Work, to be disposed of, Inquire of the Printer hereof.
 A very likely Negro Girl about 14 Years of Age, can speak good English, has been 2 Years in the Country, to be Sold, Inquire of the Printer hereof.

Reprint: New-England Weekly Journal, March 17, 1729.

Boston Gazette, July 27, 1730.

A very handy Indian Woman that can do all sorts of Household Work, to be Sold, inquire of the [Printer hereof.]

Appendix H

Boston News-Letter, October 27, 1732.

To be Sold, a very likely Indian Woman Aged Twenty Three Years, speaks good English, has had the Small Pox; fit fot Town or Country Service: She can Sew, Card, Spin, and do all sorts of Household Work: Inquire at Mr. John Harvey's Blacksmith.

Reprints: Boston News-Letter, November 2, 1732; Boston News-Letter, November 23, 1732.

New-England Weekly Journal, November 26, 1733.

To Be Sold. A Young Indian Fellow, that has serv'd his Time to a Cooper, & can work well at the Business, Inquire of Mrs. Sarah Mousell, Widow, at Charlstown [sic], or of the Printer hereof.

Reprints: New-England Weekly Journal, December 3, 1733; New-England Weekly Journal, December 10, 1733; New-England Weekly Journal, December 17, 1733.

Boston News-Letter, October 20, 1737.

To be Sold a likely Indian Man, aged about Twenty-five Years, born in the Country, and bred up to Husbandry from his Infancy: Enquire of the Printer hereof and know further.

Boston News-Letter, June 25, 1741.

A Young Indian Child to be given away; enquiry of the Printer.

Reprint: Boston News-Letter, July 9, 1741.

Boston Gazette, November 8, 1748.

To be Sold an Indian Woman, who is a very good Cook, and can wash, iron and sew, and can be well recommended. Inquire of the Printer.

Reprint: Boston Gazette, November 15, 1748.

Boston Gazette, December 19, 1749.

An Indian Servant Maids Time for two Years and half to be Sold, that can do all kind of Household Work, and can be well recommended. Inquire of the Printer.

Boston Gazette, March 26, 1759.

To Be Sold. A Spanish Indian Woman about 24 Years of Age, (and a Negro Child also about 2 Years) who can do any Household Work; is Sold because she is a notable Breeder: Enquire of the Printers hereof.

Reprint: Boston Gazette, April 2, 1759.

Newport Mercury, December 20, 1762.

To Be Sold. A new well-built Brigantine, burthen 107 Tons, now lying at the Long-Wharf. For further Particulars, enquire of Thomas Dursee at Freetown, or Israel Brayton of Newport.

Said Brayton has to sell, an Indian Wench, about 19 Years of Age, a Slave for Life.

Reprints: Newport Mercury, December 27, 1762; Newport Mercury, January 3, 1763; Newport Mercury, January 10, 1763.

MID-ATLANTIC "TO BE SOLD" NOTICES

Note: Compared to the "To Be Sold" advertisements that appeared in the newspapers printed in Massachusetts, woefully insignificant are the "To Be Sold" notices for the other British colonies.

American Weekly Mercury, January 28, 1724.

To be Sold, a likely young Indian Woman fit for all manner of House Work, as Sowing, Washing, Starching, Ironing, &c. Enquire of Andrew Bradford.

Reprint: American Weekly Mercury, February 11, 1724.

Variant Reprints: American Weekly Mercury, January 4, 1726; American Weekly Mercury, January 25, 1726; American Weekly Mercury, February 1, 1726.

American Weekly Mercury, April 10, 1729.

To be Sold by Samuel Hasell, in Front-Street, Philadelphia; an Indian Woman and her Child, a Girl about Nine years old, lately imported from Burmudas [*sic*]; she Washes, Irons and Starches very well, and is very good Cook: Any Person incli'd to Purchase, may have her upon Trail for some time, if they desire it.

Reprint: American Weekly Mercury, April 17, 1729.

Glossary

This glossary is an introduction to terms and the references to clothing fashions and local vernacular that appear in the runaway advertisements. Over time and space, spelling varies. The definitions are drawn from several sources. They are Billy G. Smith and Richard Wotowitcz, *Blacks Who Stole Themselves: Advertisement for Runaways in the Pennsylvania Gazette, 1728–1790*, Philadelphia: University of Pennsylvania Press, 1989, 179–83; Graham Russell Hodges and Alan Edward Brown, *"Pretends to Be Press": Runaway Slave Advertisements from Colonial and Revolutionary New York and New Jersey*, New York: Garland Publishing, Inc., 1994, 329–334; Antonio T. Bly, *Escaping Bondage: A Documentary History of Runaway Slaves in Eighteenth-Century New England, 1700–1789*; Antonio T. Bly and Tamia Haygood, *Escaping Servitude: A Documentary History of Runaway Servants in Colonial Virginia*; Florence M. Montgomery, *Textiles in America, 1650–1870: A Dictionary Based on Original Documents, prints, and paintings, commercial records, American merchants' papers, shopkeepers advertisements, and pattern books with original swatches of cloth*; Linda Baumgarten, *What Clothes Reveal: The Language of Clothing in Colonial and Federal America*; and, of course, the *Oxford English Dictionary*.

Apprentice: A person who works for person in order to learn a trade.
Baize: A coarse woolen material with a long nap.
Bay horse: A reddish brown horse.
Beaver: The fur of the rodent, used generally in making hats; can also refer to a heavy woolen cloth like beaver fur.
Binding: A protective covering for the raw edges of fabric.
Bodycoat: A dress coat that was worn relatively close to the body.
Brazier: An individual who manufactures and repairs objects in brass.

Brevet: A rank in the army, without the appropriate pay.

Brig: A vessel with two masts square-rigged like a ship's fore- and mainmasts, but also carrying a lower fore-and-aft sail with a graff and boom.

Brigantine: A small craft rigged for sailing and rowing, speedier and more maneuverable than larger vessels.

Broadcloth: A fine, plain-woven black cloth used primarily in men's clothing.

Brogue: A dialect or regional pronunciation; accent.

Buckskin: Leather made from a buck's skin; may also refer to a thick smooth cotton or woolen cloth.

By trade: A servant who has received training in a particular skill.

Calicoe (calico): A coarse cotton cloth used in a variety of eighteenth-century clothing.

Callimanco: A glazed linen fabric showing a pattern on one side only; described by some writers as a fashionable woolen material with a fine gloss.

Camblet (camlet): Originally an attractive, expensive fabric from the Far East, the name later referred to imitations fashioned from different materials. The raw materials for this cloth ranged from camel hair, silk, and velvet to blends of wool and silk.

Canoe: A narrow boat propelled by a paddle or paddles.

Cap: A head covering.

Cassimir: A thin, twilled woolen cloth used for making men's clothes. From Kashmir, India.

Castor: The binomial nomenclature for the North American beaver is *Castor canadensis.* Castor referred to a hat made of the fur of this animal or imitating the genuine article. As rabbit fur and other substitutes were employed in hat manufacture, the term *castor* came to be used to distinguish such models from true beaver hats.

Chemise: An undergarment usually made of linen or similar fabric and worn by women.

Cherryderry: A striped or checked woven cloth of mixed silk and cotton imported from India. Alternate word for cherryderry: charadary and carridary.

Chintz: Cotton printed in several colors.

Chitterling: A frill on the breast of a shirt. Such a frill resembled the mesentery which connects the intestine to the abdominal cavity.

Clocks: Expensive stockings were embroidered in this manner on stocking side with silk thread.

Cloth colored: Of a drab color.

Coating: Any material used to make coats.

Convict servant: A criminal transported to the New World as punishment for wrongdoings committed in the Old World.

Cooper: The manufacturer of barrels, tubs, pails, piggins, and other containers.

Crape: A thin, transparent, gauzelike fabric, plain woven, without any twill, of highly twisted raw silk or other staple, and mechanically embossed, so as to have a crisped or minutely wrinkled surface.

Cravat: Apparel worn around the neck, primarily by males.

Cue (queue): An eighteenth-century hairstyle in which hair hung down behind the head; the hair might be either one's own or a wig.

Damascus: A fabric woven in elaborate patterns of silk, wool, or linen.

Dimity: A fine ribbed cotton fabric made first in Damietta, used throughout the period.

Dowlas: A coarse sort of hefty linen employed in the fabrication of shirts and smocks.

Drawes or *Drawers:* A garment wore under breeches.

Drugget: Used primarily in work clothes, this woolen stuff might also consist of wool and silk or wool and linen mixtures.

Duck: A strong linen fabric without a twill.

Duffel (duffels): A coarse woolen cloth having a thick nap or frieze; used to produce jackets and coats.

Duroy: A variety of coarse woolen cloth formerly produced in the west of England but not synonymous with corduroy.

Everlasting: A sturdy woolen material used in clothing, including ladies' shoes.

Fearnothing (fearnought, dreadnought): A heavy woolen material often used during harsh weather abroad vessels at sea as protective outer wear.

Felt: A fabric made of wool and hair.

Ferret: A narrow ribbon or tape of cotton or silk; used mainly for binding, such as buttonholes.

Firkin (freize): A thick and warm woolen cloth in use since the fourteenth century.

Flat: A cargo boat with a flat bottom used in shallow water.

French Negro: A black servant born or raised in either a French colony or among the French.

Frock: A long gown with loose sleeves.

Fustian: A species of cloth, originally made at Fusht on the Nile, used for jackets and doublets as early as the fifteenth century. It has a warp of linen thread and a weft of thick cotton.

Fuzee: An American variant of fusee, a large-headed match for lighting a fire in the wind.

Gad: A cut on the ear of cattle or a slave as a sign of ownership.
Gaol: Variant spelling of jail.
Garlix: A sort of linen fabric originally from Gorlitz, Silesia.
Gelding: A castrated animal, particularly a horse.
Gilt: Usually specified a metal which covered an object and gave the appearance of gold.
Gingham: A kind of cotton or linen cloth, woven of dyed yarn, often in stripes, checks, and other patterns.
Great-coat (greatcoat): A topcoat or large, heavy overcoat worn as added protection from the cold.
Gunpowder (tattoo): A form of body art in which designs were made by pricking the skin and using ink that contained gunpowder.
Half joe: Slang for a Portuguese coin, the Johannes.
Halfthick: A sort of coarse cloth.
Heckling: The splitting and separating of flax and hemp fibers.
Hempen: Referring to material or cloth made of hemp.
High Dutch: An eighteenth-century term for German.
Hodden: The coarse woolen cloth produced by country weavers on hand looms.
Holland: A linen fabric named after the Netherlands' province of Holland from which it originated.
Homespun: Any cloth made of homespun yarn, also including coarse material of loose weave meant to imitate homemade cloth.
Hostler: An individual attending to horses at an inn; a stableman, a groom.
Hundred: A division of a county in the British American colonies or provinces of Virginia, Maryland, Delaware, and Pennsylvania, still existing in the state of Delaware, for example, Red Lion Hundred.
Indenture: A deed or agreement by which a person is bound to service.
Instant (Inst.): The current calendar month.
Jockey cap: A cap with a peaked front and round crown, usually decorated with a ribbon around the crown.
Joseph: A lady's riding habit buttoned down the front. When worn open this garment was popularly called a "flying Josie."
Kentish: A person or dialect from the southern counties of England and London.
Kersey: A coarse woolen cloth, often ribbed, which originated in Yorkshire, England.
Last: Shoemakers used these wooden or metal forms shaped like a human foot to produce and restore shoes for their clients.
Leggins (leggings): A pair of extra out coverings (usually of leather or cloth), used as a protection for the legs in inclement weather, and commonly reaching from the ankle to the knee, but sometimes higher.

Linsey Woolsey (lincey): A coarse woolen stuff first made at Linsey in Suffolk, England, and very popular in the colonies.

Logwood: An Indian tree, producing a substance used in dyeing.

Low Dutch: Referred to the Germans along the sea coast and the northern and northwestern flatlands, including the Netherlands and Flanders.

Lugs: Ear lobes; wattles.

Maccaroni: A nickname for a London fop, satirically based on a pretentious craving for the Italian dish. Refers to hair or hats shaped like the noodle.

Manchester velvet: A fine cotton used in making dresses.

Mare: A female horse.

Match-cloth: A coarsely woven wool often traded by Europeans to Native Americans.

Matchcoat: A type of robe prominent among Native Americans, initially consisting of fur skins and later of match-cloth.

Molatto (mulatto): The offspring of a Negro and a European. Eighteenth-century Americans freely called any person of mixed blood a mulatto if he or she resembled one.

Mustee: A person of mixed ancestry. Vernacular for molatto.

Nankeen: A sort of cotton material, initially manufactured in Nanking from a yellow variety of cotton.

Nap: Initially describing the projecting fibers found on fabric surfaces, the term subsequently described the purposeful raising of the short fibers on the surface of a textile followed by trimming and smoothing.

Napt: Any surface that has a nap.

Negro cotton: A strong coarse cloth used in making clothes for black slaves.

Nicanees (niccanee): A kind of piece goods formerly imported from India.

N.B.: The abbreviation for *nota bene*, which means to mark well and pay particular attention to that which follows.

Ozenbrig (oznaburg, oznabrig): A coarse linen made in Hanover and named for a province of that name. The commonest material purchased for slave clothing.

Pea jacket: A stout, short overcoat of coarse woolen cloth, now commonly worn by sailors.

Penniston: A coarse woolen stuff made in England.

Periauger or *Perriauger* [sic]: A small, flat bottomed vessel. A sailing barge.

Periwig: An artificial head of hair or part of one; worn formerly by women and then by men as a fashionable headdress.

Pettycoat: A woman or girl's skirted undergarment hanging from the waist or shoulders. Worn universally and made of every sort of material.

Piece of Eight: The Spanish peso of eight *reals*.

Pinchbeck: A piece of cheap jewelry.

Pistoles: Spanish gold coins often used in the specie-poor American colonies. One pistole was equal to slightly more than one Pennsylvania pound during the middle decades of the eighteenth century.

Plaited hair: Hair that has been braided.

Plush: A cloth comprised of silk, cotton, wool, and other materials, alone or in some combination, with a nap longer and softer than velvet.

Pock-fretten: "Fret" refers to a wearing away or a decayed spot. Thus, "pock-fretten" described the presence of scars resulting from a bout with smallpox.

Pomatum: An unguent used mainly for hair dressing; pomade.

Pothook: A hook over a hearth for hanging a pot.

Pretending: A derogatory term; meant to impugn.

Prunella: A lightweight stuff used for clergyman's gowns, usually a dark color.

Pumps: A shoe with a thin sole and low heel, often worn by seamen as part of their shoregoing finery.

Ratteen: A thick, twilled woolen cloth, generally friezed or with a curled nap.

Ruddy: Red of reddish hue or complexion.

Russet: A twilled woolen stuff like baize, common in the colonies.

Russia duck: A fine, imported bleached linen used for summer clothing.

Saggathy (sagathy): A woolen stuff.

Sartout (surtout): A man's greatcoat or large overcoat.

Sawyer: A worker who cuts logs into structural timbers and boards or firewood.

Schooner: A small, seagoing fore-and-aft rigged vessel, originally with only two masts.

Scutching: The beating of flax stalks necessary to separate the straw in preparation for hackling. Hemp, cotton, and silk were treated in a similar fashion.

Scythe: An agricultural implement for mowing grass or other crops, having a long, thin, curving blade fastened at an angle with the handle and wielded with both hands in a long sweeping stroke.

Serge: A durable twilled woolen cloth, sometimes blended with silk.

Shag: A heavy woolen cloth with a long nap.

Shalloon: A woolen fabric not unlike modern challis and made in Chalons, France.

Shallop (shalloop): 1. A large, heavy boat, fitted with one or more masts and carrying fore-and-aft or lug sails and sometimes furnished with guns; a sloop. 2. A boat propelled by oars or by a sail, for use in shallow waters or as a means of effecting communication between, or landings from, vessels of a large size; a dinghy.

Sheeting: A heavy fabric comprised of cotton or linen, such as is used for bed linen.

Shift: Underclothing made of cotton, linen, or other fabric.

Sloop: 1a. A small, one-masted, fore-and-aft rigged vessel, differing from a cutter in having a jib-stay and standing bowsprit. 1b. A relatively small ship-of-war, carrying guns on the upper deck only. 2. [obs.] A large open boat; a long boat.

Snuff color: The color of snuff, that is, a brownish color.

Sorrel: Of a bright chestnut color; reddish-brown.

Spanish Indian: A Native American born or raised in either a Spanish colony or among the Spanish.

Spanish Negro: A black servant born or raised in either a Spanish colony or among the Spanish.

Squaw: A Native American woman or wife.

Stroud: A coarse blanket cloth. From Stroud, in Gloucestershire, England.

Stuff: Woven material, especially wool, used to manufacture clothing.

Surtout: A man's greatcoat or large overcoat.

Swanskin: A fine, thick, fleece-like fabric; a kind of flannel.

Swarthy: Dark hued or complexioned.

Tawny: A shade of brown tinged with yellow.

Thickset: A material possessing a close-grained nap.

Thrumb'd: To make or cover with thrums, the unwoven end of a warp thread, or the whole of such ends, left when the finished web is cut away.

Ticklenburg (ticklenburgs): For Tecklenburg, from a town and county of this name is Westphalia, noted for its manufacture of linen; a kind of coarse linen cloth.

Tow: The short fibers of flax or hemp which are separated from the longer ones through heckling.

Ultimo: The last or previous month.

Viz: Namely, to wit, as follows, that is to say, viz is an abbreviation videlicet. In Latin, the meaning of viz "it is permitted to see."

Waistcoat: An underjacket or a vest.

Waiting-man: One who waited or attended on an employer or official; a personal servant.

Watch-coat: A stout coat or cloak worn in inclement weather.

Well-set: Strongly built; compact person

Wen: A lump or protuberance of the body; a knot, bunch, wart.

Wherry: 1. A light rowing boat used chiefly on rivers to carry passengers and goods. 2. A large boat of the barge kind.

Whitney: A heavy coarse stuff used for coats, cloaks, and petticoats.

Name Index

Abel, 20
Abraham, 89, 96
Abraham, Paul, 25
Allen, Elijah, 43
Allen, James, 71
Almoquit, John, 45
Amareta, 9
Anderson, John, 93
Andress, John, 90
Annis, 130
Anthony, John, 65
Arthur, 41
Attakin, Samuel, 30

Baker, John, 22
Barnabas, Isaac, 45
Ben, 69, 126
Betty, 49
Bilha, 53
Bill, 121
Bishop, William, 129
Blossom, Oliver, 56
Boston, 5
Boswell, Henry, 112
Bristow, 11
Brown, Daniel, 46
Buck, 67

Caesar, 8, 15, 32, 33, 77, 119, 124, 125
Cash, Jo, 40

Charles, 39, 51, 86, 110
Charles, Lydia, 13, 14
Charles, Silas, 25
Charles, Sylvanus (alias Venus), 27
Cheats, Joshua (alias Joshua Hazard), 68
Chin, Desiah, 9
Choho, Rachel, 9
Church, Solomon, 65
Clain, Amos, 58
Clap, Nathan, 59
Clark, Jerry, 111
Cloas, Enoch, 43
Cockchick, Anthony, 84
Col[?], Bob, 115
Commonson, Jeremiah, 34
Coochuck, James, 27
Cooly, Henry, 83
Cornet, Josiah, 70
Covy, 21
Coy, Toby, 70
Cozens, Samuel, 29
Cudjo (alias Hunk), 126
Cuff, Thomas, 48
Cuff, William, 71

Daniel, 34, 109
Daniels, Jo, 12
Daniels, John, 70
Dianah, 114
Dick, 55, 95, 97, 100

Name Index

Elishua, Hannah, 50
Elles, John, 3
Emery, Joseph, 7
Ephraim, Joshua, 35
Ephraims, Ebenezer, 40
Esther (alias Phebe), 33
Eunice, 62
Experience, 31
Ezekiel, Sampson, 63

Fanny, 85
Faulknot, Thomas, 37
Francies, John (alias Jaun Francisco), 27
Frank, 66, 97
Frost, Ephraim, 48, 96
Fuller, Ezekiel, 62
Furnace, Beneto, 12

Gardner, James, 71
George, 53, 121
George, Simon, 13
Golloway, 77
Grace, 2
Greene, Hannah, 52
Gunnitt, Isaac, 101

Hall, William, 58
Haney, Samuel, 44
Harris, Nathan, 29
Harry, 1, 42, 117, 126, 130
Harry, Jacob, 30
Hazard, Joseph, 68
Hazard, Toby, 85
Hector, 10
Hill, Vic, 61
Holborn, John, 30
Honce, John, 94
Hump, Daniel, 3
Hunley, Patrick (alias Paddy), 129

Isaac, 115

Jack, 19, 35, 79, 92, 109, 124
Jacob, 80, 82, 86, 108

James, 7, 9, 16, 28, 32, 59, 61, 80, 90
January, Peter, 67, 94
Jeffery, 78, 91
Jeffery, Daniel, 70
Jeffords, John, 58
Jenings, David, 127
Jennings, Absalom, 28
Jenny, 5, 19
Jo, 55, 68
Job, David, 54
Joe, 81, 111, 118
John, 23
John, Sarah, 33
Johns, Peter, 57
Johnson, Nathaniel, 66
Jonath, 34
Joshua, William, 110
Julian, 16
Justin, 32

Kate, 83

Larrens, Bersheba, 13
Lott, 113

Manaway, 5
Margaret, 99
Maria, 101
Mary, 24, 54, 87
Maycum, John, 107
M'Carty, James, 78
McDonald, Benjamin, 94
Micha, John, 62
Milly, 8
Moll, 5
Moses, 33
Moses, Eli, 28
Moses, Jonas, 37

Nan, 98
Nero, 15
Nevill, Samuel, 80
Newton, John, 118
Nim, 8

Name Index

Page, Comfort, 31
Page, Jack, 132
Pallas, 16
Patience, 31, 72
Patterson, James, 100
Paul, Anthony, 59
Paul, George, 66
Paul, George Tikeing, 60
Paun, Betty, 26
Pegan, Jonathan, 36
Pegg, 4, 23
Pero, 23, 44, 54, 125, 128
Peter, 6, 7, 18, 20, 42, 64, 92, 101
Peter, Moses, 44
Phelice, 123
Phillips, Sarah, 74
Phillis, 5
Phoebe, 74, 116
Pittome, John, 21
Placey, William, 69
Poheag, George, 42
Pomp, 98
Pompey, 100, 102, 104
Primus, 22, 24
Prince, 1
Pummatick, Isaac, 2
Pumsher, Williams, 108
Put, Peter (alias Pompey), 14

Quanomp, Silas, 19
Quite, Charles, 88

Robbins, James, 46
Robbins, Samuel, 41, 52, 63
Robin, 9, 95
Robin, Jeremiah, 104
Robin, Nehemiah, 104
Rose, 6
Ruth, 30
Rutter, Patience, 82

Sally, 48
Sam, 33, 118, 131
Sam (alias Job), 97
Sampson, 106

Sarah, 4, 9
Sassidillah, 11
Saunders, John, 64
Scoggins, Thomas, 29
Seedux, Sampson, 63
Shadrack, 81
Shawen, Charles, 38
Simon, 124
Simons, James, 57
Simons, Solomon (alias Solomon Silas), 71
Siscat, Samuel, 88
Skesuck, Hannah, 67
Sooduck, Ephraim, 39
Spywood, Thomas, 36
Squibb, Christopher, 49
Start, James (alias James Pratt and Jacob), 86, 87
Stephen, 52, 75
Stephen (alias Pompey), 89
Strum, Nathaniel (alias Daniel James), 31
Sy, 127
Syme (alias Symon), 91

Tallman, Joseph, 38
Tatson, Warren, 53
Tewis, Solomon, 60
Thayer, Mol, 43
Thomas, 107
Thomas, Daniel, 40
Thomas, Moses, 26
Thomas, William, 56
Thompson, William, 46
Tierce, 78
Timothy, 65
Toby, 5, 7
Toby, Peter (alias John Toby), 71
Tom, 15, 33, 88, 115, 119
Toney, 6, 125
Tony, 120
Trasher, James, 75

Umphry, Isaac, 36
Uncas, Abimeleck, 56

Valentine, Thomas, 120

Waban, Joshua, 26
Wampee, John, 46
Wamper, John, 58
Wampum, Joseph, 14
Wampum, Keziah, 18
Wampum, Solomon, 14
Wampy, John, 45
Wamscom, John, 35
Wamscomb, Louis, 35
Wan, 82, 103
Wapuck, Hannah, 3
Warhonks, Peter, 38
Warmick, 15
Warwick, Ann, 21

Watt, Primas (alias Toby), 128
Way, Fredrick, 60
Way, John, 38
White, Jonathan, 129
Wicket, Benjamin, 70
Wickett, Obadiah, 73
Will, 10, 18, 102, 107
Williams, Moses, 103, 105
Wire, Robert, 73
Wobin, Bill, 48
Wooly, Jacob, 64
Worrison, Pallas, 24
Wright, James, 25

Zipporah, 10

Subject Index

advertisement by jailers, 14, 22, 31–33, 41, 50, 51, 60, 107, 108, 120

branded, 1, 4, 9, 102, 104, 117, 130
broke or in goal, 14, 22, 31, 41, 50, 59, 60, 69, 107, 108, 120

deserters, 2, 10, 13, 23, 28, 30, 36, 37, 43–46, 48–50, 56–59, 62, 69–73, 78, 83, 96, 97

enlistment: Army, 44, 59, 73; Navy, 69. *See also* deserters
escape objectives (destinations): Bedford, 70; Boston, 72, 97, 100; Carolina, 106; Connecticut, 97; Eastward, 11, 12, 69, 72; Indian county, 96, 130; Maryland, 117; Massachusetts, 70; Mother, 118; Nantucket, 43; New York, 85, 86, 100; Northward, 71; Plainfield, 54; Rhode Island, 57, 94; Sea, 8, 11, 12, 70, 71, 85, 93; Town (in or about), 16, 20, 40, 54, 61, 94, 105, 131; Westward, 12, 69
escape strategies: change clothing, 23, 72, 94, 110, 111, 116–17, 120, 121, 129; change name, 11, 52, 66, 72, 86, 87, 89, 97, 108, 109, 121; forged pass, 39, 51, 90, 92, 105; pass, 56 (from "George Washington's Aid de Camp"); pass for free, 56, 81, 85, 108, 119
escape with others: with enslaved African Americans, 2, 4, 6–8, 18, 22, 23, 31, 71, 72, 77, 79, 80, 88, 96–98, 102, 114, 116, 117, 121, 128; with family members (with spouses or children), 4, 8, 39, 51, 97, 98, 104, 114, 116, 119, 130; with indentured servants, 10, 14, 18, 22, 46, 60, 65, 101, 103, 108; with Native Americans, 5–9, 11, 12, 30, 31, 48, 60, 61, 67, 94, 95, 101

indigenous marking: hair, 4, 6, 8, 11, 12, 14–16, 19, 25, 28, 34, 35, 39, 43, 44, 55, 58, 66, 68, 70, 79, 82, 89, 92–94, 96, 110, 115, 118; ink (tattooing), 4, 6, 11, 39, 51
irons on, 12, 13, 15, 16, 37, 41, 79, 83, 104, 112
items stolen: boat, 12, 17, 20, 63–65, 102; children, 4, 96–98, 114, 116; dog, 54; extra clothing, 5, 9–11, 14, 16, 18, 20, 23, 24, 28–30, 35, 37, 41, 51–56, 60, 62, 64–66, 74, 81, 93, 95, 98, 101, 103, 106, 108, 112, 120,

123, 126, 127, 129; fife, 96; gun, 14, 20, 40–41, 92, 106, 129–30; horse, 25, 41, 100, 118, 132; knife, 16, 39, 51; money, 5, 10, 128; saddle, 25; tools, 119, 121; Violin or Fiddle, 21, 25, 64, 67, 81, 85, 96, 103, 107, 109, 121, 128

Julian: autobiography, xvi–xvii; biography, xi–xxv; broadsides, 145–48; chronology, 157–61; court records, 161–70; newspaper accounts, 149–56

literacy: read, 21–24, 51, 80, 87, 100; read, write, and cypher, 132; read and write, 21, 23, 24, 64, 92, 95, 108, 175, 178

Martha's Vineyard Indians, 9, 37, 44, 45, 57

master's occupation: Baker, 4; Brick-maker, 101; Cordwainer, 9; Doctor, 107; Esquire, 2, 3, 6, 13, 14, 24, 35, 38, 42, 77, 79, 89, 126, 178, 179; inn-holder, 61; Mariner (seaman), 4, 5, 11, 27; Merchant, 2, 3, 7, 23; Militia, 3, 9, 15, 18, 19, 26, 27, 29, 35–37, 43–46, 48, 50, 56–58, 69–71, 78, 79, 90, 92, 96, 109, 175, 176. *See also* deserters; minister, 16, 24; Sawyer, 12; ship-carpenter, 8; Shipwright, 20; shop-keeper, 7; tailor, 15

multi-lingual, 2, 23, 32, 39, 51, 91, 95, 99, 109

musical: dancers, 97; fiddlers (includes violin players), 21, 24–25, 64, 67, 81, 85, 96, 103, 107, 109, 121, 127–28; singer, 97, 98

scars, 4, 5, 14–16, 18, 19, 21, 24, 26, 28, 30, 31, 34, 35, 37, 42, 49, 52, 56, 59, 64, 67, 72, 74, 75, 85–87, 89, 97, 100, 101, 103, 104, 108–11, 115, 116, 119, 125–27, 129–31

servant/slave's occupation: blacksmith, 115; carpenter, 8, 111; copper, 56, 116; husbandry, 66, 109; mariner (seaman), 11, 57, 85, 88, 93, 94, 97, 102; plaster, 129; shoe-maker, 116, 119, 131, 177; tailor, 78, 109; tanner, 15; weaver, 28

sex: female runaways, 2–6, 8–10, 13, 14, 18, 21, 23, 24, 26, 30, 31, 33, 35, 48–51, 54, 61, 62, 67, 72, 74, 99, 101, 116, 123, 130

sexual assault (rape), 41, 60

small-pox, 1, 2, 23, 37–39, 51, 56, 58, 64, 69, 74, 77, 88, 93, 99, 100, 107, 180, 181

taken up or captured, 6, 14, 31, 33, 36, 41, 107, 108, 117

vices: drinking, 24, 86, 94, 95, 97, 109, 111, 113, 116, 119, 121; tobacco, 86, 112

Subscribers

Abell, Samuel, 120
Acton, Benjamin, 101
Adams, Samuel, 9
Adin, John, 1
Allaen, Samuel, 18
Allen, Elijah, 43
Allen, Nehemiah, 27
Amos, Daniel, 33
Atwell, Amos, 128
Avery, Aaron, 53

Babcock, Ichabod, 67
Babcock, Joshua, 71
Bacon, Josiah, 12
Baker, Nathaniel, 4
Balding, Ezekiel, 100
Balding, Jacob, 90
Barber, William, 35
Battle, John, 35
Bayard, Nicholas, 80
Bazin, John, 26
Belcher, Andrew, 2
Beldin, John, Jr., 88
Bennet, Caleb, 28
Berry, James, 4
Biffell, William, 101
Bissel, Job, 11
Black, Nathaniel, 36
Bloodgood, Francis, 80

Bolles, Isaiah, 54
Bolling, Robert, Jr., 115
Bonnel, Isaac, 94
Borden, William, 8, 9
Bourn, Benjamin, 74
Bowen, William, 72
Breese, John, 77
Brenton, Ebenezer, 20
Brents, Adrian Van, 85
Brown, Elizabeth, 6
Brown, Jeremiah, 124
Brown, Joseph, 2
Brown, Richard, 15
Browne, William, 118
Brownejohn, William, Jr., 92
Brownell, Thomas, 124
Brownson, David, 56
Brumfield, John, 119
Buchanan, T, 93
Buchanan, William, 93
Buckman, Edward, 44
Burk, William, 129
Bush, Jost, 87
Bussing, Abraham, 98
Byles, Thomas, 11

Caldwell, John, 42, 49
Calkin, Reuben, 58
Carpenter, Nathaniel, 96

Catton, Grizel, 19
Chadwick, John, 46
Chapman, Nathaniel, 31
Chase, Job, 34
Chick, John, Jr., 107
Chickering, Daniel, 35
Choat, Thomas, Jr., 22
Clark, Daniel, 55
Clark, John, 108
Coit, William, 57
Cole, Elizabeth, 61
Concklin, Joseph, 81
Congdon, Robert, 68
Cordon, George, 42
Corney, John, 19
Cotton, William, 41, 52
Crooker, Sampson, 78
Curtis, William, 45

Dagget, James, 74
Dane, Philemon, 14
Dasheil, George, 104
Davenport, William, 97
Davis, Andrew, 25
Davis, Thomas, 109
Dayton, Henry, 71
Denison, George, Jr., 60
Dennis, Joseph, 125
Dodge, John, 49
Dolbeare, George, 23
Douglas, Ebenezer, 59
Draper, Richard, 7
Draper, Timothy, 29
Dunham, George, 44
Dwight, Seth, 40

Earle, John, 127
Eldridge, Daniel, 58
Elliot, Robert, 113
Ellis, John, 58
Ellis, Thomas, 39
Emery, Joseph, 7

Ferris, Caleb, 81
Field, Robert, 110

Fleet, Gilbert, 92
Fleet, Simon, 86
Floyd, Richard, 67, 95
Folger, Daniel, 42
Forman, Aaron, Jr., 83
Fowler, Isaac, 124
Franklin, Abel, 65
Fuller, Ezekiel, 62

Gardner, William, 4
Garner, Andrew, 28
Gilman, Andrew, 21
Gombauld, Moses, 23
Goodwin, Ichabod, 33
Gordon, George, 64
Gray, Jonathan, 60
Green, Elisha, 13
Greene, Benjamin, 128
Greene, Mary, 67
Guynn, John, 27

Hallett, Robert, 88
Hammet, Malachi, 70
Hankison, Kenneth, 114
Hardaway, Daniel, 118
Hardaway, Henry, 116
Hardaway, John, 115
Hardy, James, 61
Hargill, Christ, 62
Hassard, Stephen, 55, 68
Haszard, Enoch, 126
Hauley, Jabiel, 7
Havens, Micah, 34
Hazard, Jonathan, 75, 125, 126
Hill, Thomas, 100
Hinddell, Mahuman, 14
Hinds, Patrick, 131
Hodges, James, 105
Holbrook, Nathanael, 21
Hopkins, Roswell, 52
Howard, Thomas, 16
Howell, James, 30
Hughes, Clemant, 9
Hull, William, 127
Hussey, George, 40

Hussey, Obed, 20
Huston, James, 120

Jackson, John, 77
Jacob, Joseph, 64
Jamain, Nicholas, 2
James, Richard, 89, 110
Jenkins, John, 5
Jennison, Nathaniel, 41
Johnson, David, 72
Johnson, William, 88
Johnston, Andrew, 130
Johnston, Robert, 98
Jones, Dorothy, 116
Jones, John, 119
Jones, Lodowick, 131

Kanney, Nathanael, 10
Kellingworth, Eliot, 31
Kerlin, William, 111
Kimball, Asa, 74
Kinsman, Robert, 57
Kip, Abraham, 78, 79
Knight, John, 9

Lambert, William, 14
Laughton, Henry, 15
Leather, John, 5
Leffingwell, Christopher, 56
Leonard, Samuel, 103
Leonard, Thomas, 108
Loring, Daniel, 5
Low, Peter, 91
Lucas, Frind, 82
Lyell, David, 8

Mansfield, Joseph, 20
March, John, 24
Marcy, Moses, 35
Martin, Josiah, 80
M'Comb, John, 99
Menzies, John, 13, 14
M'Invaill, James, 119
Mitchell, Henry, 97

M'Neill, Alexander, 51
Moore, Samuel, 80
Moores, Robert, 82
Morse, Daniel, 40
Morton, Morton, 111
Mott, William, 89
Muzzy, Benjamin, 12
Myles, Samuel, 5

Nevins, David, 33
Newcomb, Zacheus, 91
Nicholson, Benjamin, 112
Niles, Jeremiah, 125
Niles, Nathan, 34
Niles, Nathaniel, 1
Niles, Samuel, 1
Ninegrett, Thomas, 63
Northup, John, 65
Norton, Thomas, 25

Oldfield, John, 66
Olney, Jeremiah, 73
Onion, Stephen, 102
Otis, John, 3

Page, William, 31
Parker, James, 71
Parkes, Thomas, 29
Parvin, Silas, 106
Patterson, James, 100
Peck, Darius, 59
Peck, Joseph, 51
Peckham, Timothy, 69
Pell, Thomas, 97
Perry, Joseph, 26
Philipps, Caleb, 26
Phillips, Christopher, 15
Phillips, Samuel, 70
Pitts, James, 3
Poe, James, 130
Potter, John, 32
Potter, Stephen, 72
Power, Nicholas, 69
Prince, James, 90

Putnam, Israel, 38, 39, 51

Randall, Job, 75
Rivers, Joseph, 132
Roach, James, 62
Robinson, Rowland, 32
Robinson, Thomas, 79
Rogers, James, 128
Ruff, Richard, 104
Ruffin, Edmund, 117
Ruggels, George, 27
Rutland, Edward, 130

Salter, Thomas, 9
Savage, Thomas, 5
Sawyer, Moses, 93
Sawyer, Stephen, 18
Sherman, Philip, 66
Shivers, Samuel, 105
Smith, Epenetus, 125
Smith, George, 59
Smith, Gilbert, 86, 88, 108
Smith, William, 55, 95
Soper, Amasa, 45, 48
Stanton, John, 85
Stanton, Joseph, Jr., 66
Stanton, Phineas, Jr., 63
Stevens, Henry, 111
Stewart, Edward, 26
Stewart, William, 53
Stone, Thomas, 30
Swan, John, 8
Swan, Thomas, 70
Swift, Ephraim, 37

Tabb, William, 117
Taylour, John, 5
Thacher, Josiah, 23
Thomas, Hannah, 127

Thomas, John, 89
Tibbits, George, 123
Tresscott, Lemuel, 43
Tripp, Thomas, 129
Turner, Samuel, 54
Tuthill, John, 79

Vernon, Samuel, 9
Vestpation, Titus, 48

Walker, Ebenezer, 53
Wall, William, 24
Wallace, Michael, 122
Ward, Isaac, 96
Ward, Stephen, 84
Wayman, Moses, 93
Welch, Francis, 85
Wendell, Henry, 30
Wentworth, Samuel, 3
Westcott, Gideon, 74
Wheeler, Abijah, 19
Wheeler, Philip, 29
White, Gideon, 44
White, Richard, 30
Whitford, Paskee, 28
Whyte, Robert, 109
Wilde, Thomas, 82
Williams, Elisha, 54
Williams, Ezekiel, 60
Wilson, John, 21
Wilson, Mary, 103
Wing, Ebenezer, 61
Woodson, William, 119
Worth, Lillibridge, 64
Wright, James, 132

Yoals, Nehemiah, 9
Young, Hamilton, 97

About the Author

Antonio T. Bly is the Peter H. Shattuck Endowed Chair in Colonial American History at California State University, Sacramento. In addition to *Escaping Slavery*, Dr. Bly is the author of *Escaping Bondage* and, with Tamia Haywood, *Escaping Servitude*.

www.ingramcontent.com/pod-product-compliance
Lightning Source LLC
Chambersburg PA
CBHW061711300426
44115CB00014B/2646